CREATIVE SLEEPOVERS FOR KIDS!

JULIE LAVENDER

CREATIVE SLEEPOVERS FOR KIDS!

Fun Activities, Themes, and Ideas for Overnight Parties for Boys or Girls

PRIMA HOME
An Imprint of Prima Publishing
3000 Lava Ridge Court ★ Roseville, CA 95661
(800) 632-8676 ★ www.primalifestyles.com

Prima Publishing and the author hope that you enjoy the projects and activities discussed in this book. Most projects and activities included in this book should be done with proper adult supervision. While we believe the projects and activities to be safe and fun if proper safety precautions are followed, all such projects are done at the reader's sole risk. Prima Publishing and the author cannot accept any responsibility or liability for any damages, loss, or injury arising from use, misuse, or misconception of the information provided in this book.

Interior Illustrations by Emily Eklund and Melanie Merz.

Library of Congress Cataloging-in-Publication Data

Lavender, Julie.
Creative sleepovers for kids! : fun activities, themes, and ideas for overnight parties for boys or girls / Julie Lavender
p. cm.
Includes index.
ISBN 0-7615-3245-8
1. Children's parties—Planning. 2. Sleepovers—Planning. 3. Entertaining—Planning. I. Title.
GV1205.L38. 2001
793.2'1—dc21 2001018518

01 02 03 04 DD 10 9 8 7 6 5 4 3 2 1
Printed in the United States of America

HOW TO ORDER

Single copies may be ordered from Prima Publishing, 3000 Lava Ridge Court, Roseville, CA 95661; telephone (800) 632-8676 ext. 4444. Quantity discounts are also available. On your letterhead, include information concerning the intended use of the books and the number of books you wish to purchase.

Visit us online at www.primalifestyles.com

To my wonderful husband, David,
and our precious children,
Jeremy, Jenifer, Jeb Daniel, and Jessica.
Words can never express my gratitude
for your unending love & support
and gracious contribution to
my work and my life.

Contents

Acknowledgments

I wish to thank the members of my extended family—the Bland, Lavender, and Callahan clan—for always supporting and encouraging my writing. This book would not have been possible without the talent and dedication of the following people at Prima Publishing: Denise Sternad (a special thanks for "keeping my name on file"), Michelle McCormack, and Jennifer Dougherty-Hart. Thank you, Prima Publishing!

Introduction

What children gain from slumber parties lasts them a lifetime. A night of laying in sleeping bags laughing, telling secrets, having pillow fights, and talking about anything and everything until the wee hours of the morning creates everlasting keepsakes. The memories made and friendships strengthened make this an event all its own—one that every youngster should be a part of.

Most children—even as men and women—will never forget their first sleepovers. Now you get the chance to create an unforgettable one for a special child in your life! Maybe you bought this book to plan your child's first sleepover, or perhaps you've hosted so many slumber parties that you've run out of ideas. Perhaps you're the grandma, uncle, aunt, or dad who's hosting the event. You may be a scout troop leader, church volunteer leader, or child care provider looking for an exciting way to entertain a group of children for a night or two.

Creative Sleepovers for Kids! contains idea after idea for fun and exciting slumber parties. So whether you're a novice or an experienced nighttime host looking for new ideas, you will have a blast creating with this book. Choose one of these ideas and start planning!

Chapter 1

Designs for Dozers

Sleepover Preparation and Planning

What makes a memorable sleepover? Well, undoubtedly the most important ingredient for a terrific sleepover is an intimate group of friends! However, to ensure success at any sleepover, the key lies with the plans. As some have said, "Prior, proper planning prevents poor performance!"

One would not think of planning a birthday party at the very last minute. The same holds true for a slumber party. Start preparing your sleepover at least two to three weeks before the party. Get your child involved in the action, and start having fun!

Before the Party

Well before the date of the sleepover, figure out the theme, guests, entertainment, food, and other elements guaranteed to make the event a night to remember.

Choose a Theme

Let the host of the party help you decide on the theme of the sleepover. Your child will probably want to choose something he or she is currently interested in, such as a favorite hobby, animal, or current event happening in the child's life. If your child is younger and has trouble deciding on a theme, guide him or her toward ideas that you know are of interest. Older children will probably have no trouble deciding on a theme, because their interests seem to be more focused. However, your child may choose a theme just because it's different or original and it may have nothing to do with current interests. The time of year of the sleepover may also influence the choice. Once the theme is selected, begin the actual planning of the sleepover.

Choose the Date and Time

Although most sleepovers tend to happen on a Friday or Saturday night, there's no hard-and-fast rule as to when a slumber party should take place. During no-school sessions, any night is fair game. When both parents in a family work, however, weekday slumber parties may not be as convenient.

Your child may choose to schedule the slumber party near his or her birthday or other holiday. Whenever you choose to have the party, allow yourself plenty of time to organize and plan the get-together.

Decide on beginning and ending times for the sleepover. More than likely, most of the guests will not get as much sleep as they are accustomed to. Therefore, party ending times should be established and held fast to allow children to regroup and catch up on rest.

Choose the Guests

Make a guest list for the sleepover. Four or five children are probably the maximum number that should be invited. Too many children can cause the party to get unruly and rowdy. Be sure the guests on the list get along well and have many things in common.

Choose the Invitations

Select store-bought invitations to your sleepover, or make your own, using a suggestion from this book. Your child and the guests will enjoy personalized invitations much better than ones from the store, although there are many store-bought ones to choose from.

If you use a suggestion from this book, prepare the invitations following the directions given. Mail or hand-deliver your invitations one to two weeks before the scheduled party. Ask the guests to RSVP so that you will have an accurate count.

Choose the Decorations

Keeping your theme in mind, choose the decorations for the slumber party. Decide how many rooms you'll decorate and what you'll need. Will you decorate only the room where the children plan to sleep? Or will you choose to have some decorations in each room in the house? Look for decorations in a party store, department store, toy store, novelty store, or grocery store.

If you choose to make your decorations according to guidelines in this book, locate the items you will need and begin making the decorations. Allow enough time to prepare the decorations without having to rush at the last minute. Most party decorations can be completed several weeks ahead of time. Store them in a place where they will not get damaged before the party.

Choose the Games and Activities

Using this book as a guide and keeping your theme in mind, choose the games and activities that you want to use for your party. Make a list of all the items needed for the games or crafts. Shop for all the items at one time to save several trips to the store. Make any props or game pieces ahead of time. Once again, many of these items can be made several weeks before the party and stored in a safe place.

In addition to the specific, theme-related activities, have several standby activities on hand. A lull in the party or bored guests can sometimes lead to disaster! Plan to have on hand one or more of these time-fillers: modeling dough and utensils; bubbles and bubble wands; art supplies such as watercolor paints, scented markers, glitter pens, colored chalks, and oil pastels; one or two puzzles with seventy-five to one hundred pieces for the children to work on in pairs; a basket of dress-up clothes; or building blocks in a variety of sizes, shapes, and colors.

Once you've determined the games and activities and have extra fillers lined up, make a written schedule for the party happenings. Be specific with times, but also be flexible. You may plan for a game to take fifteen minutes, only to find that the guests are bored after only five minutes. Or you may find that the guests are enjoying a craft so much that it consumes double the amount of time you have allotted. Be willing to bend, but keep a schedule handy regardless.

Choose the Food and Favors

Again, remember your theme as you plan this part of the slumber party. Select favorite foods of the host for the sleepover, or choose ideas from chapter 7. Decide exactly which meals you will be serving and what kinds of between-meal snacks you will provide. Establish what time the "diner" will close; will your kitchen be an all-night café or have predetermined closing hours?

Once you have decided on the foods, make a written menu and grocery list.

Next, with your child's help, determine the party favors, if any, you will give the attendees. If using suggestions from this book, add the needed items to your grocery list.

Shop ahead of time to locate the items you need. You may find that your favorite grocery store is fresh out of an important item you need if you wait until the last minute.

Once you have purchased all the necessary items, prepare as many of the foods and favors ahead of time as possible. This will prevent extra stresses as the party nears. Many foods are easily frozen weeks ahead of a scheduled need. Other foods can be refrigerated for one to two days.

Choose Related Videos and Books

You and your child may decide to rent or purchase movies or books to use as a sleepover "sedative." At the predetermined time, you could have the guests gather in their sleeping bags to look at and read aloud books related to the theme of the party. Perhaps a good children's video fits perfectly with your sleepover theme. Many libraries will let you reserve items for a particular date.

Choose Sleeping Arrangements

With the help of the party host, decide how the guests will sleep. Will all the guests sleep in one room? Will you have a room for some to crash in while others stay awake to watch the sunrise? Make these decisions ahead of time.

In addition to deciding exactly which room will house the sleeping bags, decide whether you want to sleep "creatively." Some of the suggested themes in this book lend themselves well to fun sleeping arrangements. For example, a sleepover with a beach theme calls for placing sleeping bags on top of large beach towels to create the atmosphere of "sleeping on the beach." An indoor camping party begs for a makeshift tent to be set up in the den by draping blankets across rope that has been strung from one end of the room to the other. Place heavy books on the corners of the outstretched blankets to hold the "tent" in place. A baseball party invites the sleepers to arrange their sleeping bags in a diamond shape with two heads meeting at "third base" and two heads meeting at "first base" while pairs of feet meet up at "second base" and "home plate." For the Calling All Explorers! Party, lay blue towels or a long strip of blue paper across the middle of the room, and have the "explorers" camp out next to the river.

Even if you don't sleep according to theme, you can still have fun and be creative with sleeping arrangements. Decide how the sleeping bags will be arranged by playing a game. Let the winner of the game determine how the sleeping bags will be positioned and who will sleep next to whom. For another idea, write all the guests' names on a slip of paper and place them in a basket. Let the host pull out one name at a time. That person chooses his or her spot and stretches out his or her bedding. Continue until each person has a place to sleep.

Make geometric patterns—large triangles, squares, rectangles, or circles—with the sleeping bags. Perhaps the simplest, most common position of sleepers is that of a circle with all pillows being in the inside of the circle. This position lends itself easily to sleepytime games and late-night discussions!

If none of those ideas work well for you, then let the sleeping bags fall where they may, and let children slumber in whatever position they choose!

Last-Minute Preparations for the Party

On the day of the party (so that the discussion stays fresh in the mind of the sleepover host), establish rules for the party. Remind your child that rules are for the benefit and safety of the guests and to help ensure a successful and fun party.

Set any room off limits that you do not want the children to be in. Remind the child of safety rules that you want enforced, such as no running in the house. Point out that no guest should be excluded from activities or conversations. Remind your child that preestablished family rules of the house remain intact.

If you feel comfortable doing so, discuss the sleepover rules with all of the guests when they arrive. That may eliminate unnecessary problems later in the evening.

Remove any breakable, dangerous, or valuable items from rooms that the guests will be playing, working, and sleeping in. Just as you "baby-proofed" your house when your children were younger, consider "slumber-proofing" your home for this event.

Prepare any last-minute foods, craft items, game props, or party favors. Have all party requirements handy.

Decorate the room(s) or house according to the decisions you and your child made during the planning of the party.

During the Party

As the guests arrive, put away sleeping bags and suitcases. Place them in a neat and orderly fashion out of the play and work area but handy for the guests if necessary.

Keep your written schedule handy at all times. Follow the schedule, but remember to be flexible. Encourage all guests to be involved in each activity, and keep the activities flowing without a lot of downtime. As mentioned before, this can lead to boredom and/or trouble!

A Homesick Guest

If you sense, at any time during the party, that a child is being left out or is feeling homesick, gently guide that child back with the group and make sure he or she is included in the activity taking place. This may be the first slumber party for a young child. Sometimes a sad child can be distracted with an activity or snack and will forget about being homesick. If a child seems to continue to be sad, perhaps a quick phone call to Mom or Dad may comfort the guest. If a child continues to be unhappy or cannot stop crying, politely suggest to the parents that the child might need to go home for the evening but is welcome to return the next morning. There's no reason for one of the guests to be that miserable! (And his or her unhappiness could ultimately lead to the unhappiness of the whole guest list!)

After the Party

When the party favors have been given out and the final good-byes have been said, many of the slumber party participants may want to just crash! After you've had time to catch a few winks and regroup, sit down with your child and discuss the party. Find out what he or she liked best and least about the party. Ask what the host would do differently the next time and what he or she would like to repeat. Find out any pertinent information that will be helpful for the next sleepover. Take notes, in the margins of this book, perhaps, to help you in the planning of your next slumber party. You may think you'll be able to remember all these things that pop into your head, but a couple of months from now when your child asks, "Can I have another spend-the-night party?" you just might not remember those important details!

A Final Word

Sleepovers can be some of the most special and precious times in your child's life. Plan a truly wonderful, unique slumber party for your child that he or she and all of the invited guests will remember and treasure for a long, long time!

Chapter 2

Siesta Suggestions

Themes for a Terrific Party

Want to have a sleepover that will long be remembered? The first order of business in planning a sleepover is to choose a theme. Let the host choose a theme based on his or her interests or hobbies. Once the theme has been determined, the fun begins.

Let the sleepover revolve around the theme. Choose invitations, decorations, games and activities, foods, books and movies, and favors related to the theme of the party.

Look over the lists here for ideas. You may decide to combine one or more party ideas or choose from a variety of suggestions.

All Aboard!

Transportation Party

Here's a great party for anyone who likes moving vehicles!

Invitations: Binocular Bonanzas, Cookie Cutter Creations, Equestrian Invitation, ID Invitations, Snack Sensations, Tantalizing Tickets, Toothbrush Tote, Train Treats

Decorations: Bundles of Balloons, Destination Unknown, Heaps of Horses, Paradise Party

Games: Derby Races; Musical Bus Seats; Paper Airplane Races; Twisted Tongues; Up, Up, and Away!

Activities: Bicycle Brigade, Hot Air Balloon, Pin the Car on the Map, Vehicle Boxes

Snacks and Suppers: Gelatin Boats, Palomino Pony Drink, Sailing Sandwiches, Train Track Vegetables, Wagon Wheels

Favors: Airplane Announcements, Basket of Goodies, Kooky Cookie Cutters, Wooden Spoon Someones

Awesome Autumn
Fall Party

Plan a fall party for a back-to-school celebration, football season opening, Halloween or Thanksgiving party, or just to welcome in cool, crisp autumn.

Invitations: Catchy Caterpillars, Clever Kites, Cookie Cutter Creations, Rainbow Reminders, Sleepover Sue (or Sam)

Decorations: Bundles of Balloons, Down on the Farm, Festive Fall, Play Ball!

Games: Apple Bobbing, Balloon Scrabble, Flying Bats, Haybale Hopping, Hidden Bones, Jell-O Toss, Leaf Collecting, Pass the Apple, Spider Tossing, Spiders in the Web, Spooky Stories, Stuff the Scarecrow

Activities: Fruity Links, Happy Hands, Sticky Balloons, Tree Trimming

Snacks and Suppers: Bat Cake, Breakfast Casserole, Coated Pretzel Logs, Country Crows, Orange Fizzy Sherbet, Orange Frothy Juice, Orange Pinwheel Sandwiches, Pumpkin Muffins

Favors: Candy-Coated Necklaces, Dough Delights, Munchies for the Munchkins

Big Top
Circus Party

Bring in the clowns and have a three-ring sleepover!

Invitations: Artistic Announcement, Clever Kites, Come-on-Over Clocks, Cookie Cutter Creations, Cracker Jack Jingles, Snack Sensations, Train Treats, Wiffle Words

Decorations: Bundles of Balloons, Heaps of Horses, Music in Your Ears, Under the Big Top

Games: Cannonball Catch, Clowns and Balloons, Lion Tamers, Memory of an Elephant, Water Balloon Fight

Activities: Elephant Parade, Face Painting, Fruity Links

Snacks and Suppers: Caramel Popcorn, Cheeseburger Pizza Pie, Cheese Grits, Chicken Taco Wedges, Cottage Cheese Face, Lion Cake, Mud Dunkers, Pink Lemonade

Favors: Candy-Coated Necklaces, Circus Sweets, Crayon Creations, Makeover Memories, Pom-Pom Pals

Blast Off!
Space Party

Have a party that is "out of this world"!

Invitations: Beach Balls, Clever Kites, Come-on-Over Clocks, Cookie Cutter Creations, Parachute People, Perky Pinwheels, Starry Sensation, Tantalizing Tickets, Toilet Tissue Talker, Toothbrush Tote

Decorations: Bundles of Balloons, Destination Unknown, Say "Cheese," Universal Appeal

Games: Alien Planet, Astronaut Relay, Falling Stars, Orbit Game

Activities: Ceiling Shows, Get-Away Box, Poster Board Puppets, Sleepover Times

Snacks and Suppers: Asteroid Meat Muffins, Constellation Cookies, Potato Planets, Skillet Solar System, Spaceship Dessert, Spaceship Salad

Favors: Pretty Pads of Paper, Space Samples, Toothy Treats

Boogie With the Beat
Music Party

Let the children dance and sing the night away with musical fun.

Invitations: Beach Balls, Cracker Jack Jingles, Letters and Lines, Manicures and Makeovers, Sleepover Sue (or Sam), Snack Sensations

Decorations: Bundles of Balloons, Midnight Celebration, Music in Your Ears

Games: Balloon Stomp, Fancy Fingers, Hum That Tune, Moving to the Music, Musical Bus Seats

Activities: And the Beat Goes On, Ceiling Shows, Glowing Reviews

Snacks and Suppers: Bach's Beef and Bow Ties, Breakfast Bread Score, Chocolate Chip Shake, Coated Pretzel Logs, Drum Cake, Note Bread

Favors: Basket of Goodies, Framed Favor, Happy Hula Hoops

Cactus and Sand

Desert Party

Plan a South-of-the-Border Party or Arizona Desert Party and use the following hot ideas!

Invitations: Beautiful Blooms, Camp-Out Cutouts, Cookie Cutter Creations, Party Blowers, Perky Pinwheels, Sandy Signs

Decorations: Bundles of Balloons, Destination Unknown, Fantastic Flowers, Sunny Delight

Games: Crepe Paper Cacti, Desert Dreams, Feather Flight, Flower Picking

Activities: Cactus Creation, Colored Sand Creations, Dough Critters

Snacks and Suppers: Fiesta Feast, Milk and Honey Shakes, Pretty Pretzels, Sandy Pudding, Spicy Cheese Grits, Sun Cookies

Favors: Beaded Bookmarks, Jump Rope Reminders, Munchies for the Munchkins

Calling All Explorers!

Lewis and Clark Party

Explore lands and rivers unknown with a gang of fast friends!

Invitations: Beautiful Blooms, Buckets of Fun, Camp-Out Cutouts, Catchy Caterpillars, Equestrian Invitation, Sandy Signs, Sleepover Sue (or Sam), Toilet Tissue Talker, Toothbrush Tote, Train Treats, Treasure Map Tokens

Decorations: Bundles of Balloons, Calling All Bird Watchers, Destination Unknown, Fantastic Flowers, Heaps of Horses, Paradise Party, Swamp of Critters

Games: Bird's Eggs, Derby Races, Explorer's List, Explorer's Search, Flower Picking, Gone Fishing, Lasso Contest, Leaping Frogs, Trail Riding

Activities: Get-Away Box, Horse Parade, Tree Trimming

Snacks and Suppers: Breakfast Pizza, Camp-Out Tent, Gelatin Boats, One-Pot Barbecue, Sailing Sandwiches, Swamp Water

Favors: Cute Canteens, Paratrooper Treats

Countdown!

Numbers Party

Plan a numbers party for a child who is just starting school or for older children who adore math!

Invitations: Beach Balls, Catchy Caterpillars, Come-on-Over Clocks, Eggs-tra Special Envelope, Sleepover Sue (or Sam), Snack Sensations, Toothbrush Tote

Decorations: Bundles of Balloons, Midnight Celebration, Numbers Everywhere

Games: Bucket Toss, Layers and Layers, Number Balloons, Number Game

Activities: Candy Counting, Fireworks Show

Snacks and Suppers: Chocolate Chip Milkshake, Fruity Animals, Ice Cream Balls, Train Track Vegetables

Favors: Candy-Coated Necklaces, Happy Hula Hoops

Cowboy Up! Cowgirl Up!

Rodeo Party

Ride the range with your guests as you lasso the night away!

Invitations: Come-on-Over Clocks, Cookie Cutter Creations, Cracker Jack Jingles, Equestrian Invitation, Sandy Signs, Sleepover Sue (or Sam), Toilet Tissue Talker

Decorations: Bundles of Balloons, Destination Unknown, Down on the Farm, Heaps of Horses, Pet Party

Games: Chapstick Corral, Derby Races, Horseshoes and Obstacle Courses, Lasso Contest, Wild Bull Roundup

Activities: Colorful Cows, Horse Parade, Leather Loops

Snacks and Suppers: Camp-Out Tent, Fiesta Feast, Mud Dunkers, One-Pot Barbecue, Palomino Pony Milk, Spicy Cheese Grits, Wagon Wheels

Favors: Pom-Pom Pals, Wooden Spoon Someones

Dinosaurs Delight!

Paleontology Party

Who can resist a good dinosaur party? Have your guests pretend to be dinosaurs or search for fossils as they become paleontologists and dinosaur lovers for the night.

Invitations: Buckets of Fun, Cookie Cutter Creations, Letters and Lines, Party Blowers, Perky Pinwheels, Sandy Signs, Snack Sensations

Decorations: Bundles of Balloons, Digging for Dinos, Say "Cheese," Swamp of Critters

Games: Digging for Info, Dinosaur Dig, Dinosaur Hideout, Discovering Dinosaur Eggs, Eggs in the Nest, Hidden Bones, Meat Eaters versus Plant Eaters, T-Rex Battles, Toy Tossing, Who Am I?

Activities: Gelatin Jewels, Muddy Mess, TV Time, Vegetable Landscapes

Snacks and Suppers: Breakfast Casserole, Dressed-Up Bananas, Sloppy Joes and Janes, Swamp Water

Favors: Magnificent Magnifiers, Munchies for the Munchkins, Toothy Treats

Feathers and Fun

Bird-Watching Party

Excite the ornithologists in your group with these fun bird games and ideas.

Invitations: Binocular Bonanzas, Catchy Caterpillars, Cookie Cutter Creations, Eggs-tra Special Envelope, Ladybug Letters, Perky Pinwheels

Decorations: Bundles of Balloons, Calling All Bird Watchers, Down on the Farm, Pet Party

Games: Bird Watching, Bird's Eggs, Eggs in the Nest, Feather Flight, Feathers in the Air, Rescue the Baby Birds, Robin's Feathers, Toy Tossing, Who Am I?

Activities: Feed the Birds, Sleepover Times, Vegetable Landscapes

Snacks and Suppers: Baby Chick Rolls, Bird's Nest Chocolatey Treats, Birds in the Nest, Country Crows, Eggs in a Nest, Fruity Animals, Pink Flamingo Fluff Shake

Favors: Pail of Paints and Paste, Rainy-Day Rainsticks

Happy Heartbeats

Valentine's Party

Have a festive February party and create Valentines for friends and family members.

Invitations: Bundle of Bears, Cookie Cutter Creations, Letters and Lines, Manicures and Makeovers, Party Blowers, Snack Sensations

Decorations: Bundles of Balloons, Fantastic Flowers, Heart-Felt Hangings and Decorations, Music in Your Ears

Games: Balloon Scrabble, Flower Picking, Spoken from the Heart, Stolen Heart

Activities: Fruity Links, Happy Hands, Hearts and Lace, TV Time

Snacks and Suppers: Cheeseburger Pizza Pie, Cinderella Cake, Stuffed Tomato Salad

Favors: Happy Hula Hoops, Kooky Cookie Cutters, Wooden Spoon Someones

Happy New Year!

New Year's Party

Bring in the New Year with favorite friends, food, and fun!

Invitations: Bundle of Bears, Come-on-Over Clocks, Confetti-Filled Firecracker, Letters and Lines, Manicures and Makeovers, Sleepover Sue (or Sam)

Decorations: Bundles of Balloons, Heart-Felt Hangings and Decorations, Midnight Celebration, Music in Your Ears, Numbers Everywhere

Games: Balloon Scrabble; Bucket Toss; Twelve-Tag; When, Where, and What?

Activities: Calendar Notes, Candy Cottage, Fireworks Show, Resolutions and Rhymes

Snacks and Suppers: Calendar Creation, Candlelight Salad, Clock Cake, Resolution Cookies, Train Track Vegetables, Waffle Sandwiches

Favors: Pretty Pads of Paper, Tick-Tock Take-Home

Hold the Presses!

Newspaper Party

It's a party for all the writer and journalist wanna-bes!

Invitations: Come-on-Over Clocks, Cracker Jack Jingles, ID Invitations, Letters and Lines, Newsy Notes, Snack Sensations, Toilet Tissue Talker

Decorations: Bundles of Balloons, Midnight Celebration, Say "Cheese," Stop the Presses!

Games: Headline Hunters, Interview a Friend, Newspaper Scavenger Hunt, Paper Carrier Contest, Photo Scavenger Hunt

Activities: Art in the Dark, Calendar Notes, Resolutions and Rhymes, Sleepover Times

Snacks and Suppers: Asteroid Meat Muffins, Ice Cream Balls, Waffle Sandwiches

Favors: Fancy Fountains of Ink, Pretty Pads of Paper

Hooray for the Red, White, and Blue!

Patriotic Party

Help your guests celebrate the great United States with these patriotic suggestions.

Invitations: Confetti-Filled Firecracker, Cookie Cutter Creations, Letters and Lines, Party Blowers, Snack Sensations

Decorations: Bundles of Balloons; Music in Your Ears; Say "Cheese"; Sunny Delight; True for the Red, White, and Blue

Games: Balloon Scrabble, Firecracker Exchange, Jell-O Toss, Patriotic Popping, Spinning Stars, Star-Studded Race, Water Balloon Fight

Activities: Fireworks Show, Patriotic Footprints, Resolutions and Rhymes

Snacks and Suppers: Colored Popcorn Balls, Flag Cookie, Patriotic Puffs, Stuffed Tomato Salad

Favors: Basket of Goodies, Dough Delights, Paratrooper Treats

I Spy!

Secret Agent Party

Turn your home into Sleepover Detective Agency, and let the secret agents go to work!

Invitations: Binocular Bonanzas, Confetti-Filled Firecracker, ID Invitations, Letters and Lines, Message in a Bottle, Newsy Notes, Super Sunglasses, Tantalizing Tickets

Decorations: Bundles of Balloons, Destination Unknown, Say "Cheese," Whodunit Decorations

Games: Detective Chase, Hidden Bones, I Spy, Layers and Layers, Operation Code Name, Wee Willie Winker, Who Am I?

Activities: Decorated Scarves, Poster Board Puppets, Spyglasses

Snacks and Suppers: Magic Juice, Mystery Cake, Sloppy Joes and Janes, Spyglass Bagels

Favors: Magic Moments, Magnificent Magnifiers, Toothy Treats

It's a Jungle Out There!

Rain Forest Party

Practice your Tarzan yell and make some fun memories with this party.

Invitations: Beautiful Blooms, Catchy Caterpillars, Cookie Cutter Creations, Jungle Jottings, Party Blowers

Decorations: Bundle of Balloons, Calling All Bird Watchers, Fantastic Flowers, Swamp of Critters

Games: Bird's Eggs, Flower Picking, Flying Bats, Frogs in the Pond, Leaping Frogs, Log Cabin Treehouse

Activities: Critter Catcher, Get-Away Box, Tree Trimming, Vegetable Landscapes

Snacks and Suppers: Baby Chick Rolls, Forest Salad, Fruity Animals, Funny Frogs, Rain Water Shakes, Spider Treats, Swamp Water, Tiger Cake

Favors: Dough Delights, Rainy-Day Rainsticks

It's a Mystery to Me!

Mystery Party

Create a mystery to be solved by the guests, or have them divide into teams and create a mystery of their own.

Invitations: Binocular Bonanzas, Cracker Jack Jingles, ID Invitations, Letters and Lines, Message in a Bottle, Newsy Notes, Super Sunglasses, Treasure Map Tokens

Decorations: Bundles of Balloons, Destination Unknown, Midnight Celebration, Whodunit Decorations

Games: Detective Chase, Hidden Bones, Mummy Wrap, Ransom Money Scavenger Hunt, Wee Willie Winker, What's Missing? Who Am I?

Activities: Art in the Dark, Funny Faces in a Frame, Poster Board Puppets, Spyglasses

Snacks and Suppers: Magic Juice, Mystery Cake, Sloppy Joes and Janes, Spyglass Bagels

Favors: Magic Moments, Magnificent Magnifiers

Land Ho!

Pirate Party

"Ho, ho, ho and a house full of fun!" That's what this pirate party will be for all involved!

Invitations: Binocular Bonanzas, Camp-Out Cutouts, Letters and Lines, Message in a Bottle, Perky Pinwheels, Sandy Signs, Treasure Map Tokens

Decorations: Bundles of Balloons, Destination Unknown, Paradise Party, Sunny Delight, "X" Marks the Spot

Games: Cannonball Catch, Catch the Coconuts, Feather Flight, Gold Spinning Contest, Hidden Bones, I Spy, Island Hopping, Pirate Limbo, Pirate's Plunder, Water Balloon Fight

Activities: Decorated Scarves, Glowing Reviews, Spyglasses, Sword Fighting

Snacks and Suppers: Chicken Taco Wedges, Country Crows, Fishbowl Gelatin, Fruity Animals, Luau Kabobs, Mud Dunkers, One-Pot Barbecue, Rain Water Shakes, Sailing Sandwiches, Sandy Pudding, Swamp Water

Favors: Magic Moments, Pail of Paints and Paste, Wooden Spoon Someones

Let the Sun Shine In!

Summer Party

Herald the arrival of summer, celebrate the end of school, or get rid of the winter blues with this warm, sunny party!

Invitations: Beach Balls, Beautiful Blooms, Buckets of Fun, Confetti-Filled Firecracker, Cookie Cutter Creations, Sandy Signs, Sleepover Sue (or Sam), Super Sunglasses

Decorations: Bundle of Balloons, Calling All Bird Watchers, Paradise Party, Sunny Delight

Games: Balloon Scrabble, Beach Ball Bowling, Beach Ball Volleyball, Flower Picking, Goggles and Giggles, Gone Fishing, Sit-Down Volleyball, Water Balloon Fight

Activities: Feed the Birds, Hot Air Balloon, Patriotic Footprints

Snacks and Suppers: Fishbowl Gelatin, Cheese Grits, Orange Fizzy Sherbet, Rain Water Shakes, Sandy Pudding, Sun Cookies, Sunny Sandwiches, Train Track Vegetables

Favors: Pail of Paints and Paste, Spray Bottle Sensations, Sunny Sun Visors

Lions and Tigers and Elephants, Oh My!

Safari Party

Dream of these creatures of the wild during an African Safari Party.

Invitations: Binocular Bonanzas, Camp-Out Cutouts, Cookie Cutter Creations, Jungle Jottings, Treasure Map Tokens

Decorations: Bundles of Balloons, Pet Party, Sunny Delight, Swamp of Critters

Games: Animal Answers, Lions and Lambs, Safari Search, Who Am I?

Activities: Dough Critters, Elephant Parade, Muddy Mess

Snacks and Suppers: Breakfast Pizza, Forest Salad, Funny Frogs, Frothy Orange Juice, Lion Cake, Pizza-Chicken Roll-Ups

Favors: Dough Delights, Rainy-Day Rainsticks, Toothy Treats

Luaus, Leis, and Limbos

Island Party

Turn your home into a tropical paradise with this sleepover party.

Invitations: Artistic Announcement, Beach Balls, Beautiful Blooms, Buckets of Fun, Confetti-Filled Firecracker, Message in a Bottle, Starry Sensation, Treasure Map Tokens

Decorations: Bundles of Balloons, Calling All Bird Watchers, Destination Unknown, Fantastic Flowers, Music in Your Ears, Paradise Party, Sunny Delight, Swamp of Critters

Games: Beach Ball Volleyball, Bird's Eggs, Catch the Coconuts, Feather Flight, Flower Picking, Island Hopping, Leaping Frogs, Lei Accolades

Activities: Edible Jewelry, Fuzzy Fish, Pom-Pom Puppets

Snacks and Suppers: Breakfast Pizza, Candied Apples, Dressed-Up Bananas, Fizzy Sherbet, Gelatin Boats, Luau Kabobs, Sailing Sandwiches

Favors: Happy Hula Hoops, Riveting Ribbon Skirts, Striking Straws

Luck and Leprechauns

Leprechaun Party

Celebrate this party in March or anytime you want to search for a pot of gold!

Invitations: Clever Kites, Cookie Cutter Creations, Letters and Lines, Message in a Bottle, Party Blowers, Rainbow Reminders

Decorations: Bundles of Balloons, Say "Cheese," Lucky Leprechauns

Games: Balloon Scrabble, Coin Collecting, Jell-O Toss, Lions and Lambs, Lucky Leprechauns, Scavenger Hunt, Wishes and Gold

Activities: Cupcake Cutouts, Face Painting, Fruity Links, Poster Board Puppets

Snacks and Suppers: Forest Salad, Green Pinwheel Sandwiches, Lime Fizzy Sherbet, One-Pot Barbecue, Rainbow Cake

Favors: Winning Windsock, Windy Wonders

My Favorite Pet

Pet Party

Is there a new puppy in the house? Welcome a child's new pet with this sleepover party.

Invitations: Buckets of Fun, Bundles of Bears, Catchy Caterpillars, Cookie Cutter Creations, Equestrian Invitation

Decorations: Bundles of Balloons, Calling All Bird Watchers, Heaps of Horses, Heart-Felt Hangings and Decorations, Pet Party

Games: Bird's Eggs, Doggy Run, Hidden Bones, Leaping Frogs, Lucky Horseshoes, Mousetrap, Nine Lives of a Cat, Pet Parade, Pillowcase Race, Puppy Power, Treats for the Puppy, Who Am I?

Activities: Elephant Parade, Fuzzy Fish, Horse Parade

Snacks and Suppers: Baby Chick Rolls, Doggie's Delight, Eggs in a Nest, Funny Frogs, Kitty Cookies, Pink Flamingo Fluff, Rain Water Shake

Favors: Dough Delights, Kooky Cookie Cutters, Pretty Pads of Paper

Once Upon a Time

Fairy Tale Party

Live happily ever after (well, at least for a night) when you plan this sleepover party.

Invitations: Artistic Announcement, Beautiful Blooms, Bundles of Bears, Letters and Lines, Manicures and Makeovers, Rainbow Reminders, Sleepover Sue (or Sam)

Decorations: Bundles of Balloons, Fantastic Flowers, Heaps of Horses, Heart-Felt Hangings and Decorations, Midnight Celebration

Games: Cinderella's Shoe, Fairy-Tale Fun, Flower Picking, Porridge in the Pot, Run from the Wolf, Stolen Heart

Activities: Candy Cottage, Poster Board Puppets, Sleepover Times, TV Time

Snacks and Suppers: Seven Dwarf Float, Candied Apples, Caramel Apples, Cinderella Cake, Cinderella's Pumpkin Bread, Funny Frogs, Hot Porridge Snack Mix, One-Pot Barbecue, Red Riding Hood Muffins, Snack Mix

Favors: Munchies for the Munchkins, Wooden Spoon Someones

Partying Painters
Art Party

Plan for the precocious party attendees with this creative party.

Invitations: Artistic Announcement, Beautiful Blooms, Letters and Lines, Paper Bag Puppets, Party Blowers, Rainbow Reminders, Sandy Signs

Decorations: Bundles of Balloons, Painter's Preparations, Say "Cheese"

Games: Colors of the Rainbow, Flower Picking, Jell-O Toss, Pass the Paintbrush

Activities: Art in the Dark, Artists at Work, Colored Sand Creations, Funny Faces in a Frame

Snacks and Suppers: Cheeseburger Pizza Pie, Dressed-Up Bananas, Pink Lemonade, Rainbow Cake, Rainbow Kabobs, Waffle Sandwich

Favors: Crayon Creations, Pail of Paints and Paste

Signs of Spring
Spring Party

Welcome spring with this colorful party.

Invitations: Artistic Announcement, Beautiful Blooms, Clever Kites, Cookie Cutter Creations, Eggs-tra Special Envelope, Perky Pinwheels, Rainbow Reminders

Decorations: Bundles of Balloons, Calling All Bird Watchers, Fantastic Flowers, Sunny Delight

Games: Balloon Scrabble, Bird's Eggs, Blooms in a Bowl, Colors of the Rainbow, Feather Flight, Fill the Vase, Flower Picking, Flower Twister Game, Jell-O Toss, Leaping Frogs

Activities: Happy Hands, Hot Air Balloon, Sticky Balloons, Tree Trimming

Snacks and Suppers: Baby Chick Rolls, Butterfly Cake, Fruity Animals, Funny Frogs, Pink Lemonade, Rain Water Shakes, Rainbow Cake, Springy Pinwheel Sandwiches, Sunny Sandwiches

Favors: Blooming Bouquets, Potpourri Pouches

Snakes and Snails and Alligator Tails

Critter Party

That's what little boys—and lots of girls—are fond of!

Invitations: Buckets of Fun, Bundles of Bears, Catchy Caterpillars, Eggs-tra Special Envelope, Ladybug Letters, Sandy Signs

Decorations: Bundles of Balloons, Calling All Bird Watchers, Pet Party, Swamp of Critters

Games: Alligator Chase, Frogs in the Pond, Gone Fishing, Leaping Frogs, Spiders in the Web, Toy Tossing, Twisted Tongues, Who Am I?

Activities: Critter Catcher, Dough Critters, Muddy Mess, Vegetable Landscapes

Snacks and Suppers: Forest Salad, Funny Frogs, Lizard Chocolatey Treats, Luau Kabobs, Pretty Pretzels, Snailshell Pinwheel Sandwiches, Swamp Water

Favors: Dough Delights, Magnificent Magnifiers

Summer's Torch

Summer Olympics Party

Carry the torch and bring home the gold!

Invitations: Beach Balls, Confetti-Filled Firecracker, Parachute People, Paper Bag Puppets, Party Blowers, Perky Pinwheels, Rainbow Reminders, Super Sunglasses

Decorations: Bundle of Balloons, Say "Cheese," Sunny Delight

Games: Beach Ball Volleyball, Finger Gymnastics, Gymnastic Judging, Party Blower Balloon Race, Three-Legged Sack Race, Torch Bearers, Water Balloon Fight

Activities: Bicycle Brigade, Cupcake Cutouts, Patriotic Footprints

Snacks and Suppers: Butterfly Cake, Magic Juice, Spicy Cheese Grits, Sun Cookies, Sunny Sandwiches

Favors: Jump Rope Reminders, Sunny Sun Visors

Take Me Out to the Ball Game!

Sports Party

Score a home run with this creative sleepover!

Invitations: Binocular Bonanzas, Come-on-Over Clocks, Confetti-Filled Firecracker, Cookie Cutter Creations, Cracker Jack Jingles, Snack Sensations, Super Sunglasses, Wiffle Words

Decorations: Bundles of Balloons, Festive Fall, Play Ball!

Games: Bubble-Blowing Contest; Dizzy Batters; Flag Zigzag; Inside Batting Contest; Peanuts, Get Your Peanuts!; Play Ball!; Race Around the Diamond; Racing the Bases; Stolen Ball; Wiffle Ball Instructions; Wrong-Glove Wrangling

Activities: Cupcake Cutouts, Sleepover Times

Snacks and Suppers: Football Chocolatey Treats, Ice Cream Balls, Magic Juice, Patriotic Puffs, Twisty Corn Dog

Favors: Happy Hula Hoops, Painted Paddles, Sunny Sun Visors

To the Rescue!

Superhero Party

Save the world—just make sure the guests return before bedtime!

Invitations: Artistic Announcement, Camp-Out Cutouts, Clever Kites, Cracker Jack Jingles, ID Invitations, Perky Pinwheels, Sleepover Sue (or Sam), Superhero Stand-Ups

Decorations: Bundles of Balloons, Destination Unknown, Say "Cheese"

Games: Flying Bats, Number Balloons, Spider Tossing, Superheroes, Tug-of-War

Activities: Fruity Links, Silly Socks, Superhero Cape

Snacks and Suppers: Bach's Beef and Bow Ties, Forest Salad, Fruity Links, Mud Dunkers, Magic Juice, Patriotic Puffs, Supercool Pie

Favors: Candy-Coated Necklaces, Paratrooper Treats, Wooden Spoon Someones

Under the Sea

Sea Creature Party

On land or sea, this is a way-cool party for your guests!

Invitations: Beach Balls, Buckets of Fun, Cookie Cutter Creations, Party Blowers, Perky Pinwheels, Rainbow Reminders, Sandy Signs, Snack Sensations

Decorations: Bundles of Balloons, Paradise Party, Pet Party, Under the Sea Decorations

Games: Goggles and Giggles, Gone Fishing, Octopus Race, Seashells and Sand Pails, Shark Attack, Swimming Balloons, Who Am I?

Activities: Ceiling Shows, Fuzzy Fish, Gelatin Jewels, Sticky Balloons

Snacks and Suppers: Fishbowl Gelatin, Gelatin Boats, Luau Kabobs, Rain Water Shakes, Sailing Sandwiches, Snailshell Pinwheel Sandwiches, Swamp Water

Favors: Jewelry Keepsake, Sand and Sea Symbols

With a "Moo-Moo" Here

Farm Party

Old MacDonald never had this much fun!

Invitations: Beautiful Blooms, Buckets of Fun, Cookie Cutter Creations, Eggs-tra Special Envelope, Equestrian Invitation

Decorations: Bundles of Balloons, Calling All Bird Watchers, Down on the Farm, Festive Fall, Heaps of Horses, Pet Party, Swamp of Critters

Games: Apple Bobbing, Bird's Eggs, Derby Races, Egg Toss, Farm Friends, Farmer and the Cows, Flower Picking, Gone Fishing, Haybale Hopping, Herding the Sheep, Jell-O Toss, Lasso Contest, Pigs in the Mud, Shear the Sheep, Spiders in the Web, Wild Bull Roundup, Who Am I?

Activities: Fuzzy Fish, Get-Away Box, Pom-Pom Puppets, TV Time

Snacks and Suppers: Baby Chick Rolls, Chocolate Cow Shake, Eggs in a Nest, Forest Salad, Fruity Animals, Mud Dunkers, Palomino Pony Shake, Pumpkin Muffins, Sunflower Cookies

Favors: Dough Delights, Rainy-Day Rainsticks

You Oughta Be in Pictures!

Photography Party

Smile and say, "Cheese! This sleepover's a breeze!"

Invitations: Artistic Announcement, Bundle of Bears, Cracker Jack Jingles, ID Invitations, Letters and Lines, Manicures and Makeovers, Sleepover Sue (or Sam), Toothbrush Tote

Decorations: Bundles of Balloons, Heart-Felt Hangings and Decorations, Say "Cheese"

Games: Paper Carrier Contest, Flower Picking, Number Game, Photo Scavenger Hunt

Activities: Edible Jewelry, Face Painting, Funny Faces in a Frame, TV Time

Snacks and Suppers: Cottage Cheese Face, Forest Salad, Magic Juice, Pizza-Chicken Roll-Ups, Photo Cake

Favors: Beaded Bookmarks, Framed Favor, Pom-Pom Pals

Chapter 3

Notes for Nodders

Interesting Invitations for Friends

Creative and personalized invitations will excite your slumber party guests and have them anxiously awaiting your party. Let your party host create a cute invitation using colorful construction paper; typing paper or tagboard; and markers, glitter pens, crayons, or paint. Decorate the invitation with stickers; yarn; ribbon; glitter; or natural items such as shells, small pebbles, and small cones.

Make the invitation in the style of a standard card fitting your party theme, using cookie cutters or pictures from coloring books, children's books, or magazines. For example, try a pig pattern for a farm party. Trace and cut the pig on pink construction paper such that the pig's back will be on a fold. Use puffy pink and black paint to add facial features, hooves, and a tail. On the inside, write, "You'll squeal with delight at my slumber party. Come join the fun!" Then add the pertinent party information.

If a small toy or trinket related to your theme will be part of your invitation, find a creative way to personalize the item. If the spring party will include an egg hunt, for instance, write or paint the guest's name on a plastic pail. Then write the party details on a bunny-shaped note. Place the note inside the pail, with instructions to bring the pail to the party. Hand-deliver the pail to your guests. At the party, you may allow the guests to add more decorations to the pail before the egg hunt.

For more invitation ideas, choose a suggestion in this chapter and personalize it for your party. Be sure to include the following on each invitation:

★ The host's name
★ The host's parent's name(s)
★ The address of the party
★ Specific directions or a map to the party
★ The party date
★ The beginning and ending times of the party
★ An RSVP number and date
★ Special instructions (i.e., what to bring and/or what to wear)

Once you have completed your clever invitations, be sure your guests receive their invitations one to two weeks before the party. If you mail the invitations, use a padded envelope or small box to keep three-dimensional invitations from being crushed.

Artistic Announcement

Stir the creative juices of your future slumber party attendees with these clever invitations.

Materials

★ Scissors
★ Oaktag, cut in the shape of an artist's palette, one per guest
★ Paintbrush for decorating
★ Paint in a variety of colors
★ Tape
★ Small paintbrushes, one per guest
★ Pen

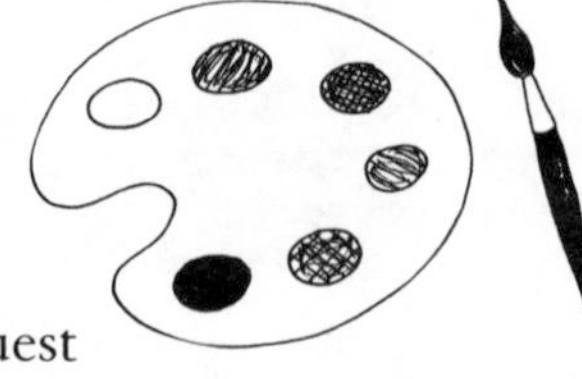

Directions

Cut a hole in each palette for the artist's thumb. Using the paintbrush, dab spots of paint around the edge, to make the palette look realistic. Tape a small paintbrush on the edge of the palette. When the paint is dry, write the details of the sleepover on the back of the palette.

Beach Balls

Give your guests a constant reminder of the upcoming sleepover as they play with this party invitation.

Materials

★ One beach ball per guest
★ Permanent black marker
★ Padded envelopes

Directions

Inflate the beach ball. Write the sleepover details and instructions on the ball. When the marker is dry, deflate the ball and place it in a padded envelope. Add a note to your guest, instructing him or her to inflate the ball and read the message. Also, remind your guest to bring the ball to the sleepover, if you choose to use it in some of your games.

Beautiful Blooms

Welcome spring with these blooming invitations. Use these invitations for a garden slumber party, spring slumber party, or all-occasion party.

Materials

- ★ Scissors
- ★ Yellow construction paper
- ★ Glue
- ★ Small white paper plate, one per guest
- ★ Pen
- ★ Envelopes

Directions

Cut petals from the yellow construction paper and glue around the outside of the paper plate. When the glue is dry, write the party details on the paper plate. Fold the flower carefully, place it in an envelope, and mail it to your guests. Or, glue the flower onto a green pencil or green-painted dowel rod and hand-deliver the flower invitation.

Binocular Bonanzas

Looking for a new invitation idea? Try this on for size! Use this idea for a bird-watching party, spy party, mystery party, or all-occasion party.

Materials

- ★ Colored markers
- ★ Typing or construction paper
- ★ Hole punchers
- ★ Pair of toy binoculars, one per guest
- ★ Ribbon or yarn

Directions

Write the details of the slumber party on the paper, using one of the colored markers. Punch a hole in the corner of the note. Attach the note to the binoculars with the ribbon or yarn.

Buckets of Fun

Personalize this invitation and use it for a beach party, explorer's party, paleontologist slumber party, Easter sleepover, or any number of fun get-togethers.

Materials

★ Puffy paints or permanent markers
★ Pail and shovel for each guest
★ Colored typing paper
★ Ribbon or yarn

Directions

Write the guest's name on the pail, using the paints or markers. Then decorate with flowers, squiggly lines, hearts, animals, and so on. Decorate the shovel, also. Tie a note using ribbon or yarn to the handle of the pail, supplying the slumber party details.

Bundle of Bears

Have this adorable bear invite your guests to a stuffed animal slumber party, puppet party, zoo party, or wild animal party. You can finish the bear completely for the invitation, or simply make an outline and have the guests bring the bear to the party to add the finishing touches.

Materials

★ Pen or pencil
★ Large bear pattern
★ Felt
★ Scissors
★ Puffy paints
★ Buttons, craft eyes, rick-rack, ribbon
★ Safety pins

Directions

Trace the outline of a bear onto the felt. Cut out. Add facial features, clothing, and/or decorations with the paints and other craft items. When the bear is dry, pin a note to the bear with party details and this message: "I just couldn't bear it if you didn't come to my slumber party!"

Variation: Trace only the outline of the bear. Cut two shapes for each guest, but only deliver one. Pin a note on the bear shape with party details and a message to bring the bear to the party. At the party, have each guest decorate his or her own bear. Use a hot-glue gun under adult supervision to glue the decorated bear to another bear shape, leaving a small opening at the bottom. Stuff the bear with batting mate-

rial, then glue closed. Take the stuffed animal home as a party favor.

Camp-Out Cutouts

Whether you're having an outdoor or indoor camp-out, use these invitations to excite and invite your guests.

Materials

- ★ Scissors
- ★ Construction paper in browns and greens
- ★ Glue or stapler
- ★ Black felt-tip pen

Directions

Cut the construction paper into tent shapes. Cut an extra triangle for the tent flap. Glue or staple the tent flap into place. Write the details of the party on the front or back of the tent. Be sure to note whether the party will be inside or outside so the kids will come prepared for the weather, if necessary.

Catchy Caterpillars

Make these caterpillar puzzles for your guests to assemble and read.

Materials

- ★ Plastic cup or drinking glass
- ★ Pen or pencil
- ★ Colored construction paper
- ★ Scissors
- ★ Colored markers
- ★ Envelopes

Directions

Using the cup or glass, trace enough circles on construction paper to make a lengthy caterpillar, five or six, perhaps. Trace each circle unattached to the other circles. Add two legs to all but one of the circles. Add antennae and eyes to the legless circle. Cut all of the circles out. Write the party details on the circles, one detail per circle, if possible. Then put all the pieces in an envelope, with a short note to tell your guest to assemble the caterpillar for a surprise message.

Clever Kites

Plan to use this invitation for a spring or fall slumber party when the trees are swaying, breezes are blowing, and kites are flying.

Materials

- ★ Colorful permanent markers

* White cotton material (e.g., an old sheet or pillowcase), cut into strips for kite tails
* One kite per guest

Directions

Write the details of the party on the strip of white material. Attach the tail to the kite. Include a small note that asks the guests to bring the kites to the party. Plan to fly the kites in the late afternoon of the party or the early morning of the next day.

Come-on-Over Clocks

"It's time for a party," announces this clock! Have your guests counting the minutes until the party begins with this cute invitation.

Materials

* White typing paper, construction paper, or tagboard
* Drinking glass or cup for pattern
* Black felt-tip pen
* Scissors
* Black construction paper
* Paper fasteners

Directions

Fold the white paper. Using the glass or cup for a pattern, draw a circle such that an area of the circle is on the fold. On the front, draw lines or numbers with the black pen to resemble a clock. On the inside, write, "It's time for a party!" and give the details. Cut hands for the clock from the black construction paper and add the hands to the front of the clock with the paper fasteners.

Variation: Purchase small clocks or inexpensive watches at a dollar store, and attach a note with the party details.

Confetti-Filled Firecracker

Your sleepover will explode with fun when the party begins with these exciting invitations! Use this idea for a New Year's Eve sleepover, Fourth of July sleepover, or any time you're planning an electrifying slumber party!

Materials

* Hole punchers
* Colored construction paper
* One empty paper towel roll per guest
* Masking tape
* Spoon

- ★ Pen or pencil
- ★ Typing paper
- ★ Paintbrushes
- ★ Red, black, and white paint
- ★ Red felt-tip pens

Directions

If you plan to use this invitation for a patriotic theme, punch holes from red, white, and blue construction paper. For any other theme, use an appropriate color or a variety of colors. Punch lots of holes for gobs of fun confetti! Close one end of the paper towel roll with masking tape. Use a spoon to put the confetti into the roll. Write the sleepover details on a sheet of paper. Roll the paper and place it inside the tube. Then close the other end of the roll with masking tape. Paint the firecracker with red, black, and white paint. When the paint is dry, tape a note on the outside of the firecracker instructing the guest to cut off one end of the firecracker to receive the message inside.

Cookie Cutter Creations

Cookie cutters make simple, easy patterns for invitations. Or the cookie cutter itself may be part of the invitation. Look for cookie cutters in department stores, party stores, or grocery stores. Choose one in a pattern related to your party and get cooking!

Materials

- ★ Cookie cutters
- ★ Pen or pencil
- ★ Typing paper, construction paper, or tagboard
- ★ Scissors
- ★ Stickers, glitter, paints, or markers

Directions

Choose a cookie cutter to go with your theme. Trace the shape on an appropriate color of paper. Cut out the shape and decorate using stickers, glitter, paints, or markers. Then write the details of the party on the back of the shape or inside of the shape if you've cut the pattern on a fold.

Variation: Use the cookie cutter itself as part of the invitation. Write the details of the party on a small piece of paper, and attach the note with ribbon to a cookie cutter. You could even use more than one cookie cutter per guest. For example, if you're having an under-the-sea party, locate cookie cutters in these various shapes: octopus, seahorses, whales, and dolphins. Use the ribbon to tie one of each shape together and attach a note with party details. The guest will have a remembrance of the slumber party as well as stencils to use for future art projects. Or, let the host of the party help you make your favorite sugar cookie recipe in a theme-related shape. Frost; then wrap in cellophane paper. Attach a note with the party details and deliver the cookies in person to each guest.

Cracker Jack Jingles

Let the guests find double surprises in their box of Cracker Jacks as you hide the sleepover invitation in the box of peanuts and popcorn.

Materials

- ★ Colorful, fine-tip pens
- ★ Colored typing paper
- ★ One box of Cracker Jacks per guest
- ★ Glue

Directions

Write the sleepover information on a small piece of typing paper. Carefully open the box of Cracker Jacks, so as not to tear the end of the box. Fold the note so that you can slide it into the box of popcorn. Close the popcorn box, and put a dab of glue on the end to reseal it.

Eggs-tra Special Envelope

Use this unique envelope for your invitation to a farm slumber party, Easter slumber party, or all-occasion party.

Materials

- ★ Typing paper (white or colored, according to theme)
- ★ Colored pens
- ★ One egg carton per guest

Directions

For this invitation, you can use white or colored typing paper. If you are using this idea for a farm party, use white paper. If the idea will be used for a party that includes an egg hunt, use a variety of colors. Decide on the words that will be included in the invitation. Try dividing the message into twelve sentences or notes. Write each sentence on half of a sheet of typing paper. (You may decide to print the message using a computer.) Wad each paper into an egg shape, and put one "egg" note in each section.

Variation: Write the invitation on eleven pieces of paper and include a small toy or trinket related to the party theme in the twelfth spot. Write the guest's name on the outside of the egg carton as well as instructions to read each note inside. Hand-deliver the invitation.

Equestrian Invitation

Invite your horse-loving friends over with these clever cutouts. This invitation works great for a western party, horse-show party, or farm party.

Materials

- ★ Pattern for horseshoe, cowboy boot, or cowboy hat
- ★ Pen or pencil
- ★ Brown or black construction paper
- ★ Scissors
- ★ White chalk

Directions

Decide which pattern you'd like to use. Trace one outline for each guest onto the construction paper. Cut out; then add the party details with white chalk.

ID Invitations

Make these identification cards for each guest to stir their imaginations and get them ready for the community theme slumber party.

Materials

- ★ Scissors
- ★ Colored oaktag
- ★ Ruler
- ★ Fine-tip markers
- ★ Polaroid camera
- ★ Clear Con-Tact or self-adhesive paper

Directions

Cut oaktag into three- by five-inch rectangles. Make one identification card per guest. Write information, such as name, age, eye color, and so on. Leave a place for a small head shot to be taken at the party. If you are doing a community or neighborhood sleepover theme, give each child an occupation to fit into the community and list that occupation on the card. Write a note giving the details of the sleepover. Ask the guest to bring the ID card to gain admittance to the party. At the party, take a Polaroid snapshot of each guest. Cut out just the head shot and glue it to the identification card. Have each child sign his or her card, and then cover the cards with clear self-adhesive paper during the party.

Jungle Jottings

Have a roaring good time at your slumber party! Start off with this lovable lion sleepover invitation.

Materials

- ★ Scissors
- ★ Yellow and brown construction paper
- ★ Ruler
- ★ Glue
- ★ Yellow paper plate, one per guest
- ★ Pencil
- ★ Bits of colored construction paper
- ★ Black marker

Directions

Cut strips of yellow and brown construction paper, three-quarter inch by three inches. Glue one end of each strip of paper around the outside of the plate rim. When the glue is dry, use a pencil to "curl" the lion's "mane" by rolling the unglued end of each strip of paper around a pencil and gently removing the pencil. Use the bits of colored construction paper to give the lion facial features. On the back of the lion, write, "Come to my slumber party for the adventure of a lifetime!"

Ladybug Letters

Make these cute insects for a creepy-crawly slumber party.

Materials

- ★ Red and black paint
- ★ Paintbrushes
- ★ Two large and one small paper plates per guest
- ★ Scissors
- ★ Stapler
- ★ Paper fasteners
- ★ Pen
- ★ Large envelopes

Directions

Using red, paint the small paper plate and one of the large paper plates. Paint the other large paper plate black. When the paint is dry, add black spots to the large red plate and add eyes to the small plate. Cut two wings from the black paper plate. With the left-over scraps, cut two antennae. Staple the head to the body. Staple the antennae to the head also. Attach the wings to the body with the paper fasteners. Write the sleepover details on the back of the ladybug. Slip the ladybug into a large envelope, and mail to your guests.

Letters and Lines

Your host will have fun spelling out this invitation! Find the food items at a grocery store or large department store.

Materials

★ Alphabet-shaped pasta, cereal, or cookies
★ Glue
★ Colored construction paper or tagboard
★ Padded envelopes

Directions

Decide what you want to say on the invitation. Make a prototype on a piece of paper to use as a guide. Then choose the letters you need to write the message. Glue the letters in place on the paper or tagboard. After the glue is dry, carefully place the note in a padded envelope to mail or hand-deliver.

Manicures and Makeovers

Who needs a beauty salon when you've got friends at a sleepover? Start the makeover evening off with these cute invitations.

Materials

★ Pen or pencil
★ Colored oaktag
★ Scissors
★ Fingernail polish
★ Toy ring
★ Padded envelopes

Directions

Trace a hand shape onto the oaktag and cut out for each sleepover guest. Paint the fingernails on the hand shape, using the fingernail polish. Place a toy ring on the fourth finger of the invitation. List the party details on the back of the hand. Tuck the hand-shaped invitations in padded envelopes, and send them to your guests.

Message in a Bottle

Use this fun invitation for a mystery, beach, pirate, or all-occasion party.

Materials

★ One clear plastic water bottle per guest
★ Scissors
★ White or colored typing paper
★ Permanent markers
★ Colorful ribbon

Directions

Empty, clean, and peel labels off of plastic water bottles. Allow the bottles to dry completely. Cut paper to fit inside the bottle. You want the paper to fit around the inside of the bottle, without overlapping. It may take a couple of tries to get the paper the right size. Use tweezers to retrieve the paper from the bottle, if necessary. After you have determined the correct size, write the slumber party details on the paper with the markers. Roll the paper and carefully slide it into the bottle, with the words on the outside. Use the tweezers, if necessary, to help the paper uncurl and fit inside the bottle. Be sure you can read the note from the outside of the bottle. Put the cap back on the bottle, and tie a ribbon around the neck of the bottle.

Newsy Notes

These notes are fun to make, fun to read, and especially nice for a mystery or detective party.

Materials

★ Scissors
★ Newspapers and old magazines
★ Glue
★ Construction paper or typing paper

Directions

Cut out letters from newspaper or magazine headlines to spell out the details of the party. Glue the letters onto construction or typing paper. Make one copy per guest.

Paper Bag Puppets

Deliver the materials to your guests to make a paper bag puppet. Encourage the friends to make a puppet at home to bring to the slumber party where the puppet productions will begin!

Materials

★ One lunch-sized paper bag per guest
★ Bits of construction paper
★ Yarn pieces
★ Pen
★ Paper

Directions

Open the paper bag and place bits of construction paper and yarn pieces inside. Include a note that gives the details of the party and encourages each guest to create a puppet using the materials provided. Ask the guest to bring the puppet to the party, and plan to put on a puppet show while at the slumber party.

Parachute People

These invitations fold and fit nicely into a small padded envelope. What a nice treat for the guest to receive a toy and party invitation, all in one!

Materials

★ Black permanent marker
★ White handkerchief, one per guest
★ Scissors
★ Yarn
★ Toy figurine, one per guest
★ Padded envelopes

Directions

Write the party details on each handkerchief. Use scissors to cut a small hole in each corner of the handkerchief. Cut yarn into four strips equal in length. Attach one strip of yarn to each corner of the handkerchief. Then attach the other end of each strip of yarn to the toy figurine. Fold the handkerchief and carefully roll the toy, wrapping the yarn and handkerchief around it. Place the parachutist in a padded envelope and mail to your guests.

Party Blowers

Herald your slumber party using party blowers found at department or party stores. Try to find a design related to the theme of your party.

Materials

★ Party blowers, one per guest
★ Black felt-tip pen
★ Small square of white or colored typing paper
★ Small strip of ribbon per party blower

Directions

Carefully unroll the party blower. Have an assistant hold the ends of the blower while you write the party invitation on the blower. Give the ink a chance to dry before letting the blower recurl. There will probably not be enough room to write the details of the party on the blower itself. Write those important details on a smaller piece of paper, and attach it to the blower using the strip of ribbon.

Perky Pinwheels

Delight your guests with these pinwheel party invitations. Hand-deliver them to your guests, or poke them into the grass at the guest's front door, ring the doorbell, and "blow away."

Materials

- ★ Black permanent marker
- ★ Pinwheels

Directions

Using the permanent marker, write the details of the party on the petals of the pinwheel. Be careful not to touch the petals until after the marker has had time to dry.

Rainbow Reminders

Use a rainbow of colors to remind your guest of the slumber party.

Materials

- ★ Black permanent marker
- ★ One box of crayons or markers per guest
- ★ Padded envelopes

Directions

Use the black marker to write the sleepover details on the back of the box of crayons or markers. Place the invitations in padded envelopes and mail to your guests.

Sandy Signs

Give your guests a hint of the fun to be had at the sleepover with this original invitation.

Materials

- ★ Powdered paint or colored drink mix (several colors)
- ★ Clean sand
- ★ Bowl
- ★ Small funnel
- ★ Clean, clear plastic water bottles, one per guest
- ★ Colored typing paper
- ★ Colorful ribbons
- ★ Colorful pens

Directions

Use the powdered paint or colored drink mix to give your sand vibrant hues. Pour some of the sand into a bowl and stir in a color. Make a variety of colors. Using a funnel, fill each empty, dry water bottle with different colors of sand and reseal the cap. Attach a note to the bottle with colored ribbon that says something to the effect of "Come help me watch for Mr. Sandman at my beach sleepover."

Sleepover Sue (or Sam)

Make each guest a paper doll complete with sleeping bag for an invitation and as part of the sleepover entertainment.

Materials

★ Store-bought paper doll, one per guest
★ Scissors
★ Colorful construction paper
★ Cotton balls
★ Glue
★ Colorful markers

Directions

Purchase paper dolls, or buy one doll and then use it as a guide for other patterns. Your host might have fun trying to make the dolls look like his or her guests. Cut rectangles out of the construction paper in the shape of sleeping bags, according to size of the dolls. Cut the sleeping bag with a flap on three-quarters of one side to fold over for the top of the sleeping bag. Stretch a cotton ball into a rectangular shape and glue it in place for a pillow. Fold over the top of the sleeping bag and glue just the bottom closed so that you can slip the paper doll inside. Write the sleepover details on the front of the sleeping bag. Be sure to remind the guests to bring the paper dolls to the sleepover. Save the clothes that come with the doll for play time during the slumber party.

Snack Sensations

Look in the snack and candy section of the grocery store to find creative ways to invite your guests.

Materials

★ An individually wrapped pack of chips, crackers, or candy, one per guest
★ Black felt-tip pen
★ Typing or construction paper

Directions

Decide on the snack you want to use. Write a clever message, along with the party details on the package or on a piece of paper attached to the snack item. Some examples of catchy phrases to use are provided here. Write your own message, according to the theme of your party.

★ Fish-shaped crackers: "There's nothing fishy about it! You're invited to a sea creature slumber party!"

★ Almond Joy candy bar: "It will be a joy to have you at my party!"
★ Popcorn: "Pop on over to my house for a slumber party."

Starry Sensations

Your guests will have as much fun deciphering this message as you will have making it! This idea is especially cute for a sleepover with a space theme or an outdoor camp-out.

Materials

★ Black construction paper, one sheet per child
★ Sharp-pointed pencil
★ Sticky notes
★ Long envelopes
★ Star stickers

Directions

On each sheet of paper, lightly write the sleepover details with the pencil. Then, using the point of the pencil, poke holes along the lines of each letter. Attach a sticky note to the front of the paper instructing your guests to hold the black paper up near a lamp to read the message. Fold the paper carefully and enclose in a long envelope. Add star stickers to the outside of the envelope.

Superhero Stand-Ups

Personalize these invitations to fit each one of the guests of the sleepover.

Materials

★ Crayons or fine-tipped markers
★ Tagboard
★ Scissors
★ White cotton material
★ Stapler

Directions

Draw a paper-doll-style superhero for each child on tagboard. Cut out. Add the word "Super" across the top of the doll's chest and the guest's name across the waist with a superhero symbol between the two words. Draw and cut out a cape from the white cotton material for the paper doll. The cape will need to be large enough to write sleepover information but small enough to fit the paper doll. Write the sleepover details on the back of the cape. Then, staple the cape onto the superhero paper doll.

Super Sunglasses

Enjoy a cool party with these personalized shades! Purchase cheap sunglasses at a department store or dollar store; add a little paint and a party invitation, and you'll surely brighten someone's day!

Materials

- ★ Puffy paints in a variety of colors
- ★ Plastic sunglasses, one pair per guest
- ★ Yellow construction paper
- ★ Scissors
- ★ Black felt-tip pen
- ★ Yellow ribbon or yarn

Directions

Use puffy paints to add dots, squiggles, or flowers around the rims and sidepieces of each pair of glasses. You may want to add each child's initials to the glasses, then have the guests add the decorations as part of the party activities. Use the yellow paper to cut out a sun shape. Write the party details on the sun shape and attach it to the glasses with the yellow yarn or ribbon.

Tantalizing Tickets

Give your guests permission to fly over to your house for an exciting slumber party.

Materials

- ★ White typing paper
- ★ Scissors
- ★ Ruler
- ★ Colorful construction paper
- ★ Black fine-tip marker
- ★ Envelopes

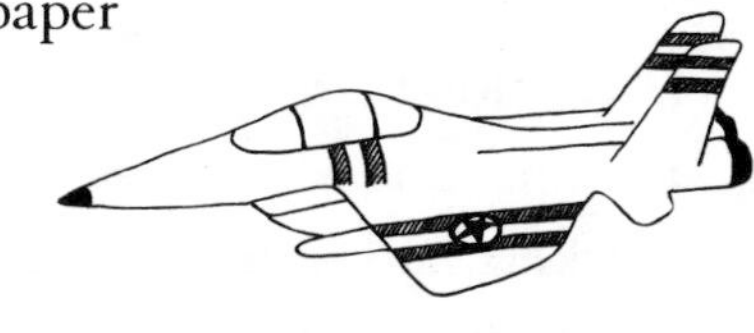

Directions

Use a computer, if possible, to print the sleepover invitation and details on white paper. Print several on each sheet, such that when cut apart, the invitation is about three and a half inches by eight and a half inches. Then cut construction paper into pieces seven inches wide by nine inches long. Fold the paper in half, matching the seven-inch sides to form a ticket envelope. Write the host's name, followed by the word "Airlines" on the envelope. Place these tickets to fun in an envelope, and mail them to your guests.

Toilet Tissue Talker

Here's one of those invitations that borders on the yucky!

Materials

★ One roll of toilet tissue per guest
★ Colorful markers
★ Gift bags or cellophane

Directions

Unroll some of the toilet tissue. Using the colorful markers and beginning at the end of the roll, write the party details and instructions. On the paper, ask the guests to bring the roll of tissue to the party. When the marker has had time to dry, carefully reroll the paper around the tube. Put the tube in a small gift bag or wrap it in colored cellophane for delivery. When the guests come to the slumber party, play a tossing game with the rolls or have a mummy-making relay.

Toothbrush Tote

Give an invitation that can be used by your guest at the sleepover and then taken home as a reminder of the fun.

Materials

★ Puffy paints
★ One plastic toothbrush holder per guest
★ Typing paper or construction paper
★ Colorful ribbon
★ Pen

Directions

Use the puffy paints to decorate and personalize a toothbrush holder for each guest. When the paint is dry, attach a note with the ribbon, detailing the sleepover instructions.

Train Treats

"All aboard for the Slumber Party Express!" Invite your guests with these terrific train invitations.

Materials

★ Train car patterns
★ Pen or pencil
★ Colorful construction paper
★ Scissors
★ Safety pins
★ Black felt-tip markers

Directions

Use train car patterns to trace an engine, several cars, and a caboose. If you do not have a pattern, simply make rectangles for the cars and caboose and a rectangle for the engine with a small square added to the top. Make sure each train car has two wheels on the bottom. Cut out and hook one engine, several cars, and a caboose together, using safety pins. Insert the pin in one car, then in the other car to allow the cars to move. (In other words, do not pin the two cars on top of one another.) Write the party details on the train cars using the markers.

Treasure Map Tokens

Invite your guests to come to a treasure-filled slumber party with this invitation. Use this idea for a pirate, mystery, detective, or all-occasion party.

Materials

- ★ White typing paper
- ★ Black felt-tip pen
- ★ Matches
- ★ Candle
- ★ Yarn
- ★ Small bag of chocolate coins wrapped in gold foil, one bag per guest

Directions

Make a map to your house on a sheet of typing paper, including the sleepover details. Make a large *X* at the location of the party. With adult assistance, light the candle and burn just the edges of the paper. Make one map for each guest. Roll both ends of map, meeting in the middle, to form a scroll. Tie the scroll closed with the yarn, attaching a bag of gold chocolate coins to the tie.

Wiffle Words

Sports fans of both genders will love this invitation!

Materials

- ★ Colorful markers
- ★ Typing paper
- ★ One Wiffle ball per guest
- ★ Permanent black marker

Directions

Write the party details on the paper with a colorful marker. Fold the paper such that you can slip it into one of the holes in the ball, but not so small that the paper will fall out. Using the permanent marker, write the guest's name on the outside of the ball.

Chapter 4

Dreamy Decorations

Dandy Decor Ideas

With some imagination and a few supplies, creatively transport your sleepover guests to anywhere in this world—and beyond! Take your guests to the jungles of Africa, the depths of the sea, tropical islands, or outer space. Transform your den into a fairy-tale land, newspaper editing room, or tropical rain forest. Using homemade or store-bought decorations, you can create the perfect ambiance for your sleepover.

Your decorations may be as simple as cutouts from construction paper, balloons, and streamers or as detailed as giant animal posters, palm trees, and cornfields. If you choose not to make your own decorations, look for them in party stores, department stores, or rental stores.

Decide on a theme two to three weeks before the party. Use the tips in this chapter or other ideas suggested by your host to decorate the house. Make as many decorations ahead of time as possible and store them in a safe place until the day of the party. Allow enough time to decorate the house so that you will not be rushed before the party. Remember, though, that balloons inflated too early will wilt, and streamers hung too soon may droop.

Use fishing line or yarn to hang cutouts and shapes from the ceiling. Tie a knot in one end of the line or yarn, and then use a pushpin or tape to secure the line to the ceiling. Attach the cutout, shape, or balloon to the other end of the line. Use double-sided tape or pushpins to secure pictures and items to the wall. A dab of toothpaste will also hold streamers in place and washes off the wall easily.

Top the table with a theme-related tablecloth and centerpiece. Make homemade place mats and place cards for each child attending. Decorate the table with small toys or trinkets related to the theme of the party. Then send each guest home with these personalized goodies as a party reminder.

Decorate one room, two rooms, the entire house—transform as much or as little of the house as you desire. And don't forget to set the mood outside your home, too. Use lights and tiki torches to decorate the entryway of the house. Tie balloons and streamers on the mailbox and front door. Hang glow-in-the-dark stars in trees and bushes.

Look for theme-related music to play during the party. Or, find favorite songs of your host or guests to serenade the group.

Colored light bulbs (found in some department, party, hardware, or lighting stores) can spotlight the theme of your sleepover, too. Bulbs come in blue, green, orange, red, and yellow. Use green light bulbs around Saint Patrick's Day, for example, red ones around Valentine's Day, or yellow ones for a summery party. Once you and the host have transformed the home to another time or place, you're ready for the guests to arrive!

Bundles of Balloons

Save your breath by using a helium tank and bicycle pump, for you will be using lots and lots of balloons for this festive party!

Materials

★ Helium tank (check with your local party store)
★ Bicycle pump
★ Balloons

Directions

Use the helium tank and bicycle pump to inflate many balloons. Fill the ceiling with helium balloons and cover the floor with air balloons.

Calling All Bird Watchers

Fascinate the feathered-friend lovers in the bunch with these fun decorations.

Materials

- ★ Scissors
- ★ Bird-shaped templates (optional)
- ★ Construction paper in a variety of colors
- ★ Fishing line
- ★ Pen or pencil
- ★ Tree-shaped templates (optional)
- ★ Brown and green bulletin board paper
- ★ Tape
- ★ Blue crepe paper
- ★ Plastic eggs
- ★ Wicker baskets
- ★ Stuffed or plastic bird toys
- ★ Brightly colored tablecloth
- ★ Small wooden birdhouse
- ★ ⅓ cup butterscotch chips
- ★ Cupcake liners
- ★ Decorator's spatula or paintbrush
- ★ Cupcake pan
- ★ Jelly beans

Directions

Cut bird shapes from different colors of construction paper. Hang the birds from the ceiling using fishing line. Draw and cut large trees from the bulletin board paper, and tape them securely to the wall. Attach blue crepe paper to one side of the ceiling. Twist the paper loosely and stretch it across to the other side of the ceiling, attaching the other end of the paper with tape. Make rows completely across the ceiling to resemble the sky. Put a few plastic eggs in each wicker basket, and place them in various locations of your home. Place a stuffed or plastic bird in the basket with the eggs.

Top the table with the tablecloth, and use the birdhouse for a centerpiece. To make an edible place marker, melt one-third cup of butterscotch chips and coat the bottom and sides of a cupcake liner. Use a decorator's spatula or small paintbrush to make a layer of melted butterscotch. Make one decorated cupcake liner for each child and place each in a cupcake pan. Place the pan in the refrigerator until the melted chips have hardened. Once the butterscotch has completely hardened, carefully peel off the cupcake liner. Put four or five jellybean "eggs" in the butterscotch "nest" and place one at each child's place.

Nature and specialty stores sell tapes and CDs with birdcalls and songs. If you desire, locate one to set a chirpy mood during a meal or early evening.

Destination Unknown

Use these decorations for any would-be travelers or explorers.

Materials

- ★ Travel brochures
- ★ Maps
- ★ Toy vehicles
- ★ Tablecloth
- ★ Pen
- ★ Postcards

Directions

Attach travel brochures and maps to the walls. Scatter toy vehicles in various rooms in the house.

Cover the table with a tablecloth, and use toy cars, boats, trucks, and other vehicles for tabletop decorations. Write each guest's name on a postcard, and use the cards for place markers. (Choose postcards from nearby sights or sights easily recognized by the children.)

Digging for Dinos

Fill your house with evidence of large and amazing reptiles for the dinosaur lover or future paleontologist on the guest list.

Materials

- ★ Dinosaur pictures
- ★ Construction paper
- ★ Scissors
- ★ Glue
- ★ Cardboard
- ★ Crayons or paint
- ★ Ruler
- ★ Plastic dinosaur toys
- ★ Green tablecloth
- ★ Puffy pens
- ★ Green crepe paper
- ★ Plastic shovels
- ★ Dinosaur-shaped gummy snacks

Directions

Enlarge pictures of dinosaurs onto construction paper. Cut out and glue onto cardboard. Have the host (or guests during the party) color or paint the dinosaurs. Make two slits in the bottom of the cardboard and insert eight- by three-inch rectangles of cardboard to form a stand. Complete the decor of the room by following the directions in the "Swamp of Critters" decoration suggestion, replacing the toy reptiles with toy dinosaurs.

Top the table with a green tablecloth, and stand plastic dinosaurs on the table. Write each guest's name on a plastic shovel with a puffy pen. Lay the shovel at each guest's spot at the table, placing a snack-size bag of dinosaur-shaped gummy pieces in each shovel.

Down on the Farm

Have your guests crowing with delight when you take them "down on the farm."

Materials

- ★ Scarecrow
- ★ Overalls
- ★ Straw hat
- ★ Markers
- ★ Poster paper
- ★ Green paint
- ★ Paintbrush
- ★ Dowel rods
- ★ Pen or pencil
- ★ Scissors
- ★ Sunflower patterns (optional)
- ★ Yellow and green construction paper
- ★ Sunflower seeds
- ★ Tape
- ★ Green construction paper
- ★ Flowerpots
- ★ Flower-arranging Styrofoam
- ★ Green crepe paper
- ★ Corn templates (optional)
- ★ Green tablecloth
- ★ Farm animal–shaped cookie cutters
- ★ Ribbon
- ★ Paper

Directions

Dress a scarecrow in overalls and a straw hat; stand the scarecrow outside next to the front door. Write "Welcome, Y'all!" on the sheet of poster paper and stand the sign next to the scarecrow. Paint the dowel rods with green paint. Draw and cut out sunflower shapes from the yellow construction paper. Glue sunflower seeds in the center of the flower. Tape the flower to the dowel rod; add green construction paper leaves. Stand the flowers in the flowerpots using floral Styrofoam to hold the flowers in place. Place the flowerpots in various places in the house.

Draw and cut out large cornstalks from green construction paper. Secure the cornstalks to the walls. Twist crepe paper to form the husks of the corn. Attach the husks to the corn plants. Cut corn shapes from yellow construction paper and tuck them inside the cornhusks.

Top the table with a green tablecloth. Tie several farm animal–shaped cookie cutters together with ribbons and a nametag, and use these as place markers.

Fantastic Flowers

Fill the room with blossoms and blooms and create a springtime celebration.

Materials

- ★ Construction paper
- ★ Artificial flowers
- ★ Flowerpots
- ★ Plastic vases
- ★ Helium tank (check with your local party store)
- ★ Balloons in springtime colors
- ★ Yarn or ribbon
- ★ Pastel-colored tablecloth
- ★ Small flowerpots
- ★ Puffy pen
- ★ Potting soil
- ★ Resealable plastic bags
- ★ Flower seed packages
- ★ Glue
- ★ Cupcake liners
- ★ Large craft sticks

Directions

Use the construction paper to make large flowers to tape on the walls. Arrange artificial flowers in flowerpots and vases; place these throughout the house. Use helium to inflate the pastel-colored balloons. Tie the balloons about twelve inches apart onto a long piece of ribbon that will stretch from one side of the room to the other. Use something heavy to tie down the ends of the ribbon, allowing the helium to lift the balloons and form a rainbow shape.

Top the table with a pastel-colored tablecloth. Use a pretty floral arrangement for a centerpiece. Make a place marker for each guest by writing children's names on small flowerpots with the puffy pen. Place a handful of potting soil in enough resealable bags for each guest to have one. Place the soil and a seed packet in each flowerpot. Glue a cupcake liner on the top of a craft stick and place in the flowerpot.

Festive Fall

Use delightful shades of orange, yellow, red, and gold to create a festive fall atmosphere in your home.

Materials

- ★ Pumpkins and squashes
- ★ Ears of corn
- ★ Pen or pencil
- ★ Scissors
- ★ Tree templates (optional)
- ★ Brown and green bulletin board paper

- ★ Fall-colored crepe paper
- ★ Fall-colored construction paper
- ★ Scissors
- ★ Tape
- ★ Scarecrow
- ★ Fall-colored balloons
- ★ Black yarn
- ★ Pushpins
- ★ Plastic spider(s)
- ★ Orange light bulbs
- ★ Red or yellow tablecloth
- ★ Basket
- ★ Nuts in shells
- ★ Pumpkin templates (optional)
- ★ Orange construction paper

Directions

Place the pumpkins, squashes, and corn on tabletops throughout the house. Draw and cut out a tree from the bulletin board paper. Secure the tree to the wall. Hang fall-colored crepe paper streamers from the ceiling. As the guests arrive for the sleepover, have them trace their hands on fall-colored sheets of construction paper. Have each child make and cut out five or more hand patterns. Use tape to stick the hand-shaped "leaves" on the tree hanging on the wall.

Stand the scarecrow outside near the front door. Tie fall-colored balloons on the mailbox or around the door.

Use black yarn to make a large spider web in one corner of the room. Make a large *X* in the corner with the yarn and pushpins. Cut another strip of yarn and stretch it across the center of the *X* pinning each end to a wall. Then form a circle with a diameter of about twelve inches in the center of the *X* tying the yarn to each crosspiece as you go around. Make another circle, much larger, near the outer edge of the web. Tie one or more plastic spiders to the web.

Replace some of the bulbs in your home with orange bulbs. Top the table with a fall-colored tablecloth. Fill a basket with squashes, corn, and nuts, and use for a centerpiece. Make large pumpkin shapes from orange paper, one shape per child. Write a child's name on each pumpkin and use for place mats.

Heaps of Horses

Use these ideas for your little equestrian. Decorate with horses and horse paraphernalia for a rodeo party, desert party, or farm party.

Materials

- ★ Hay bales
- ★ Rope
- ★ Stick horses
- ★ Pictures of horses (draw or find in magazine)
- ★ Tablecloth
- ★ Bandannas
- ★ Markers
- ★ Construction paper
- ★ Tape
- ★ Toy sheriff's badges

Directions

Place the hay bales outside near a tree. Use the rope to tie the stick horses to the tree. Draw or find pictures of horses. Secure the horse pictures on the wall. If you have other horse equipment, such as reins, bridles, saddles, and horseshoes, place these in various locations throughout the house.

Top the table with a tablecloth. Fold bandannas in a triangle and use one for each child's place mat. Write each child's name on a small strip of construction paper. Tape the name strip on the top of a toy badge and use the badge as a place marker. (If you choose not to purchase toy badges, make one per child from construction paper, writing the name in the center of the badge.)

Check the library for a tape of cowboy songs, or play country and western music during the sleepover.

Heart-Felt Hangings and Decorations

Turn everything blush-red with hearts and balloons, and have a *love*ly evening!

Materials

- ★ Helium tank (check with your local party store)
- ★ Red balloons
- ★ Thin red ribbon
- ★ Scissors
- ★ Red construction paper
- ★ Red crepe paper
- ★ Red light bulbs
- ★ Pink or white tablecloth
- ★ Glitter pen
- ★ Heart-shaped dish
- ★ Red cinnamon candies

Directions

Use the helium tank to inflate enough red balloons to cover the ceiling. Tie the balloons and attach a red ribbon to each one. Tie enough length of ribbon to hang just above the guests' heads. Cut hearts from the construction paper and attach each heart to a strip of red crepe paper. Attach the other end of the crepe paper to the ceiling such that the hearts hang about the same height as the end of the ribbons. Purchase red light bulbs from a lighting or party store; change some bulbs around your home for a nice red glow.

Top the table with a pink or white tablecloth. Cut a large red construction paper heart for each child. Write each child's name on a heart with the glitter pen; use the heart as a place mat for each guest. Fill a heart-shaped dish with red cinnamon candies for a centerpiece.

Lucky Leprechauns

Bring the luck of the Irish into your home for this sleepover. Cloverleaves, green paper chains, and even some leprechaun footprints will guarantee a night of luck and fun.

Materials

- ★ Scissors
- ★ White sheet or long strip of butcher paper
- ★ Tape or weights
- ★ Green paint
- ★ Gold glitter (optional)
- ★ Scissors
- ★ Green construction paper
- ★ Stapler
- ★ Green balloons
- ★ Helium tank (check with your local party store)
- ★ Green ribbon
- ★ Metal washers
- ★ Green plastic flowerpots
- ★ Green tissue paper
- ★ Green light bulbs
- ★ Light green tablecloth
- ★ Empty green liter bottle
- ★ Ivy or other greenery
- ★ Dark green construction paper
- ★ Black paint
- ★ Paintbrushes
- ★ Disposable cardboard bowls (one for each guest)
- ★ Gold pen
- ★ Gold foil–wrapped chocolate candy coins

Directions

Cut a piece of butcher paper long enough to cover the sidewalk or entryway into your home. Tape the paper or weigh it down with weights. Create small "leprechaun" footprints: Make a fist, and dip the side of your hand and your pinkie into the green paint. Make a print on the white paper; then dip your index finger in green paint, and make a small dot above the "foot," on the inside of the print, to be the big toe. Then dip your pinkie in the green paint and add four more toe prints next to the big toe print. Continue this pattern with both hands all along the path to make tiny footprints. Sprinkle gold glitter along the trail, too, if desired.

Cut the green construction paper along the long side into one and a half-inch strips. Staple the ends of the first strip together to form a circle. Then stick the next strip through the circle, and staple the ends together to form another circle. Continue linking the strips together to form a long paper chain. Secure the end of the chain to the ceiling or wall, and swag the chain all around the room.

Inflate the green balloons with helium and attach green ribbon strips, varying in length between twenty-four and thirty-six inches, to each balloon. Tie the ends of five or six balloons to a metal washer. Place the washer in a flowerpot, and fill the flowerpot with green tissue paper. Make several balloon bouquets and place them throughout the house. Locate green light bulbs from a lighting store, and replace some bulbs in your home.

Top the table with a light green tablecloth. For a centerpiece, cut the top out of a green plastic liter bottle to make a vase. Fill this vase with ivy or other greenery. Cut a large cloverleaf from green construction paper for each person to use as a place mat. Paint a cardboard bowl with black paint and allow to dry. When the paint is dry, use a gold pen to write a person's name on each bowl. Fill the bowl with gold foil–wrapped chocolate candy coins.

Check the library for Irish music tapes or CDs to play during the sleepover.

Midnight Celebration

Welcome in a new year, new month, birthday, or any other special day with this celebration.

Materials

- ★ Black, gold, and white balloons
- ★ Funnel
- ★ Confetti
- ★ White paint
- ★ Paintbrush
- ★ Black yarn or fishing line
- ★ Black and gold tinsel
- ★ Alarm clocks
- ★ Black tablecloth
- ★ Party blowers
- ★ Party hats
- ★ Gold marker (or other bright color)

Directions

Before inflating the gold and white balloons, use a funnel to put about three tablespoons of confetti in each balloon. Inflate the balloons and tie the ends. Scatter them around on the floor. Inflate the black balloons. Using white paint, paint the face of a clock on each black balloon. Allow to dry, then hang the clock-face balloons from the ceiling with black yarn or fishing line. Hang black and gold tinsel in the doorways. Set several alarm clocks to sound at midnight, and place them in various locations of the house.

Place a black tablecloth on the table, and sprinkle gold confetti on top. Place a party blower and party hats at each child's place at the table. Using a bright-colored or gold marker, label each hat with a child's name.

Music in Your Ears

Guests will be humming and singing when surrounded by musical notes and instruments.

Materials

- ★ Scissors
- ★ Music note templates (optional)
- ★ Black construction paper
- ★ Silver tinsel
- ★ White tablecloth
- ★ Musical instruments or tape or CD player
- ★ Markers
- ★ Old forty-five-speed records

Directions

Cut large musical notes from black construction paper. Hang the notes on the walls and from the ceiling. Hang silver tinsel in the doorways of doors that will be used by the guests.

Top the table with a white tablecloth. Use musical instruments or a tape or CD player for a centerpiece. (If you use the musical instruments, have the tape or CD player nearby, playing the host's and guests' favorite music.) Write each guest's name on an old forty-five record to use as a place marker.

Numbers Everywhere

Use these decorations for a back-to-school party, end-of-school party, or any "number" of party ideas!

Materials

- ★ Markers
- ★ Construction paper
- ★ Scissors
- ★ Con-Tact or other self-adhesive paper
- ★ Fishing line

- ★ Balloons
- ★ Large stand-alone clock
- ★ Dice

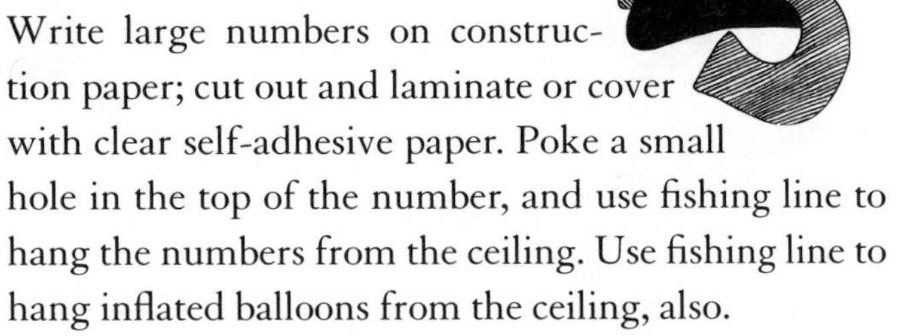

Directions

Write large numbers on construction paper; cut out and laminate or cover with clear self-adhesive paper. Poke a small hole in the top of the number, and use fishing line to hang the numbers from the ceiling. Use fishing line to hang inflated balloons from the ceiling, also.

Place a large clock in the center of the table for a centerpiece, and place two dice at each person's place.

Painter's Preparations

Prepare the house for your budding artists with these colorful expressions.

Materials

- ★ Balloons in a variety of colors
- ★ Colorful ribbons
- ★ Crepe paper in a variety of colors
- ★ Easels
- ★ Blank paper
- ★ Drop cloth
- ★ Basket
- ★ Paints, markers, and other art supplies
- ★ Paintbrushes
- ★ Permanent marker

Directions

Inflate the balloons, and tie a colorful ribbon strip to each one; attach the other end of the ribbon to the ceiling. Hang the balloons at varying heights. Hang strips of crepe paper from the walls and ceiling, too. Stand easels around the house with blank paper for the guests to doodle on or with copies of famous prints.

Use an artist's drop cloth for a tablecloth. Fill a basket with art supplies to use as a centerpiece. Write each guest's name on a paintbrush, and place brushes on the table as place markers.

Paradise Party

Take your guests to a tropical island, and hula your way through the night.

Materials

- ★ Tiki torches or strings of colored lights
- ★ Cupcake liners
- ★ Plastic, colored beads
- ★ Colored yarn

- ★ Large-eyed needle
- ★ Pens
- ★ Scissors
- ★ Palm tree templates (optional)
- ★ Brown and green bulletin board paper
- ★ Fish shower curtain
- ★ Fisherman's net
- ★ Seashells
- ★ Coconuts
- ★ Pineapples
- ★ Leis (store-bought)
- ★ Colorful tablecloth
- ★ Live or artificial flowers

Directions

Stand tiki torches near or string colored lights in the walkway or around the front door. Make lei strips to hang from the ceiling by stringing cupcake liners and beads onto a length of yarn and securing them to the ceiling to just above the guests' heads: Cut strips of yarn the necessary length; tie a knot in one end. Thread the yarn onto the needle, and poke the needle through the center of a cupcake liner, carefully pushing it down to the knot. String a bead next. Alternate liners and beads until the yarn is full, leaving several inches to knot and attach to the ceiling with a push-pin. Make many lei-strips to hang from the ceiling.

Draw and cut out palm trees from the brown and green bulletin board paper; attach these to the wall. Secure the fish-patterned shower curtain to one wall. Attach a fisherman's net to another wall. Push seashells into the holes and lay seashells on the floor. Place the coconuts and pineapples in various locations around the house. Lay store-bought leis around the rooms, also.

Top the table with a colorful tablecloth; stand a pineapple and two coconuts in the center of the table. Wrap a lei around the centerpiece. Place a live or artificial flower at each child's place. Girls may choose to wear the flowers above their ears. Be sure to have Hawaiian or Polynesian music playing throughout the evening.

Pet Party

Treat the animal lovers in your group to these fun decorations.

Materials

- ★ Pictures of animals
- ★ Stuffed animals
- ★ Large appliance box
- ★ Tape
- ★ Scissors

- ★ Paints
- ★ Paintbrush
- ★ Tablecloth
- ★ Plastic dog food bowls
- ★ Puffy pens

Directions

Hang pictures of animals throughout the house; place stuffed animals throughout the house. Open two of the top flaps of the appliance box and tape them together to form a roof. (If the roof tends to droop, use cardboard strips as support beams.) Cut a doggie door in the front of the box. Let the host paint the "doghouse." When the paint is dry, stand the "doghouse" in the room where the guests will sleep.

Cover the table with a tablecloth; use stuffed animals for the centerpiece. Write each guest's name on a dog food bowl with a puffy pen, and use these for place markers.

Play Ball!

Decorate the house for your ball enthusiasts using just a few sports supplies.

Materials

- ★ Variety of sports balls
- ★ Baseball caps
- ★ Football helmets
- ★ Sports mitts or gloves
- ★ Team pennants
- ★ Fishing line
- ★ Plastic Wiffle baseballs
- ★ Markers
- ★ White paper tablecloth

Directions

Place the balls, caps, helmets, and gloves or mitts around the house to decorate each room that will be used by the guests. Secure the team pennants to the wall, or use fishing line to hang them from the ceiling. Tie fishing line to Wiffle balls and hang them from the ceiling.

Top the table with the decorated tablecloth. Give the guests markers and encourage them to draw the flag or mascot of their favorite ball team. Write each guest's name on a Wiffle ball (or small plastic football) with a permanent marker, and use the balls for place markers.

Say "Cheese"

With the help of the guests' parents, everyone will be smiling at this sleepover!

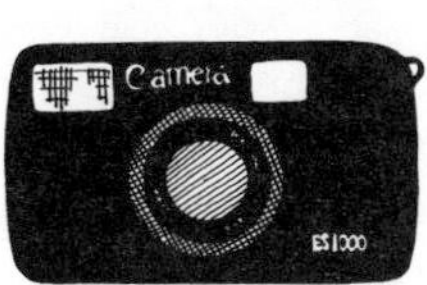

Materials

- ★ Pictures of guests
- ★ Black construction paper
- ★ Tablecloth
- ★ Camera

Directions

Several weeks before the party, ask the parents of your guests for several photographs of their child, reminding them not to tell the children about your request. Make copies of the pictures, enlarging them to be about eight and a half by eleven inches. Make one four- by six-inch copy of each child's picture to use as a place marker. Glue the pictures onto sheets of construction paper, leaving a border for a frame; secure the pictures to the walls.

Top the table with a tablecloth, and use a camera for a centerpiece. Set each child's picture on the table as a place marker.

Stop the Presses!

Turn your house into a newsroom for the future reporters and columnists in the sleepover bunch.

Materials

- ★ Black and white balloons
- ★ White yarn
- ★ Tape
- ★ Newspapers
- ★ Old typewriter
- ★ Comic strips from newspapers
- ★ Black construction paper
- ★ Scissors
- ★ Glue
- ★ Con-Tact or clear self-adhesive paper

Directions

Inflate balloons and tie white yarn to each one. Secure the yarn to the ceiling, or tie the balloons around the house. Tape newspapers onto lots of walls in the house, especially the room where the guests will be sleeping.

Tape several newspaper pages together to make a tablecloth for your table. Place an old typewriter in the center of the table. Tape or glue several comic strips to a large sheet of black construction paper, leaving a border. Cut out large letters from newspaper headlines to spell out guests' names. Glue each guest's name on one of the sheets of construction paper. Cover the sheet with clear self-adhesive paper, and use it as a place mat.

Sunny Delight

Use these bright, warm decorations to welcome summer, to warm hearts during the middle of winter, or to create the feeling of a day spent in the desert or steamy jungle. A few supplies are all you need to create this sunny climate!

Materials

★ Pen or pencil
★ Butcher paper
★ Yellow paint
★ Paintbrushes
★ Orange and yellow construction paper
★ Glue or stapler
★ Newspaper for stuffing
★ Fishing line
★ Yellow crepe paper
★ Yellow balloons
★ Yellow ribbon
★ Yellow light bulbs
★ Fan
★ Yellow tablecloth
★ Cactus plants (use for desert-themed party)

Directions

Make a sun decoration by drawing two large circles on a sheet of butcher paper. Paint the circles yellow. Let dry. Cut strips of orange and yellow construction paper for the sun's rays. After the yellow paint has dried, glue or staple the two sides together, painted side outward. Leave a hole for stuffing. Use newspaper to stuff the circle for a three-dimensional effect. Glue or staple the opening closed, then attach the sun's rays by gluing or stapling. Poke two small holes and tie fishing line to the sun; hang it from the ceiling.

Hang strips of yellow crepe paper and balloons attached to yellow ribbons from the ceiling. Replace light bulbs with yellow bulbs, and aim a fan toward the ceiling to cause the streamers and balloons to be in constant motion.

For a desert party, place cactus plants around the house, and use a cactus for a table centerpiece.

Variation: Top the table with a bright yellow tablecloth. For place markers, personalize a water bottle or hand-held, battery-operated fan by writing a child's name with puffy paint, and place one next to each child's place. For a centerpiece, set a vase of sunflowers or daisies in the center of the table.

Swamp of Critters

Create this swamp that only kids and creepy critters could enjoy!

Materials

- ★ Green and brown bulletin board paper
- ★ Pen or pencil
- ★ Scissors
- ★ Tree templates (optional)
- ★ Green crepe paper
- ★ Green poster board
- ★ Markers
- ★ Scissors
- ★ Wooden stake
- ★ Brown tissue paper
- ★ Plastic reptiles and amphibians
- ★ Green tablecloth
- ★ Dark green construction paper

Directions

Using the green and brown bulletin board paper, draw and cut out large trees; secure these to the wall. Hang strips of green crepe paper from the ceiling, just above the guests' heads. On the poster board, write "[Host's name]'s Swamp." Staple the poster paper to the stake and stand or prop the sign in one corner of the room. Crumple the brown tissue paper somewhat and lay it near the sign. Scatter plastic snakes, frogs, alligators, and lizards in the brown "mud" and around your home.

Top the table with a green tablecloth. Cut lily pad shapes from the green construction paper. Write a child's name on each lily pad for place markers. Put a small, plastic frog on each lily pad.

True for the Red, White, and Blue

Let your guests' hearts beat true for that grand ol' flag with these patriotic decorations. Turn the house into a rainbow of red, white, and blue!

Materials

- ★ Red, white, and blue balloons
- ★ Helium tank (check with your local party store)
- ★ Red yarn
- ★ Metal washers
- ★ Small and large American flags
- ★ Small vases

- ★ Red tablecloth
- ★ Confetti (or scraps of red, white, and blue construction paper and a hole puncher to make your own)
- ★ Toilet paper tubes
- ★ Individually wrapped candies or other trinkets
- ★ Red tissue paper
- ★ Blue and white ribbons
- ★ Pen or marker

Directions

Inflate the red, white, and blue balloons with helium. Tie the ends closed. Starting with blue balloons and the red yarn, tie the balloons onto the yarn, about twelve inches apart. Tie about seven balloons (or enough to reach from the floor to almost the top of the ceiling) on the yarn. Then tie ten or more red and white balloons, alternating each one, and keeping them about twelve inches apart. (The number of balloons will vary according to the height of your ceiling. You want the balloons to form a rainbow shape that will stretch from one side of the room to the other.) Tie metal washers to each end of the yarn to weigh down the ends. Make several rainbows, enough to make a canopy of rainbows, if desired.

Secure large flags on the wall; place two or three small flags in a vase, and set several vases throughout your home.

Top the table with a red tablecloth. Scatter red, white, and blue confetti all over the tabletop. (Make your own confetti by using a hole puncher and scrap construction paper pieces. Some department stores and craft stores sell star-shaped punchers that might be fun.) Place one of the vases with small flags in the center of the table.

Make firecracker place markers for each guest: Fill a toilet paper tube with individually wrapped candies and/or trinkets, and wrap red tissue paper around the tube, leaving three or four inches on each end. Twist both ends, and tie them closed with blue ribbon. Write a child's name on a firecracker, and place one for each guest on the table.

Many patriotic tapes and CDs are available. Locate a selection of music from the library or a music store to treat your guests.

Under the Big Top

Gather your gang under a circus tent for fun and excitement.

Materials

- ★ Three brightly colored sheets (with polka dots or stripes, if possible)
- ★ Brightly colored streamers
- ★ Brightly colored balloons
- ★ Helium tank
- ★ Ribbon
- ★ Metal washers
- ★ Stuffed animals
- ★ Tablecloth (circus theme or brightly colored)
- ★ Silver, aluminum pail
- ★ Dry-roasted peanuts in shells
- ★ Clown toys
- ★ Clown noses

Directions

Choose three brightly colored sheets. Secure the sheets to the ceiling, leaving some slack between secured areas such that the sheets droop some. Cover the entire ceiling, if possible, adding more sheets if necessary.

Cut strips of streamers to cover the walls. The strips will need to be about one and a half times the length of the wall. Attach one end of the strip to the top of the wall, near the ceiling. Loosely twist the streamer, securing the other end at the bottom of the wall, near the floor. Alternate the colors; attach streamers close together to cover an entire wall.

Inflate the balloons with helium and tie with ribbons. Attach the other end of four or five ribbons to a washer to form a balloon bouquet. Make several bouquets and place them in various rooms. Scatter stuffed animals (preferably elephants, tigers, or other circus animals) throughout your home.

Top the table with a tablecloth. Fill an aluminum pail with dry-roasted peanuts in the shell and use for a centerpiece. (If any of the guests are allergic to peanuts, use marshmallow circus peanuts, usually found with candy in the grocery store.) Prop a clown toy next to the bucket. Place a clown nose at each child's place, with a note attached to each nose that says, "[Guest's name]'s nose goes here."

Under the Sea

Let your guests think they have discovered Atlantis with these sea creature decorations.

Materials

- ★ Scissors
- ★ Sea-creature–shaped templates
- ★ Construction paper

- ★ Tape
- ★ Blue clear plastic wrap
- ★ Fisherman's net
- ★ Large seashells
- ★ Butcher paper
- ★ Paints
- ★ Paintbrushes
- ★ Newspaper for stuffing
- ★ Glue
- ★ Fishing line
- ★ Sea creature–shaped sponges
- ★ Blue paper tablecloth or sheet
- ★ Goldfish bowl
- ★ Blue food coloring
- ★ Fish-shaped crackers
- ★ Typing paper
- ★ Pen, pencil, or markers
- ★ Plastic sea creature toys
- ★ Toothpicks

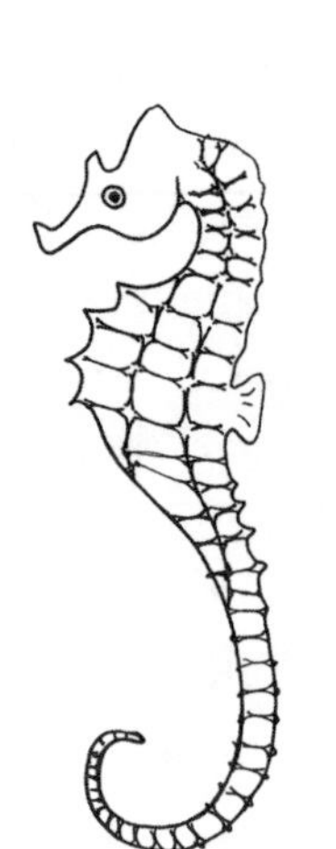

Directions

Cut sea creature shapes out of the construction paper. Tape the cutouts on one wall. Then loosely tape the blue plastic wrap over the cutouts. (As an alternate idea, look for a shower curtain with a fish or ocean animals scene, and use pushpins to secure the shower curtain to the wall.) On another wall, secure the fisherman's net. Push some of the seashells into the holes of the net. Use the butcher paper to make large fish and sea creature shapes, creating a front and back of each pattern. Paint the shapes; glue the shapes together around the edges, leaving an opening. Carefully stuff the shapes with newspaper; then glue the opening closed. Hang the sea creature shapes from the ceiling with fishing line.

Early during the party, have the guests help decorate the tablecloth. Have the guests use the fish and sea creature sponges dipped in paint to make prints on the paper tablecloth or blue sheet. Let the paint dry, then place the tablecloth on the table. Fill the goldfish bowl with water and add blue food-coloring. Place a large, clean shell at each child's place, and fill it with fish-shaped crackers. Cut a small rectangle of typing paper and write a child's name on it. Thread the nametag onto a toothpick, and stand the "flag" inside the shell with the crackers for a place holder.

Nature or specialty stores sell tapes or CDs with ocean sounds and whale songs. This would be a nice addition to an Under the Sea sleepover.

Universal Appeal

Make these decorations for a space party using mostly aluminum foil, trinkets, and tinsel.

Materials

- ★ Aluminum foil
- ★ Silver tinsel
- ★ Individually wrapped candies
- ★ Small treats or trinkets
- ★ Blue light bulbs
- ★ Plastic glow-in-the-dark stars (found in party or department stores)
- ★ Fishing line
- ★ Toy spaceship and astronauts
- ★ Permanent marker

Directions

Cover doors with aluminum foil. Hang silver tinsel in doorways, from the ceiling, and along the walls. Make asteroids by wrapping a piece of candy or small treat with aluminum foil. Continue wadding aluminum foil around the candy to make a baseball-sized "asteroid." Place the "asteroids" in various locations in the house, but do not reveal that they contain a hidden treat until the appropriate time.

Purchase blue light bulbs and replace some bulbs in your home. Hang glow-in-the-dark stars from the ceiling with fishing line.

Cover the table with aluminum foil, and place a toy spaceship and plastic astronauts in the center of the table. Using a permanent marker, write a child's name on a glow-in-the-dark star and place ... each guest at the table.

Whodunit Decorations

Keep your guests guessing at this mystery or detective party.

Materials

- ★ Tiki torches or strings of colored lights
- ★ Scissors
- ★ Cardboard
- ★ Gold paint
- ★ Paintbrushes
- ★ Fishing line
- ★ Black tablecloth
- ★ Unlined index cards
- ★ Black ink pad
- ★ Magnifying glasses

Directions

Stand the tiki torches along the driveway or walkway, or string colored lights along the outside of the house or front door. Cut question marks out of cardboard, and paint with gold. Use fishing line to hang the question marks from the ceiling.

with a black tablecloth. On an un-
d, make a thumbprint by having the
r her thumb in the black inkpad and
the paper. Then write a child's name
l use for a place marker. Place a magnifying glass next to each person's name card.

"X" Marks the Spot

Let the guests pretend to be pirates for a day and search for treasure with these fun decorations.

Materials

- ★ Glow-in-the-dark paint
- ★ Pen or pencil
- ★ Paintbrushes
- ★ Dark-colored sheet
- ★ Scissors
- ★ Star templates (optional)
- ★ Construction paper
- ★ Fishing line
- ★ Box and black paint, or black chest
- ★ Toy or costume jewelry
- ★ Plastic gold coins
- ★ Tiki torches or strings of colored lights
- ★ Black tablecloth
- ★ Black felt-tipped pen
- ★ White construction paper
- ★ Con-Tact or clear self-adhesive paper
- ★ Balloons
- ★ Helium tank
- ★ Yarn
- ★ Bandannas
- ★ Pirate eye patches

Directions

Using glow-in-the-dark paint, outline and paint stars on the dark-colored sheet. Cut stars from construction paper, and paint each star with glow-in-the-dark paint. Secure the sheet to the ceiling. Use fishing line to hang the star cutouts from the ceiling. Paint a box black or use a black chest. Put some toy or costume jewelry and plastic coins inside the box or chest, with the lid open and jewelry spilling out. Also scatter jewelry in other places of the house. Stand the tiki torches outside along the driveway or walkway or string the colored lights around the doorway of the house.

Top the table with a black tablecloth. Place loose jewelry pieces all over the table. On sheets of white construction paper, draw a pirate's map. Draw a large *X* in one spot and write, "'X' marks the spot for [guest's name]'s seat." Cover the map with clear self-adhesive paper, and use for a place mat and place marker.

Let each child add a pirate buddy at his or her place, also. Inflate a balloon with helium for each child. Attach yarn to the balloon and tie the balloon to the back of the child's chair. Let the child use a medium-point black pen (not felt-tipped, as that will smear) to draw a pirate face and hair. Give each child a bandanna and eye patch for his or her pirate pal.

Chapter 5

Recreation for Resters

Grand Games for Guests

Game time can be the most memorable part of a sleepover or party. Pick activities that are both fun and challenging for your guests, matching them, if you can, to the party's theme. (A word of caution: Look closely at all of these recreational activities before choosing games for your party. Some of the activities may not be appropriate for certain rooms in your home. Messy games and those with lots of physical activity may not work well on plush carpets or hardwood floors. Also be aware that some of the games are more girl-oriented or boy-oriented and choose the games accordingly.)

Ask the host to decide on the games at least two to three weeks before the party, so that you may collect and make the supplies needed for each game well in advance. Make a list of all games and supplies. You'll probably want to have a couple of extra game ideas to use as alternates in case you have too much time on your hands or the children are just too excited to stop playing!

Remembering the old saying "Everyone's a winner" will certainly keep everyone happier at the party, too. Make sure every guest is included in every game, and find a way to make everyone at the party a winner. Give prizes for all who participate, have winner prizes and runner-up prizes, or do not keep score at all.

Change teams and partners throughout game time to give the guests the opportunity to play with a different group of friends. Do not allow unkind comments; encourage and foster a team spirit, and help each child cheer his or her teammates as well as opponents throughout playtime.

Games are suggested here in three categories: outside games, inside games, and bedtime games. Play the outside games in the afternoon or early evening of the sleepover or the next morning before the guests leave. Play the inside games throughout the evening or next morning. Settle the guests into their sleeping bags and introduce a bedtime game.

Most important, have fun! Now, let the games begin!

Outside Games

Use both outside games as well as inside games for a variety of sleepover fun!

Alligator Chase

Materials

- ★ No materials needed

Directions

Choose one player to be the "alligator"; the rest of the players are the "frogs." Have the alligator chase the frogs, opening and closing his or her arms like alligator jaws as he or she runs. When a person is tagged, he or she is out until all the frogs have been "eaten." The last player eaten becomes the next alligator.

Apple Bobbing

Materials

- ★ Apples
- ★ Large tub of water
- ★ Scarf or handkerchief to use as blindfold

Directions

Place apples in the tub of water. Blindfold a guest and have him or her bob for an apple.

Astronaut Relay

Materials

★ Two large towels or one sheet
★ Adult-sized coats and pants (a jumpsuit would work even better), one set per team

Directions

Divide the children into two teams. Have the children form two lines. Put the towels or sheet about twenty feet away from the teams. If you use towels, each team will have its own "moon." If you use a sheet, both teams will use the same moon. Give the jumpsuits or adult coats and pants to the first person in each line. On "Go," the first person in each line puts on the "spacesuit" and begins to run to the moon. After walking on the moon, the players run back to the next player in line. The astronaut removes the suit and gives it to that player. The game continues until each astronaut has walked on the moon. The first team to complete the game is the winner.

Beach Ball Volleyball

Materials

★ Volleyball net
★ Inflated beach ball

Directions

(*Hint:* If you do not have a volleyball net, set two chairs about ten feet apart and tie a rope from one chair to the other.)

Divide the guests into two teams, and play volleyball with a beach ball. The ball must not land on the ground, and each team may only hit the ball twice before it must go to the other side of the net.

Bird's Eggs

Materials

★ Plastic eggs, filled with candy
★ Baskets for each child

Directions

Before the game, hide the candy-filled eggs in the yard. Give each child a basket and have an egg hunt.

Bucket Toss

Materials

★ Twelve plastic sand pails or buckets
★ Twelve Ping-Pong balls

Directions

Line the twelve buckets on the ground. Line up the guests facing the buckets, about four feet away. Give the first player a sack of twelve Ping-Pong balls. The player starts by tossing a ball into the bucket closest to him or her. If he or she makes that bucket, then the guest chooses another ball and aims for the second bucket. If the child misses, he or she sits out to cheer on the others. The guest who gets to the farthest bucket is the winner.

Cannonball Catch

Materials

- ★ Scissors
- ★ Twenty-four inches of elastic
- ★ Sewing machine or needle and thread
- ★ Twelve- by twelve-inch square of felt
- ★ Wiffle balls

Directions

Before the sleepover, make a large slingshot. Cut the elastic into two twelve-inch pieces. Sew each end of the elastic to a corner of the felt, making two handles. To play the game, have two people hold the slingshot, one on each handle. Have a third person place a Wiffle ball inside the felt square, close the square, and pull backward to stretch the elastic. A fourth child stands in front of the slingshot, about ten feet away. The child releases the square of material, shooting the ball forward. The child in front tries to catch the ball. If he or she catches the ball before it hits the ground, the child gets a point. The person with the most points at the end of the game is the winner.

Derby Races

Materials

- ★ At least two stick hobbyhorses
- ★ Orange plastic cones or folding chairs

Directions

(*Hint:* If you do not have store-bought stick horses, draw a horse head on construction paper. Make four identical heads. Add the facial features to the horse outlines, making sure to turn two of the heads in the other direction. Match the heads and glue around the outside edges, leaving the bottom open. Glue or tape a strip of yarn on either side of the horse's head to be the reins. Slip each head over a yardstick.)

Divide the children into two teams. Set up cones or the folding chairs to follow for a trail. You will need two identical trails about six feet apart. Give each team a horse. On "Go," the first person in line races the horse along the trail and then returns to his or her team, handing off the horse. The game continues until each person has had a turn to race the horse. The first team to complete the race wins.

Detective Chase

Materials

★ Adult-sized trench coat (raincoat will do)
★ Toy, plastic magnifying glass

Directions

Choose one person to be the "detective." The detective puts on the trench coat and carries the magnifying glass. The other guests are "villains." The detective chases the villains until one is tagged. That person becomes the detective and puts on the detective coat. Play continues until each person has had a turn being the detective.

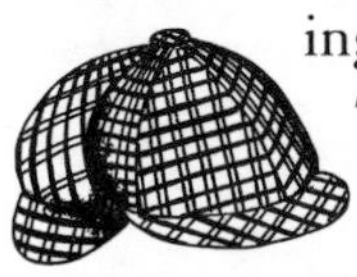

Discovering Dinosaur Eggs

Materials

★ Plastic eggs
★ Small dinosaur toys or candies
★ One basket per child

Directions

Before the sleepover, fill the eggs with dinosaur toys and candies and hide them in the yard. To play the game, give each child a basket and have him or her search for dinosaur eggs.

Dizzy Batters

Materials

★ Two baseball bats
★ Two Wiffle balls

Directions

Divide the guests into two teams. Place a bat on the ground about ten feet away from each team and a Wiffle ball next to each bat. On "Go," the first person in line runs to the bat, stands the bat on end, places his or her forehead on the handle of the bat, and spins around the bat five times. After spinning, the child replaces the bat on the ground, picks up the ball, and throws it to the next player. The next player retrieves the ball, then runs to the bat with the ball in hand. Play continues until each player has had a turn. (To prolong the game, have each player run twice.) The team who completes the game first is the winning team.

Doggy Run

Materials

- ★ Two dog leashes
- ★ Two old T-shirts

Directions

Divide the guests into two teams. Have each person on the team find a partner. Give the first pair of players on the team a leash and a T-shirt. Have one of the players put on the T-shirt, and hook the leash onto the T-shirt. Have that player get on all fours, with his or her partner holding the leash. On "Go," the first pair of children run to the boundary line and then run back. The "doggy" removes the leash and T-shirt and hands the material to the next pair. That pair then goes for a "doggy run," with the first pair going to the end of the line. When the first pair moves back up to the front of the line, they will run again, this time reversing roles. Play continues until each person has had a turn being the doggy and the owner.

Farmer and the Cows

Materials

- ★ Ropes

Directions

Use ropes to mark off an area that will be the cow's pen. Choose one player to be the "farmer"; the other players are "cows." The farmer chases the cows. When a cow is tagged, he or she has to go inside the fence. The cow must stay inside the fence until all the cows are tagged or until another cow moves the rope and allows the cows to go free. After a farmer has caught two or three cows, change farmers and give someone else a turn.

Feather Flight

Materials

- ★ Rope
- ★ Feather for each child

Directions

Stretch the rope on the ground for a boundary line. Divide the guests into two teams. Give each player a feather to place on his or her head. On "Go," the first player in line walks to the boundary line with the feather on his or her head. The player may not touch the feather while walking. If the feather falls off, the player has to start back at the beginning. After crossing the boundary line, the player removes the feather, runs back, and tags the next player. Play continues until each person has had a turn. The team who completes the relay first is the winning team.

Flag Zigzag

Materials

★ Small flags on twelve-inch wooden dowel rods

★ Two soccer balls

Directions

Place the flags in the ground in a straight line about a yard apart. Make two rows of flags, one for each team. Divide the guests into two teams and give each team a ball; have them line up facing a row of flags. On "Go," the first person in line dribbles the ball (giving small kicks with alternating feet to keep it rolling) in and out of the flags in a zigzag fashion until he or she reaches the last flag. The child then turns the ball and dribbles it back through the flags. When the player returns with the ball, the next person begins. The first team to have all the players complete the course is the winning team.

Flower Picking

Materials

★ Cupcake liners in a variety of colors

★ One basket per child

Directions

Before the game begins, scatter the cupcake liners in the yard. Give each child a basket. Choose a color for each child to be searching for. On "Go," each player "picks flowers" by collecting cupcake liners only in the color he or she has been given. The player to collect all of his or her liners first is the winner. If you have more children than colors of liners, let the children collect any color and give prizes for the most of each color.

Frogs in the Pond

Materials

★ Scissors

★ Blue poster paper (one less sheet than number of players)

Directions

Before the sleepover, cut the blue poster paper into large pond shapes. For the game, scatter the ponds on the ground. There should be one less pond than number of players. Choose one person to be the "bullfrog." The bullfrog squats like a frog in front of the ponds. The other children squat like frogs on the pond shapes, one "frog" per pond. The bullfrog announces, "Leap, little frogs, leap!" Each frog on a pond has to leap to another pond; the bullfrog tries to get to a pond first. The "frog" that is left without a pond becomes the next bullfrog. Play continues until each player has had at least one turn as bullfrog.

Gone Fishing

Materials

- ★ Fish-shaped crackers
- ★ Large blue towel (e.g., a beach towel)
- ★ Kitchen tongs, one per team
- ★ Two plastic beach pails

Directions

Pour the crackers onto the towel. Divide the guests into two teams and have them line up on either side of the towel. Place two beach pails about fifteen feet in front of the teams. Give each team a pair of tongs. On "Go," the first person in line uses the tongs to "catch a fish," by carefully picking up a cracker. Instruct the children to be gentle, or the crackers will crack. The child takes the fish to the team's bucket, drops it in, and then runs back to the team, handing off the tongs. The team with the most fish in the bucket after an allotted amount of time is the winning team.

Gymnastic Judging

Materials

- ★ No materials needed

Directions

Have each child take turns doing somersaults and cartwheels. Let each of the other children be judges, reminding them not to be hurtful with their comments. Require that each person give some kind of award to each person, such as "Most interesting way to land," "Most creative cartwheel," and so on.

Haybale Hopping

Materials

- ★ Three bales of hay
- ★ Stopwatch

Directions

(*Hint:* If you choose not to use hay bales, use piles of straw or leaves.)

Spread the hay bales out such that guests can jump from one to the other with some extra effort. Divide the guests into teams. Have one team race first; time the race using a stopwatch. Then have the other team race and compare times. The object of the game is for each child to hop from bale to bale and run back to tag the next person.

Hidden Bones

Materials

★ Bone-shaped dog treats
★ Paintbrushes
★ Glow-in-the-dark paint

Directions

This game can be adapted for a variety of themes. For a pet, animal, puppy, or dinosaur theme, hide the bones in the yard and have the guests search for them. For a fall, mystery, or secret agent theme, paint the bones with glow-in-the-dark paint and let them dry. Then hide the bones and have the guests look for them in the dark.

Island Hopping

Materials

★ Fourteen old dishcloths

Directions

Before the game begins, randomly place seven dishcloths in an area of the yard, about a yard apart. (The guests should be able to jump from one to the other without landing on the ground.) Make another path of seven dishcloths nearby. To play the game, divide the guests into two teams. Have the teams line up in front of the dishcloth paths. On "Go," the first person in the line hops from one dishcloth to the other until he or she reaches the last dishcloth. The player then turns around and runs back to the team, moving his or her arms as if swimming while running. The first team to complete the relay wins.

Jell-O Toss

Materials

★ Box of Jell-O (prepared according to box's directions)

Directions

(*Hint:* You may want to suggest on the party invitation that guests bring a change of clothes if you'll be playing this game, so they can change out of Jell-O–covered clothes afterward.)

This game can be altered to fit any theme by changing the flavor, thus color, of the Jell-O (red and blue for a patriotic party, green for St. Patrick's Day, orange for a fall party, etc.) and by using gelatin molds in party theme–related shapes. If you're not using molds, cut the Jell-O into large chunks just before the game. Divide the guests into groups of two, providing old shirts to wear as smocks. Have the pairs line up about five feet apart, facing one another. The first person throws the Jell-O to his or her partner. If the person catches it, he or she takes one step backward. Play continues until everyone is out of Jell-O or everyone is a mess! The pair who moved the farthest apart and kept their Jell-O together wins.

Lasso Contest

Materials

★ Two stuffed animals or small chairs
★ Two hula hoops

Directions

Have the children form two teams. Place the two stuffed animals or small chairs about six feet apart. Give the first person in each line a hula hoop. The object of the game is to attempt to "lasso" the "cow" (stuffed animal or small chair) with the hoop. Points are awarded each time the hula hoop lands flat on the ground and is completely around the stuffed animal or chair.

Layers and Layers

Materials

★ Clothing articles
★ One die
★ Hose

Directions

Make a pile of clothing in the yard (on cement works best). Spray the clothing with the hose. Take turns rolling the die. The number of the die is the number of items of wet clothing that person must put on. See how many pieces you can put on before you fall down.

Leaping Frogs

Materials

★ Rope

Directions

Place the rope on the ground to be a finish line. Divide the guests into two teams and have them form two lines. On "Go," have the first person in the line leap forward like a frog and squat on all fours on the ground. Remind each player to duck his or her head during the game. The next player puts his or her hands on the squatted player's back and leaps over that player. The second player then squats on all fours on the ground. Each child on the team continues leaping over his or her teammates. When the last person has leaped over each player, the first player then stands and begins to leap over the fellow teammates. Play continues until each person on the team is across the finish line.

Lions and Lambs

Materials

★ No materials needed

Directions

Choose one player to be the "lion." Establish boundaries on all four sides. Have all the other players line up at one end of the boundaries. Have the lion stand in the middle. The lion shouts, "Run, lambs, run!" The players run from one side to the other, trying not to get tagged. The players must not go out of bounds on either side. If a "lamb" is tagged, he or she waits on the outside of the boundaries until all the lambs have been tagged.

Meat Eaters versus Plant Eaters

Materials

★ No materials needed

Directions

Choose two players to be the meat-eating dinosaurs. The rest of the players are the plant-eating dinosaurs. The meat eaters chase the plant eaters. When a plant eater is tagged, he or she becomes a meat eater and chases the remaining players. The last plant eater to be tagged becomes the next meat eater and chooses a partner to play with him or her.

Moving to the Music

Materials

★ Tape player or CD player
★ Favorite tapes or CDs

Directions

Have the children spread out in the yard. Place the tape player or CD player in the center of the group. Play the music loudly for all to hear. Each child

dances and moves to the music. Stop the music in the middle of a song. Children must freeze immediately. Anyone spotted moving receives a point. The first person with ten points must sit out until someone else reaches ten points. That person then sits out and the first person resumes dancing.

Octopus Race

Materials

★ Rope

Directions

Stretch the rope on the ground for a boundary line. Pair the children. Have one child in each pair lean over on the ground such that hands and feet are touching the ground. Then have his or her partner lean criss-crossed over that person such that his or her hands and feet are touching the ground. On "Go," each "octopus" pair move their hands and feet forward to the finish line. The first pair to cross the line is the winner.

Orbit Game

Materials

★ No supplies needed

Directions

Choose one person to be "it." Have that person stand about twenty feet away from the rest of the players. Each player lines up facing "it" with about two yards between each player. "It" turns his or her back to the other players and yells, "Orbit!" The players spin around with outstretched arms until "it" yells, "Stop." At that point, each person stops immediately and tries to stand very still. If "it" sees any person moving, he or she may direct that person to start back at the beginning. "It" continues to turn back and forth, until someone tags him or her on the back. That person then becomes "it," and play starts all over again.

Paper Carrier Contest

Materials

★ Newspapers
★ Rubber bands

Directions

Roll each newspaper and secure each with a rubber band. Have each child pick a newspaper and fling it as far as he or she can. The winning newspaper is the one that travels the farthest.

Pass the Apple

Materials

- ★ Two or more apples

Directions

Divide the children into two teams, and give an apple to the first person in each line. On "Go," the first person in line tucks the apple under his or her chin. The player must pass the apple to the next player; neither player may use anything but chin and neck. If a player drops an apple, he or she must pick up the apple using only his or her chin and neck. The last player to receive the apple runs to the front of the line and starts passing again. When the original first player returns to the front of the line, the team is finished. The team to complete the game first is the winning team.

Pass the Paintbrush

Materials

- ★ Rope
- ★ Two large paintbrushes

Directions

Divide the guests into two teams. Station each player about ten feet from another player on his or her team. Stretch a rope about ten feet from the last player to be the finish line. Give a paintbrush to the first person in line. On "Go," the first person runs to the next person, passing the paintbrush to that person, who then begins to run. The team whose player crosses the finish line first is the winning team.

Photo Scavenger Hunt

Materials

- ★ List of items to be found, one list per team
- ★ Disposable instant cameras, one per two or three children

Directions

Before the sleepover, create a list of items to be found and photographed. The list could include such easily located items as flower, tree, plant with red berries, mound of dirt, swing set, and more difficult-to-find items such as an insect, animal, cloud shaped like an animal, and so on. Decide how you will divide the guests according to how many will attend and how many cameras you wish to purchase. Make a list for each team. To play the game, give each team an instant camera and a list of items to photograph. Decide how long you want the game to last, and send the photographers on their way. The team with the most items found and photographed wins. (This game lends itself easily to awarding each team. In addition to the team who finds the most items, choose pictures that are "most creative," "fluffiest cloud," "prettiest flower," etc.)

Play Ball!

Materials

★ Mitts for each player
★ Plastic bat
★ Wiffle ball
★ Batting tee (if necessary)

Directions

Play a game of baseball or tee-ball.

Porridge in the Pot

Materials

★ One large bowl
★ Large container of oatmeal
★ Two plastic spoons
★ Two small cereal-sized bowls

Directions

Place the large bowl on the ground. Pour the oatmeal and place two spoons into the bowl. Divide the children into two teams, and have them stand in a line on either side of the bowl. About ten feet away from the teams, place the small cereal bowls on the ground. The first player scoops up a spoonful of oatmeal on the word "Go" and carries it to the bowl opposite his or her team. The player empties the oatmeal into the bowl and runs back to his or her team, passing the spoon to the next person in line and stepping to the back of the line. Play continues for a predetermined number of rounds; the team with the most oatmeal in the bowl wins.

Puppy Power

Materials

★ No materials needed

Directions

Choose one person to be the "dog;" the remaining guests are the "cats." The dog chases the cats until all are caught. The last cat becomes the next dog.

Racing the Bases

Materials

★ Baseball bases

Directions

Place the bases (use real ones or make out of card-board and secure to the ground with small stakes) on the ground in a diamond shape. Have the children form a line behind home plate. Have an adult stand at home plate, instructing the guests when to go. On "Go," the first player begins running around the bases, tagging each base. The adult should let one child start running about every ten seconds. Each child attempts to catch the person in front of him or her.

Ransom Money Scavenger Hunt

Materials

★ Toy dollar bills
★ Markers
★ Toy purse
★ Plastic gold coins

Directions

Before the sleepover, decide several places in your home to hide a toy dollar bill. Write notes on each dollar bill, leading the children to the next dollar bill. Have the last spot contain the toy purse with the rest of the "ransom money" dollar bills and gold coins. Give the children the first bill with a clue written on it, and have them search as a team to find the rest of the money.

Run from the Wolf

Materials

★ One basket for each child
★ Paper wadded into balls (three balls per player)
★ Red towel or cape for each player (optional)

Directions

Choose one player to be the "wolf." Give each of the other players a basket with three wads of paper; these will be the "muffins." Choose a spot, called "Granny's House," to be the base. If you are using the optional red towels or capes, pin or tie one to each of the players with baskets. Have all the players run around the yard. The wolf tries to catch "Little Red Riding Hood." If the wolf tags a player, he or she loses one muffin. The first player to lose all of his or her muffins is out of the game. Play continues until only one player is left; then that player becomes the wolf.

Scavenger Hunt

Materials

- ★ Items to hide, such as pair of socks, empty cups, ticket stubs, marbles, dice, old keys, and so on (have two of each item)
- ★ Two lists of the hidden items

Directions

Before the sleepover, hide the items to be found in the yard. Make some of the items easy to find and some more difficult. Make identical lists for each team of the items to look for. To play the game, divide the guests into two teams. Establish boundaries so the children will know where to look. Giving each team a list and telling them there are two of each item, have them search for the items on the list. If one team finds another item that they have already located, the team should leave the item there and not tell the other team its location. The first team with all the items on the list or the team with the most items after an allotted time is the winning team.

Shark Attack

Materials

- ★ No materials needed

Directions

Establish boundaries for playing this chase game. Choose one person to be the "shark;" the other players are "fish." Have the children run and move their arms in a swimming motion. When the shark tags a child, that person becomes a shark also. Play continues until all children have been caught. The last fish to be tagged becomes the next shark.

Spiders in the Web

Materials

- ★ Black balloons
- ★ White paint
- ★ Paintbrushes
- ★ Scissors
- ★ Black crepe paper
- ★ Tape
- ★ Large black marker
- ★ Large sheet

Directions

Before the party, inflate the black balloons. Use the white paint to add two eyes to each balloon. Cut crepe paper in strips of about twelve inches in length. Tape eight "legs" onto each balloon. Use the marker to draw a spider web on the sheet. Stretch the sheet out flat. Start in the center and draw a spiral extending to the edge of the sheet. Then draw lines from the inside to the outside, perpendicular to the spiraled lines. To play the game, have the children gather around the outside of the sheet and lift it about waist high. Place the spiders "in the web" and have the children shake the sheet. The object is to keep the spiders on the sheet as long as possible. You may choose to tape or paint a number on each spider's back, and the children can try to guess which spider will last the longest on the sheet.

Torch Bearers

Materials

- ★ Two cardboard paper towel tubes
- ★ Paintbrush
- ★ Black paint
- ★ Scissors
- ★ Red construction paper
- ★ Tape
- ★ Rope

Directions

Before the sleepover, make two torches using the paper towel tubes. Paint the torches with black paint and let dry. Cut a flame shape from the red construction paper. Tape it to the top of the paper towel tube.

For the game, divide the guests into two teams. Stretch the rope on the ground for the finish line. Station each player from one team about twenty feet apart, with the last player being about twenty feet from the finish line. Do the same with the other team, keeping the teams separated by about six feet.

Give the torch to the first player on the team. That person runs to the next person and hands off the torch. The play continues, delivering the torch to the next player, until the last player has the torch. That player runs to the finish line. The first team to have a player cross the finish line is the winning team.

Tug-of-War

Materials

- ★ Long rope
- ★ Two stuffed animals, beanbags, or other toys

Directions

Divide the children into two teams, with each team lined up on opposite ends of the rope. Use beanbags or choose items related to the party as markers for each team (e.g., for a stuffed animal party, use two stuffed animals as markers; for a reptile party, use two large plastic snakes; for a fall party, use two small pumpkins). Place one marker six feet behind the last player of each team. On "Go," both teams tug on the rope, trying to move back toward their marker. The first team to pick up their marker is the winning team.

Twelve-Tag

Materials

- ★ Twelve hula hoops, baseball bases, or old rags
- ★ Alarm clock

Directions

Place the twelve items you've selected randomly on the ground. Spread the bases out throughout the yard as far as you want the boundaries of the tag game. Choose one child to be "it." Place the alarm clock, with the alarm set for two minutes, in the middle of the play area so that the children will be able to hear the alarm. Have the children skip or walk around inside the boundaries; each child must keep moving. "It" walks around inside the boundaries. When the alarm rings, all the players run to stand on a base. If "it" tags a player before he or she reaches a base, that person is the next "it." If a player is not tagged, reset the alarm and have the players start over again.

Up, Up, and Away!

Materials

★ Twelve plastic cones or folding chairs

Directions

Before the game, write or tape a number on each cone or chair from one to six. Make two sets. Place the cones or chairs on the ground randomly, not in numerical order. Divide the guests into two teams. Have each team choose a team name by selecting an airline name. Instruct the children that they are to stretch out their arms like wings. On "Go," have the first child in each line begin running to the cones or chairs in order, from one to six, tagging each one along the way. After he or she has successfully flown to all six destinations in order, he or she returns to the team. The next player then takes off. The game is over when a team is completely finished.

Water Balloon Fight

Materials

★ Balloons (choose a color to fit your theme)

Directions

(*Hint:* You may want to suggest on the party invitation that guests bring a change of clothes if you'll be playing this game, so they can change out of wet clothes afterward.)

Before the party, fill many balloons with water in a theme-related color and load them in a basket. For the game, give each player two balloons. Have the players chase one another, attempting to hit a friend with a water balloon. When a player has thrown both balloons, he or she may get two more from the basket. The wettest guest is the loser!

Wild Bull Roundup

Materials

★ No materials needed

Directions

Choose two children to be the horse riders; the rest of the guests will be the "wild bulls." Establish boundary lines before the game. The bulls place their hands on either side of their heads with the index finger pointing up for a horn. The bulls run around inside the "pen," and the riders, galloping, try to catch them. If a bull is tagged, he or she is out until only one bull remains. The last bull gets to be the next rider, and he or she chooses a friend to be the second rider (encourage this child to pick someone who has not had a turn).

Wrong-Glove Wrangling

Materials

★ Mitts (right- and left-handed)
★ Two Wiffle balls

Directions

Divide the children into two teams. Choose one player from each team to be the "pitcher." Give the first person in each line a mitt that oppositely fits his or her throwing hand (give a right-handed person a left-handed mitt and vice versa). On "Go," have the pitcher pitch to the first person in line. That player must catch the ball, throw it back to the pitcher, hand the mitt to the next person, and then run to the end of the line. Once each child has had a turn, the first person in line becomes the pitcher, and the original pitcher runs to the end of the line. Play continues until each player has had a turn as pitcher. The winning team is the team who finishes first.

Inside Games

Play inside games any time of the night, or even the morning after the sleepover. Select only games that will work for the appropriate age group and gender of your guests.

Balloon Scrabble

Materials

★ Balloons
★ Medium-point ink pens
★ Large trash bags

Directions

Using balloons in a color related to your theme, inflate them and tie the ends shortly before the sleepover, so they won't deflate before game time. Decide on a message you will want the guests to search for, such as "Happy Birthday," "Happy New Year," or "Welcome Spring." Write one large letter on each balloon to spell out the message. You will need to write the message as many times as you have children participating. Stuff the balloons in trash bags and put in a safe place until the sleepover. Then write extra letters also. To play the game, dump the balloons on the floor, tell the children the message they are hunting to create, and give each child a trash bag. Have each child search for balloons to spell the message, stuffing the balloons in the bag as they collect them. The first person to spell the message is the winner.

Balloon Stomp

Materials

★ Balloons in theme-related colors

Directions

Inflate the balloons. Give each player or pair of players a color. The children try to stomp other colors of balloons. The player or team with the last balloon is the winner.

Beach Ball Bowling

Materials

★ Ten empty water bottles
★ Inflated beach ball

Directions

Line the water bottles up like bowling pins: one bottle in front, two bottles in the second row, three bottles in the third row, and four bottles in the fourth row. Let each child take turns rolling the beach ball toward the bottles to see how many bottles he or she can knock down.

Blooms in a Bowl

Materials

★ Miniature marshmallows
★ One large bowl
★ Two small bowls
★ Two small spoons

Directions

Divide the children in two teams; have the teams line up one behind the other. Pour the bag of miniature marshmallows in the big bowl. Place the bowl between the lines of children. Set the small bowls on the floor about six feet in front of the teams. Give the first player in each line a spoon. On "Go," the first person scoops a spoonful of mini marshmallow "blooms" and runs to the small bowl. After pouring the marshmallows in the bowl, the player runs back to the line, handing off the spoon. Play continues until one team fills a bowl. The first team to fill its bowl is the winning team.

Bubble-Blowing Contest

Materials

★ Bubble gum for each player

Directions

Choose a bubble gum to fit your theme. If this is a sports or baseball party, for example, buy the shredded bubble gum that comes in a sports pack. For a springtime theme, choose pink and blue bubble gum. Find red, white, and blue gums for a summer theme. To play the game, give each player some gum to chew. At a determined time, see who can blow the biggest bubble without it bursting.

Catch the Coconuts

Materials

★ Burlap sacks, one per two players
★ Wiffle balls

Directions

Have each player choose a partner for this game. Give each pair a burlap sack and five Wiffle balls. One player holds the sack open; the other person tosses the balls into the sack. Let the pairs take turns "catching the coconuts."

Cinderella's Shoe

Materials

★ A pair of bedroom slippers for each child
★ Timer

Directions

(*Hint:* On the invitation, be sure to request that the guest bring a pair of bedroom slippers to the sleepover.)

To play the game, have each guest put on slippers. Each guest should remove one slipper and put it in a pile in the middle of the floor. Set the timer for thirty seconds. The guests close their eyes, and on "Go," they search for their matching slipper while keeping their eyes closed. When the timer goes off, guests must grab a slipper, even if it is not their own slipper. The guests put on the other slipper and walk around the room. Play the game again and model the next pair of shoes each "Cinderella" receives.

Clowns and Balloons

Materials

- ★ Old adult-size coat, pants, and belt for shirt for each child
- ★ Small inflated balloons
- ★ Yarn

Directions

Have each child put on an adult-sized coat, pants, and belt. Tie balloons to each child's ankle, one balloon per ankle. The object of the game is to try to pop each other's balloons. The last player with an unpopped balloon is the winner.

Coin Collecting

Materials

- ★ Foil-wrapped chocolate candy coins
- ★ Two small pots (preferably black ones)
- ★ Two pair of kitchen tongs

Directions

Scatter coins on the floor. Set the two pots away from the coins. Divide the children into two teams, giving each team a pair of tongs. On "Go," have the first player pick up a coin with the tongs and take it to the pot. Then the player returns to the team and hands off the tongs to the next player. The first team to fill the pot is the winning team.

Crepe Paper Cacti

Materials

- ★ Green crepe paper rolls, one roll per two people

Directions

Group the children in pairs. Give each pair a roll of crepe paper. Have one child stand with one arm up, bent at the elbow, and one arm down, bent at the elbow. Have his or her partner wrap the crepe paper around his or her body, arms and head, but not the face. After all the children have finished creating their cacti, give prizes for the neatest cactus, bushiest cactus, silliest cactus, and so on.

Dinosaur Dig

Materials

- ★ Large sheet or shower curtain
- ★ Large plastic container
- ★ Large bags of rice to fill the container

- ★ Small plastic or rubber dinosaur toys
- ★ Plastic spoons

Directions

Spread the sheet or shower curtain on the floor. Place the container in the middle of the sheet. Pour the rice into the container. Hide the dinosaur toys in the rice, burying some of the toys at the bottom. Give two children spoons and have them search for the toys. No hands may be used, only spoons. The child who finds the most dinosaurs wins out of that pair. Repeat the game for other pairs.

Dinosaur Hideout

Materials

- ★ Large sheet
- ★ Card table

Directions

Drape the sheet over the card table to make a cave. Choose one player to be the *Tyrannosaurus rex* dinosaur. Have the other dinosaurs crawl around the room on hands and knees. When the T-rex roars, all the dinosaurs run to the "cave." The last player to get in the cave is the next T-rex.

Egg Toss

Materials

- ★ Towels, one per three children
- ★ Plastic eggs

Directions

Divide the children into teams of three. Have two children in each team hold either end of a towel. Have the third child stand about six feet away and toss five eggs, one at a time, in the direction of his or her partners. The two children with the towel should use the towel to catch the eggs. Award points for the number of eggs that land in the towel.

Eggs in the Nest

Materials

- ★ Plastic eggs
- ★ Basket

Directions

Have a contest to see who can toss the most eggs into the basket. Move the basket varying distances from the players, and see who has the best aim.

Explorer's Search

Materials

- ★ Scissors
- ★ Construction paper
- ★ Tape
- ★ Pair of dice

Directions

Cut footprints out of construction paper. On each footprint, write instructions such as, "Met friendly Native Americans; move ahead two spaces," "Fell into the river; go back one space," "No food available; go back three spaces," and so on. Tape the footprints in a path to the bathroom tub. Label the tub "Columbia River." Have all of the "explorers" stand at the beginning of the footprint path. Choose a player to go first. The first player rolls the dice, and then moves along the path the sum of the numbers on the dice. The player must follow the instructions on the footprint. The first person to reach the Columbia River is the winner.

Falling Stars

Materials

- ★ Balloons
- ★ Markers
- ★ Tape player or CD player
- ★ Favorite tapes or CDs

Directions

Before the sleepover, inflate balloons and draw a large star on each balloon. Write a number inside the star from one to ten. To play the game, give each child a balloon. Have the children bat the balloons in the air with music playing in the background. The children do not have to hit only their own balloon. The object is to keep all the balloons in the air until the music stops. When the music stops, each child should catch a balloon. The number written on each balloon is the score for that person. Keep a tally of the scores throughout the game to see who has the most points at the end of the game.

Feathers in the Air

Materials

- ★ One feather per player

Directions

Give each person a feather. On "Go," each person blows his or her feather into the air. The object is to see which person can keep the feather in the air the longest without touching it with his or her hands. You may choose to play music in the background as you do this game.

Fill the Vase

Materials

- ★ Two vases
- ★ Real or artificial flowers

Directions

Divide the children into two teams. Place the vases on the floor about six feet from each team. Carefully lay the flowers on the floor in between both teams. On "Go," the first person in line chooses one stem of flowers and runs to the vase. The player puts the stem in the vase, then runs quickly to tag the next player. If you have enough flowers, have each player take two or three turns to create a beautiful arrangement of flowers. The first team to complete the game is the winning team.

Firecracker Exchange

Materials

- ★ Paintbrushes
- ★ Empty toilet paper tubes, one per child
- ★ Red paint
- ★ Small toy prizes or candy
- ★ Orange, yellow and red tissue paper
- ★ Rubber bands
- ★ Two dice

Directions

Before the sleepover, paint the tubes red. When dry, add a toy surprise and/or candy. Cover both ends with small squares of orange, red, and yellow tissue paper. Wrap rubber bands around the tissue paper to secure it. Write a small number, one to six, on the bottom of the tube. To play the game, give each player a "firecracker." Let each child take a turn rolling the two dice. Have the children holding the firecrackers with the two numbers that show up on the dice switch firecrackers. Play until each child has had a turn rolling the dice. Then let each child "pop" the firecracker he or she is holding by punching a hole in one end of the tissue paper and emptying the contents.

Flower Twister Game

Materials

- ★ Paint
- ★ Paintbrushes
- ★ Large white sheet
- ★ Game spinner

Directions

Before the sleepover, paint a large flower on the sheet with different-colored petals. Use the colors that are on the game spinner. (If you do not have a spinner, make one from cardboard, cutting out a cardboard arrow and securing it with a paper fastener to a separate piece of cardboard.) Paint several petals of each color. To play the game, spread the sheet on the floor. Choose a child to be the caller. The child spins the spinner and calls out a body part. For example, as the arrow is spinning, the caller may yell out, "Right foot," and the arrow lands on yellow. Each child must put his or her right foot on a yellow petal. The play continues until one child loses his or her balance and topples. Then a new caller is chosen and the play begins again.

Flying Bats

Materials

- ★ Black balloons, one per player
- ★ Marker
- ★ Black construction paper
- ★ Scissors
- ★ Tape
- ★ White paint
- ★ Paintbrush

Directions

Just before the party, make a "bat" for each player. Inflate a balloon. Draw wing-shapes on the construction paper and cut out. Tape the wings onto either side of the balloon. (Have the tied end at the front for the bat's nose.) Use the white paint to add eyes and teeth to the bat's face. Store the bats in a safe place until the sleepover. (The bats shouldn't be made too far in advance, as the balloons will wilt as air seeps out.) To play the game, give each player a bat, and have him or her see how long he or she can keep it in the air.

Headline Hunters

Materials

- ★ Drawing paper
- ★ Crayons
- ★ Newspapers

Directions

Give each child a sheet of drawing paper and some crayons. Read one of the headlines in the newspaper. Read several headlines and have the children illustrate. Tell the children not to put their names on their papers. Gather all the papers and let the children choose the best picture to go with each headline.

Herding the Sheep

Materials

★ Cotton balls in at least two different colors
★ Straws, one for each player

Directions

Play this game on a table in pairs. Scatter cotton balls of two different colors on the table; make sure there are equal numbers of each color. Give each person a straw. Let two children challenge each other. Determine a color for each person and designate which end of the table will be each child's "pen." Using the straw, the kids blow the cotton balls to opposite sides of the table. The first child to "herd" all of his or her "sheep" to his or her pen is the winner. Continue playing until each pair has had a turn. You can continue the game by switching partners.

Horseshoes and Obstacle Courses

Materials

★ Pillows
★ Jump ropes
★ Two pair of adult-sized shoes
★ Stopwatch

Directions

Use the pillows and jump ropes to create an obstacle course in two or three rooms of the house. Have a guest put an adult-sized pair of shoes on his or her feet, then lean over and put his or her hands into another pair of adult-sized shoes. The "horse" runs the obstacle course on the word "Go," and someone times the race. Time the race with a stopwatch and compare times of the players. Let the players run the course again to try to beat their former time.

Hum That Tune

Materials

★ No materials needed

Directions

Have the children take turns humming favorite songs for their friends to guess the tune.

I Spy

Materials

★ Paintbrushes
★ Empty paper towel tubes, one per player
★ Black paint

Directions

Before the sleepover, paint each cardboard tube with black paint. Allow time to dry. Store in a safe place until the sleepover. To play the game, give each player an empty paper towel tube. Choose one person to start the game. The player must look through his or her "spy glass" until he or she finds something to start the game. The child says, "I spy something . . ." and gives the colors of the object. (Remind the child to keep moving the spy glass so as not to give away the chosen object.) The other children use their own spy glasses to search for the object, guessing what it is by the hints the lead player is dropping.

Inside Batting Contest

Materials

★ Newspaper, wadded into balls
★ Fly swatter

Directions

Have a batting contest by pitching wadded newspaper balls to a batter, using a fly swatter as a bat. See who can hit the most balls and who can hit the balls the farthest.

Leaf Collecting

Materials

★ Scissors
★ Tissue paper
★ Straws, one for each player
★ Two baskets

Directions

Play this game on a table. Cut leaf shapes from tissue paper and spread the leaves on the table. (If you are using this with a fall theme, use orange, red, brown, and gold leaves. For a spring or summer theme, use green leaves.) Give each player a straw. Have two players challenge each other at a time. On "Go," each player puts one end of his or her straw on top of a leaf shape. Then, the player puts the other end of the straw in his or her mouth and inhales, sucking the leaf onto the end of the straw. The player holds his or her breath while walking the leaf to the basket. The child should lean over the basket with the leaf and exhale. The leaf should fall into the basket. The child who collects the most leaves after an allotted amount of time is the winner.

Lion Tamers

Materials

★ Two pillows for each player

Directions

Have each player put both pillows on carpeted floor (to keep pillows from slipping) in front of him or her, about twelve inches apart. Have the players pretend to be lions and leap back and forth on their pillows, moving the pillows farther apart with each jump. The player must land on the pillow and not on the carpet. If he or she touches the carpet with hands or feet, the game stops for that player. The player who moves the pillows the farthest is the winner. (Be sure to separate the players enough so that there will be no crashes!

Lucky Horseshoes

Materials

★ Index cards
★ Markers
★ One die

Directions

Give each guest an even number of index cards. Have each guest write a phrase that might be on a board game and is related to the sleepover theme. For example, at a horse party, the guests might write, "Horse stopped to eat hay; lose one turn." Or "Horse stung by a bee; gallop ahead three spaces." Let each guest write an equal number of forward and backward instructions. Place all the cards on the floor in a horseshoe shape. Use plastic, toy horses for markers. Roll the die and move your marker to the correct card for direction, and play the game to see which horse wins.

Mousetrap

Materials

★ Small cheese crackers in a bowl
★ Scissors
★ Clear Con-Tact or self-adhesive paper

Directions

Place a bowl of cheese crackers at the front of the room. Cut the self-adhesive paper into rectangles about three inches by four inches. Peel the lining off and place the paper, sticky side up, on the floor in random order. Let each child take a turn being a "mouse." The child must run quickly through the "mousetraps," trying not to get "caught in a trap"; pick up a cracker with his or her fingers; eat the cracker; and run back through the "traps." You may need to replace some of the pieces of adhesive paper if some get stuck onto the children.

Mummy Wrap

Materials

★ Toilet paper, one roll per pair of children

Directions

Divide the children into pairs. On "Go," have one child in the pair proceed to wrap the other child with the toilet paper, making a mummy. Be sure to have the pairs leave the face uncovered. The first pair to complete the mummy is the winning team. Play the game again, and have pairs switch roles.

Musical Bus Seats

Materials

★ One less chair than number of players
★ Tape player or CD player
★ Favorite tapes or CDs

Directions

Line the chairs one behind the other, like seats on a bus. Play the music as the guests walk around the chairs in a circle. When the music stops, each player quickly sits in a chair. The player without a chair is temporarily out of the game. Remove one chair and play the game again. The winner is the person who sits in the very last chair on the last round.

Newspaper Scavenger Hunt

Materials

★ List of words to search for (two identical copies)
★ Newspapers
★ Pens

Directions

Before the sleepover, make two identical lists of words that children are apt to find in a newspaper. To play the game, divide the guests into two teams. Give each team a stack of newspapers, a pen, and a scavenger hunt list. Have the teams search for the words on the list, and circle them when they find them. The first team to find all the words is the winning team.

Nine Lives of a Cat

Materials

- ★ Pillows, one less than the number of players
- ★ Stickers (preferably cat stickers, but small office dots will work fine)
- ★ Tape player or CD player
- ★ Favorite tapes or CDs

Directions

Put the pillows on the floor in a circle. Give each player nine stickers to wear on his or her pajamas. Play musical pillows, just like musical chairs. Each time a person is without a pillow, that person loses a sticker. When a person loses all nine stickers, that person is out of the game.

Number Balloons

Materials

- ★ Balloons
- ★ Permanent markers
- ★ Two dice
- ★ Pair of socks, rolled together

Directions

Inflate the balloons and write numbers, one through twelve, on each balloon. You may have more than one of each number, but only write numbers through twelve. Have the guests rub the balloons in their hair, causing static electricity, and then stick the balloons to the wall with the numbers showing. Have the guests take turns rolling the dice, adding the numbers together, and trying to knock that balloon off the wall by throwing the rolled-up socks at the balloon.

Paper Airplane Races

Materials

- ★ Sheets of typing paper

Directions

Give each child a sheet of paper to create a paper airplane. Have pairs of children race their planes to see which one travels the farthest or turns the most flips.

Party Blower Balloon Race

Materials

- ★ Balloons
- ★ Party blowers for each child
- ★ Crepe paper strip

Directions

Before the sleepover, inflate two balloons. To play the game, give each child his or her own blower. Divide the children in two teams, and give each team a balloon. Stretch the crepe paper strip on the floor for a finish line. On "Go," have the first person in line use his or her blower to push the balloon across the floor to the finish line. The balloon must cross the finish line, then the player turns around and pushes the balloon back to the next teammate, only using the party blower to make the balloon go. The children may not touch the balloon at any time with their hands or other body parts. Play continues until each player has had a turn. The first team to complete the game is the winner.

Party Hat Race

Materials

- ★ Styrofoam packing pieces
- ★ Two party hats
- ★ Two plastic beach pails

Directions

Scatter the Styrofoam packing pieces all over the floor. Divide the players into two teams. Give the first person in each team a party hat. On "Go," the first player scoops up a hatful of Styrofoam pieces and takes them to his or her team's pail. After emptying the packing pieces, the player gives the hat to the next person on the team. Each person continues to take a turn until the pail is full. The first team to fill their pail is the winning team. Play the game long enough to collect all the packing pieces off the floor!

Patriotic Popping

Materials

- ★ Equal numbers of red, white, and blue inflated balloons

Directions

Divide the children into three teams. Give each team a color. On "Go," the players try to pop their team's color of balloons. The team who pops its balloons first is the winning team.

Pigs in the Mud

Materials

- ★ Chocolate pudding
- ★ Large tray
- ★ Plastic tablecloth
- ★ Miniature marshmallows

Directions

Prepare the pudding according to the directions on the box. To play the game, spread pudding onto the tray, like a mud puddle. Cover the table with a plastic tablecloth and place the tray in the middle of the table. Have the children gather around the table. Give each child ten mini marshmallows. Have the children place a marshmallow on the table in front of him or her and flick the marshmallow with his or her fingers toward the tray. The child who gets the most "pigs in the mud" is the winner.

Pillowcase Race

Materials

★ Pillowcases
★ Favorite stuffed animal

Directions

(*Hint:* Be sure to include on the invitation a reminder to bring a pillow and favorite stuffed animal to the sleepover.)

Have each child remove his or her pillowcase and step inside. Have the child hold his or her favorite stuffed animal with both hands while also holding the pillowcase. Establish a door or wall for a boundary. Have the children hop to the boundary line, touch the door or wall, and then hop back to the starting point. If a player drops the stuffed animal, he or she must start over again. The first person back to the starting point is the winner.

Pirate Limbo

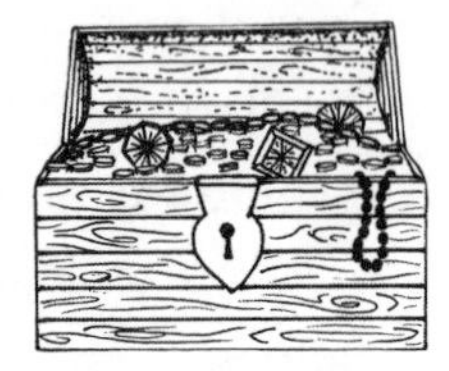

Materials

★ Rope
★ Pirate's patch for each player
★ Handkerchief for each player
★ Tape player or CD player
★ Favorite tapes or CDs (beach music is preferable)

Directions

Choose two players to hold the rope. The players stretch the rope taut and hold it above their heads. Each of the other players put on a patch and bandanna and do the limbo to music. The players holding the rope gradually lower it after each child has had a turn at one level. Repeat the game often to allow the players holding the rope to get a turn.

Pirate's Plunder

Materials

- ★ Gold plastic coins
- ★ Paper
- ★ Black markers

Directions

Divide the guests into two teams. Give each team a handful of gold coins and specify one room for each team. Send the teams to their designated room to determine a good hiding place for the coins. After the teams have hidden the coins, the children return to a table to draw a treasure map. When both teams have completed the treasure maps, the teams exchange maps and race to see who can find the treasure the quickest.

Race Around the Diamond

Materials

- ★ Markers
- ★ Index cards
- ★ Buttons or miniature helmets, caps, or sports balls for markers
- ★ One die

Directions

Have each player write four or five cards with board-game type instructions, related to a sports activity, such as, "Dropped the ball; go back one space" or "Kicked a field goal; move ahead two spaces." Line the cards up in a diamond shape, and use markers and a die to play the game.

Rescue the Baby Birds

Materials

- ★ Beanbags, five per team
- ★ Two pairs of kitchen tongs
- ★ Two baskets

Directions

Divide the children into two teams. Give each team five beanbags and a pair of kitchen tongs. Place the baskets about six feet away from the teams. On "Go," the first person in line uses the tongs to take one beanbag "birdie" to the basket "nest." The player then runs back to get the next bird. After the player has taken all five birds to the nest, the player brings all five beanbags back to the team and hands off the tongs. The next player then begins taking the birds to the nest. The game is over when each player on the team has taken all five birds to the nest. The team who completes the game first is the winning team.

Robin's Feathers

Materials

- ★ Feathers, one for each child
- ★ Tape player or CD player
- ★ Favorite tapes or CDs

Directions

Give each child a feather to put on his or her head. Play a favorite tape or CD. Have the guests dance to the music, trying to keep the feather from falling off.

Seashells and Sand Pails

Materials

- ★ Styrofoam packing pieces
- ★ Two plastic sand pails
- ★ Two plastic beach shovels

Directions

Scatter the Styrofoam packing pieces on the floor to be "seashells." Place the sand pails at the front of the room. Divide the children into two teams and have each team line up near the scattered seashells. Give the first person in line a shovel. On "Go," the first person scoops a shovel full of seashells and takes them to the pail. The first team to fill the pail with seashells is the winner.

Shear the Sheep

Materials

- ★ Pillows with cases
- ★ Stopwatch

Directions

Place all the pillows in the middle of the floor. Have each child take a turn "shearing the sheep": To "shear," a person removes all the pillowcases from the pillows as quickly as possible. Then he or she replaces all of the pillowcases onto the pillows. Time each person with the stopwatch to see who can work the fastest.

Sit-Down Volleyball

Materials

- ★ One small chair or tray per two people
- ★ One inflated balloon per two people

Directions

Have children choose a partner and sit cross-legged on the floor, facing one another. Have the partners sit about three and a half feet apart. Place a chair or tray on the floor between the partners for the net. Give each pair a balloon. The children bat the balloon back and forth over the net. If one person misses the balloon and it touches the ground, the other person gets a point. Or if one person uncrosses his or her legs, the other person gets a point, also. The first person to reach twenty-one is the winner.

Spider Tossing

Materials

- ★ Scissors
- ★ Black felt
- ★ Sewing machine, needle and thread, or hot-glue gun
- ★ Dried beans or stuffing beads
- ★ Sheet with painted web (used in "Spiders in the Web" in the Outside Games section)
- ★ Black marker

Directions

Before the sleepover, make several spider beanbag toys. Cut the felt into circles with a six-inch diameter. Hot-glue or stitch the circles together, leaving an opening for stuffing. Stuff the circles with dried beans or stuffing beads, found in a craft store or department store. Hot-glue or stitch the opening closed. Cut eight strips of felt for legs and hot-glue four on each side of the circle. Using the sheet painted to resemble a web, add points to each spot on the web by writing numbers one to ten in each area.

To play the game, lay the sheet flat on the floor. Give each child three beanbags to toss into the web. Give the child the sum of the three numbers nearest to his or her spiders for a score. Keep score for several rounds, and then compare numbers.

Star-Studded Race

Materials

- ★ Red or blue markers
- ★ Fifty stars cut from white construction paper
- ★ Tape
- ★ Two dice

Directions

Before the sleepover, write notes on each star, such as "Move forward two spaces," "Skip two spaces," "Stay here until a six is rolled," and so on. Tape each star on the floor in a meandering path. To play the game, have each player stand at the beginning of the path. The first player rolls the dice. The number of the two dice added together is the number of stars that that person will walk over. The player must do what is written on the last star the person lands on. The first person to get to the end of the fifty stars is the winner.

Stolen Ball

Materials

- Mitt for each player
- Chair
- Ball

Directions

Have the guests sit on the floor with their mitts turned upside down in front of them. Place a chair, turned around backward, in front of the guests. Choose one player to sit in the chair; place the ball on the floor under the chair. Decide on a player to crawl quietly to the ball and remove it from under the chair while the person in the chair has his or her eyes closed. The person takes the ball back to his or her spot and puts the ball under his or her mitt. The person who took the ball says in a disguised voice, "Play ball!" The person in the chair opens his or her eyes and has three guesses to determine who stole the ball.

Stolen Heart

Materials

- Chair
- Small heart-shaped Mylar balloon

Directions

Have the guests sit cross-legged on the floor on top of their sleeping bags. Turn a chair away from the children. Choose one person to start the game and have that person sit in the chair. Place the heart-shaped balloon under the chair. Decide on one person to take the heart quietly while the person in the chair closes his or her eyes. That person should hide the heart inside his or her sleeping bag and cross legs over the heart to hide it. Then the person with the heart giggles in a disguised voice. The person in the chair turns around and tries to guess who stole the heart.

Stuff the Scarecrow

Materials

- ★ Two adult-sized shirts
- ★ Two pairs of adult-sized pants
- ★ Newspapers

Directions

Divide the children into two teams. Choose one person to be the "scarecrow." On "Go," the scarecrow dons the adult-sized clothes. His or her teammates wad up the newspaper and stuff the inside of the shirt and pants. The first team to complete their scarecrow is the winning team.

Swimming Balloons

Materials

- ★ Swimming goggles, one per player
- ★ Inflated balloons, one per player

Directions

(*Hint:* Use the goggles as party favors at the end of the sleepover.)

Just before the party, carefully slip a
gles on each balloon, tightening or loosen
sary. To play the game, give each child a
balloon. On "Go," have the players bat
into the air. See who can keep his or her balloon "swimming" in the air the longest.

Three-Legged Sack Race

Materials

- ★ Pillowcases
- ★ Stopwatch

Directions

Have the children choose a partner. Each pair will need one pillowcase. The pairs stand side by side, each putting his or her inside leg in the pillowcase. Establish a course for each pair to follow, such as "Go to the kitchen to get a spoon, go to the bathroom to get a tissue, and go to the den to get a pencil." Have one pair go at a time and use the stopwatch to time the length of the trip. The pair who completes the course in the shortest length of time is the winning team.

Toy Tossing

Materials

★ Small toy minnow net for each of two players
★ Small toys, related to the party's theme

Directions

Purchase toys appropriate for the theme (e.g., dinosaurs, reptiles, birds, etc.). Pair the children, and give each pair a minnow net and handful of small toys. One of the members of the pair holds the minnow net. The other player tosses the toys, one at a time, to his or her partner. The winning pair is the pair who catches the most toys in the net.

Treats for the Puppy

Materials

★ Two small dog bowls
★ Spoon-Size Shredded Wheat cereal

Directions

Divide the children into two teams. Choose one person to be the "puppy owner" for each team. Place the small bowls on the floor about six feet away from the teams. Each of the team members gets on hands and knees on the floor. On "Go," have the puppy owner give a "treat" (cereal piece) to the first "puppy" in line. That puppy takes the treat in his or her mouth and runs to the dog bowl. After dropping the treat in the bowl, without touching it, the puppy runs back to the end of the line. Play continues until each child has had a turn. The first team to complete the game is the winner. Play the game again to give the "owner" a chance to be a "puppy"; however, do not reuse the cereal pieces that children have had in their mouths.

T-Rex Battles

Materials

★ Eight-inch lightweight balls, one per two players

Directions

Have each child pull his or her elbows into the sleeves of his or her shirt such that only the wrist and hand extend. Pair the children and give each pair a ball. Have the pairs stand about three feet apart. The person with the ball tosses the ball to his or her partner. The partner catches the ball without removing his or her elbows from the sleeves. If the person catches the ball, he or she takes one step backward. The pair who moves the farthest apart is the winning team.

Who Am I?

Materials

- ★ Markers
- ★ Index cards
- ★ Safety pins

Directions

Write the names of birds, reptiles, amphibians, farm animals, or another category related to the theme of your party on index cards. Pin the cards to the backs of the guests, not allowing the children to see their own cards. The children must ask "yes" or "no" questions of their friends to try to guess what is on their own card.

Wiffle Ball Instru

Materials

- ★ Markers
- ★ Strips of paper
- ★ Enough Wiffle balls for at least three per player
- ★ Tweezers
- ★ Trash bag or paper bag

Directions

Before the sleepover, let the host help you think of silly instructions, such as, "Oink like a pig," "Turn a flip and sing 'Twinkle, Twinkle, Little Star,'" and "Make a monster face." Using markers, write each silly instruction on a strip of paper. Fold the pieces of paper and put one in each Wiffle ball. Use tweezers to open the notes back out just enough to keep them from falling back out of the holes. Put all of the balls in the bag, and keep in a safe place until the sleepover. To play the game, have the guests gather around the host, who pours the balls out of the bag onto the floor. As the balls roll, each player should quickly grab a ball. After each player has a ball, let the children take turns removing the paper and obeying the command. After each child has followed his or her instructions, put the rest of the balls back into the bag and play the game again.

Alien Planet

Materials

★ No materials needed

Directions

Have the children tell a cumulative story about landing on another planet. Let the host start the story and talk for about three minutes. Then let the next player start where the host left off and continue the story. Go all the way around the circle, with the host ending the story.

Animal Answers

Materials

★ No materials needed

Directions

Start with letter *A*. Have the players name as many animals that begin with that letter as they can think of. When players have exhausted all the *A* animals, have them begin with letter *B*. Continue all the way through the alphabet.

Bird Watching

Materials

★ No materials needed

Directions

Have the children play this listening game while resting in sleeping bags. The first child begins with this line: "I went bird watching. I saw a [fill in with a bird]." The next person repeats the exact words of the first person, then adds another bird name. The third person has to say the line, both birds and add another one. The cumulative listening game continues all the way around the circle two or three times, or as long as the players can still remember the names of the birds called.

Chapstick Corral

Materials

★ A different flavor of Chapstick for each guest
★ One yard of yarn

Directions

Have the children stretch out their sleeping bags in a circle, leaving the center open to play this game. Have the guests crawl into their bags with their heads in the middle. Give each child a tube of Chapstick. Tell the children to remember their own flavor. Use the yarn to make a circle in the empty place on the floor. Place all the tubes inside the circle. Each child will take a turn thumping his or her tube of Chapstick. The object is to try to get your friends' tubes out of the circle, without your own tube going out. If a tube goes out of the circle, that tube is out of the game for that round. When there is only one tube left, that person is the winner, and play can begin again with all the tubes. Have the children keep their tubes as a sleepover favor.

Colors of the Rainbow

Materials

★ Game spinner with colors

Directions

Have a child spin the spinner. The child who did the spinning names one thing that is the color on which the arrow landed. Each person in the circle names something that color. Then the next person takes a turn spinning and starting the answers. Go around the circle, giving each person a turn to start the game.

Desert Dreams

Materials

★ No materials needed

Directions

Let the children describe a make-believe mirage. Have each child say, "In the desert where it's hot and dry, I saw a mirage right before my eyes." Then have the child tell about his or her mirage.

Digging for Info

Materials

★ No materials needed

Directions

Have the children take turns telling an old memory about one of the friends at the sleepover. If some of the children have not known each other for very long, have the guests tell an old memory of their own childhood.

Explorer's List

Materials

★ No materials needed

Directions

Have the guests rest in a circle. Choose one person to start the game. Have that person say, "When I go exploring the oceans and the seas, I'll bring with me . . . ," naming one thing he or she will bring. The next person in the circle repeats the same words of the first person, then adds another item to the list. The third person does the same, repeating the sentence, two items, and his or her own item. Play continues for as long as the children can remember the list of words. Then have another child start the game and play again.

Fairy-Tale Fun

Materials

★ No materials needed

Directions

Have the host and guests crawl into their sleeping bags. Take turns making up a fairy tale, using the sleepover friends as characters.

Fancy Fingers

Materials

★ Tape player or CD player
★ Favorite tapes or CDs

Directions

Have the guests place their sleeping bags in a circle on the floor, leaving the center open. Let the children climb into their sleeping bags, heads facing inside the circle. Play music, and have the guests use their fingers to perform dances and tricks.

Farm Friends

Materials

★ No materials needed

Directions

Sing this song to the tune of "Ten Little Indians." "One little, two little, three little donkeys; four little, five little, six little donkeys; seven little, eight little, nine little donkeys; ten little donkeys going, 'Hee-haw, hee-haw.'" Let each child choose a farm animal to be. When the friends sing that verse, that person will give the animal sound at the end of the song.

Finger Gymnastics

Materials

★ Black ink pen

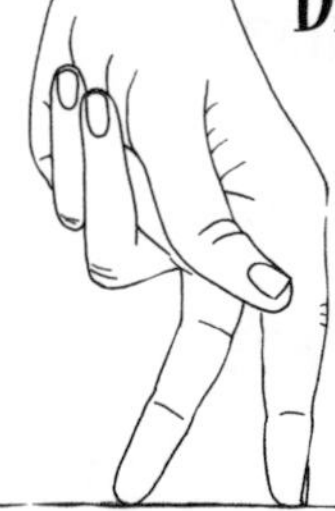

Directions

Have the children stretch out in sleeping bags in a circle, leaving an open space in the middle. Have the children form pairs with a person next to them. Each pair should work together to give their "finger gymnast" a face. Have the child point his or her first and second finger, like rabbit ears. Then have the child turn his or her hand so that the rabbit ears are touching the ground and all the other fingers are closed. These two fingers are the "gymnast's" legs. Let a child use the pen to draw eyes, nose and a mouth on his or her partner's hand, around the knuckle area. Then give the pen to the other person and have him or her do the same for that person. When everyone has added a face to his or her "gymnast," let the show begin! Take turns doing gymnastic tricks and shows on the floor by using only those two fingers.

Goggles and Giggles

Materials

★ One pair of swimming goggles

Directions

Let each child take a turn wearing the goggles. When a person wears the goggles, the remaining friends have to tell three funny things that happened to that person. If someone cannot think of three funny events for that friend, he or she can make up a funny story.

Gold Spinning Contest

Materials

★ Three gold toy coins per person
★ Cookie sheet

Directions

Give each person three gold coins. Place a cookie sheet in the middle of the floor for a flat surface. (If you do not have carpet, this step is not necessary.) Let two children oppose each other at a time. Have the two children stand one of their coins on end, holding with only the index finger. Then use the other hand to thump the coin so that it spins. The person whose coin spins the longest is the winner, and he or she collects both coins. Play continues until only one player has all the coins. Then play again.

Interview a Friend

Materials

★ Hand-held toy microphone

Directions

(*Hint:* If you do not have a toy microphone, make one from a cardboard paper towel tube before the sleepover. Cut off about three inches from the empty tube. Wad one sheet of typing paper into a ball. Use a hot-glue gun to glue the wad of paper to the top of the empty tube. When the glue is dry, spray-paint the entire tube with black spray paint.)

Take turns pretending to be reporters. Have one child hold the microphone and "interview" a friend by asking him or her questions. The questions can be serious, silly, true, or fictitious.

Lei Accolades

Materials

★ One Hawaiian lei

Directions

Let each child take turns wearing the lei. When a person has on the lei, each of the rest of the friends must tell three nice things about that person.

Log Cabin Treehouse

Materials

★ Tray
★ Pretzel logs
★ Pretzel sticks
★ Unwrapped Tootsie Rolls

Directions

Let the children work in pairs or threesomes to build treehouses on the tray with the pretzels and Tootsie Rolls.

Memory of an Elephant

Materials

★ No materials needed

Directions

Let each child take a turn telling a true story about someone in the room, without saying the person's name. See whether the other friends can guess whom the story is about.

Number Game

Materials

★ One die

Directions

Let each child take a turn rolling the die. The player must quickly name something that relates or comes in the number showing on top of the die. For example, if the child rolls a one, he or she could say, "The wheel of a unicycle."

Operation Code Name

Materials

★ No materials needed

Directions

Let the children brainstorm secret agent code names for all of their family members, friends, and neighbors.

Peanuts, Get Your Peanuts!

Materials

★ Baseball cap

★ Roasted peanuts in the shell

Directions

Have the children stretch out their sleeping bags in a circle, leaving the center open, where you set the cap. Have the guests crawl into their bags with their heads in the middle. Give each child a handful of peanuts. Take turns tossing the peanuts in the cap. See who can get the most peanuts in the cap.

Pet Parade

Materials

★ Hand-held toy microphone

Directions

(*Hint:* If you do not have a toy microphone, see the instructions on how to make one under the "Interview a Friend" bedtime game.)

Let each child take a turn being the Pet Parade emcee. The emcee holds the microphone and narrates the pet parade, using each guest and a made-up pet as parade participants.

Safari Search

Materials

★ No materials needed

Directions

Choose one child to start this listening game. Have that child complete this sentence: "I went on a safari and I saw a(n) . . . ." The next person repeats what the first person said and then adds another jungle animal. The third person repeats the words and two jungle animals, and adds a third animal. The game continues until the children forget the animals or run out of jungle animals to name.

Spinning Stars

Materials

- ★ A set of jacks
- ★ Cookie sheet

Directions

Have the children take turns spinning the jacks on the cookie sheet. See who can spin their jack the longest. (If you do not have carpet, the cookie sheet is not necessary.)

Spoken from the Heart

Materials

- ★ Bowl of candy hearts inscribed with words and phrases

Directions

After snuggling into sleeping bags, have the children pick five hearts from the bowl and make a sentence using as many of the words on the hearts as possible. Replace the hearts, stir the bowl, choose five more hearts, and make a new sentence.

Spooky Stories

Materials

- ★ No materials needed

Directions

Tell a scary story in a round. Have one person start the story. After three minutes, have the next person continue the story.

Superheroes

Materials

- ★ No materials needed

Directions

Have each person complete this sentence: "If I were a superhero, I would . . . ."

Trail Riding

Materials

★ No materials needed

Directions

Have the children close their eyes and pretend to be on a trail ride. Have them name the things that they see. The answers can be real or imaginary.

Twisted Tongues

Materials

★ No materials needed

Directions

Let each child make up a tongue twister for the other friends to attempt. Start with this one: "The sixth sick sailor sent to Seattle bought six slick shirts."

Wee Willie Winker

Materials

★ Scissors
★ Dark-colored sheet of construction paper
★ Marker
★ Basket

Directions

Before the sleepover, cut enough strips of paper for each child in the group to have one. On one strip of paper, make an *X;* leave all the other strips blank. Fold the papers several times, and put them in the basket. Have the children stretch the sleeping bags on the floor in a circle, with heads facing the middle of the circle. Put the basket in the middle of the circle, and have each child draw a piece of paper. Have them open it such that no one else can see their paper. The child who picks the *X* is the winker. He or she tries to wink at one other person without being seen. When a person is winked, he or she waits a few seconds, then says, "I'm asleep," and puts his or her head down. The winker tries to put everyone to sleep before someone guesses who it is. The children can guess at any time who the winker is, but if they guess incorrectly, they are then asleep and out of the game. Once the winker has been found out or puts all children to sleep, fold the papers up again, place them in the basket, and play again.

What's Missing?

Materials

★ Two dozen or more small items that will fit on a tray
★ Tray

Directions

Have all the children snuggle into their sleeping bags, stretched out in a circle with their heads facing the middle. Place twelve of the items on the tray, and put the tray in the middle of the circle. Let the host begin the game. Allow time for the children to observe the tray. Then ask all the guests to close their eyes while the host removes one item and puts it in his or her sleeping bag. The host then tells the children to open their eyes and calls on one child to try to guess what's missing. If the person guesses correctly, that person gets a turn to remove an item. If the person misses, the guest to the right of the host goes next. Play several rounds of removing one item, then change items and remove two at a time.

When, Where, and What?

Materials

★ No materials needed

Directions

Have the children crawl into their sleeping bags to play this word game. The game begins with the month of January. Each person takes a turn saying, "In January, I went to [name a place that begins with a *J*] and ate [a food that begins with a *J*]." The children may not repeat the same place or same food. After each person has had a turn with January, move to February, naming *F* places and foods. Continue with each month of the year.

Wishes and Gold

Materials

★ Black pot
★ Gold foil–wrapped chocolate candy coins

Directions

Have the children crawl into their sleeping bags, positioned in a circle, with their heads facing the inside of the circle. Leave room in the middle for a pot. Place the black pot in the middle of the circle and give each player five gold candy coins. Have the children take turns making a wish aloud, then tossing a coin in the pot.

Chapter 6

Nocturnal Notions

Amazing Crafts and Activities for Attendees

Intersperse fun crafts and activities with exciting games to provide a little rest time, challenge the creativity of your brood, and keep them busy for several hours of the party! Look over the suggestions in this chapter to find activities that match the theme of the party or interests of the host and guests. Make a list of the activities you would like to use, as well as the supplies you will need. Shop for the supplies and prepare any items that need to be made well before the sleepover.

Don't forget to have a few extra "goodies" on hand, just in case you have idle minutes: bubbles and bubble wands, building blocks, bricks and manipulatives, puzzles with lots of pieces, modeling dough and other art supplies, dress-up clothes and jewelry, puppets, balsa-wood airplanes, and/or crossword puzzle books and dictionaries.

And the Beat Goes On . . .

Materials

★ Oatmeal boxes

★ Glue

★ Construction paper

- ★ Permanent markers
- ★ Empty paper towel holders
- ★ Masking tape
- ★ Uncooked rice
- ★ Hot-glue gun and glue
- ★ Empty thread spools
- ★ Small pieces of wood (about three inches by five inches)
- ★ Sandpaper
- ★ Wooden spoons
- ★ Kazoos (optional)

Directions

Let the guests make homemade musical instruments and then have a parade. Make drums with the oatmeal boxes by gluing construction paper around the outside of the box and decorating with markers. Make maracas with paper towel holders by taping one end closed, pouring one-fourth cup uncooked rice in, taping other end closed, and then decorating the outside with markers. Make sand blocks by hot-gluing (with adult help) thread spools on one side of two wooden blocks. Cut sandpaper the size of the blocks; glue on the opposite sides of the blocks. Make clackers by decorating the wooden spoons with permanent markers. Form a parade with banging drums, rattling maracas, swishing sand blocks, and tapping clackers. If desired, give each child a kazoo as a party favor and have him or her play that during the parade, also.

Art in the Dark

Materials

- ★ Large sheet of white bulletin board paper
- ★ Washable markers

Directions

Cover the table completely with the white paper. Have the guests sit around the table with the markers in the middle of the table. Turn off the lights and let the children draw in the dark. After an allotted amount of time, turn on the lights and look at the artwork!

Artists at Work

Materials

- ★ Varied selection of art supplies, such as markers, paints, colored pens, oil pastels, and colored pencils
- ★ Easels with paper or tables covered with paper
- ★ Glue and any materials you choose

Directions

Set out as many art supplies as you choose to use. Let the children create as many projects and pieces as they desire.

Bicycle Brigade

Materials

- ★ Crepe paper streamers
- ★ Ribbons

Directions

Be sure to include a note on the invitations to ask the guests to bring their bikes to the sleepover. Have the guests use streamers and ribbons to decorate their bikes. Then have a parade or race, or go on a neighborhood field trip.

Cactus Creation

Materials

- ★ Acrylic paint
- ★ Paintbrushes
- ★ Small clay flowerpot, one per guest
- ★ Medium Styrofoam ball, one per guest
- ★ Green tissue paper
- ★ Glue
- ★ Green or wooden toothpicks

Directions

Have each guest paint and decorate a clay pot. While the paint is drying, have each guest wrap a Styrofoam ball with green tissue paper. Squeeze a small dab of glue on the back to secure the loose ends. Insert toothpicks about halfway into the Styrofoam ball. When the paint dries, set the "cactus" in the flowerpot.

Calendar Notes

Materials

- ★ Large hanging calendars, one per guest
- ★ Stickers
- ★ Pens and thin-lined markers

Directions

Before the sleepover, have the host choose a calendar for each guest. For this activity, give each guest his or her calendar and set out the stickers, pens, and markers. Have the children gather around a table and take turns writing personal notes and placing stickers on each guest's calendar, writing, doodling and marking throughout the calendar year. Let each child take home the calendar as a party favor and a remembrance of good friends for an entire year.

Candy Cottage

Materials (for one candy cottage)

- ★ Vanilla frosting in decorating bag with writing tip
- ★ Seven (1½-inch) shortbread cookies
- ★ Serrated knife
- ★ Assorted candies, such as cinnamons, shaped sprinkles, miniature candy-coated chocolate pieces, miniature chocolate chips

Directions

Pipe a line of frosting on opposite edges of two cookies. Attach two more cookies to form four walls of house. With serrated knife and gentle sawing motion, carefully cut one cookie in half diagonally. Generously pipe frosting on cut edge of each half. Attach to long sides of house. Generously frost slanted edges of cookies; attach two cookies to form roof. Allow houses to stand several hours or overnight before decorating. To decorate, use frosting as "glue" and attach candies and sprinkles.

Candy Counting

Materials

- ★ Colored, small paper bags
- ★ Theme-related stickers
- ★ Assorted individually wrapped candies in separate bowls
- ★ One die

Directions

Give each guest a paper bag to decorate with stickers. When guests are finished, set out the bowls of candy. Let one child roll the die. The child chooses the number of candy pieces that matches the number showing on the die. Let each child take a turn rolling the die, collecting candy to put in his or her bag. Decide whether the children will snack on the candy during the sleepover or will take the candy home as a party favor.

Ceiling Shows

Materials

- ★ Oatmeal boxes
- ★ Scissors
- ★ Poster board
- ★ Cookie cutters, preferably theme-related ones
- ★ Flashlights

Directions

Give each guest an empty oatmeal box. Help the guest cut out the bottom of the box. Cut out the top of the box, leaving the plastic rim and a narrow border. Cut a circle from the poster board the same size as the bottom of the box. Trace around a cookie cutter, such as a star, animal, or other shape in the center of the circle. Cut out the shape, under adult supervision, if necessary. Place the cutout stencil inside the plastic rim and replace the top. Give each child a flashlight to hold inside the oatmeal box. Turn off the lights; point the light and oatmeal box cutouts toward the ceiling; and put on a play, tell a story, or let the characters "dance."

Colored Sand Creations

Materials

- ★ Poster board, cut into ten- by twelve-inch pieces
- ★ Paintbrushes
- ★ Paint
- ★ Glue
- ★ Colored sand, available at toy stores or craft stores

Directions

Give each child a piece of poster board. Have the children paint a picture or abstract design; squirt on glue in interesting designs and sprinkle on different colors of sand for a beautiful creation.

Colorful Cows

Materials

- ★ Liquid food coloring
- ★ Spoons
- ★ Eight ounces of milk (for each child) in clear glasses

Directions

Let the children drop one or two drops of food coloring in their glasses of milk and stir to create beautiful shades of milk for a bedtime drink.

Critter Catcher

Materials

- ★ White sheet
- ★ Safety pins or rope for tying
- ★ Flashlights

Directions

In the early evening or nighttime, hang or drape a sheet from a tree or over a swing set. Shine flashlights on one side of the sheet and watch for insects that will be attracted to the light.

Cupcake Cutouts

Materials

- ★ Pen or pencil
- ★ Gingerbread boy or girl (or both) cookie cutters
- ★ Oaktag
- ★ Markers
- ★ Scissors
- ★ Drinking straws

Directions

Trace gingerbread cookie cutter onto the oaktag to make a boy or girl. Use the markers to turn the cutouts into Olympians, leprechauns, fairy-tale characters, athletes, or kids at the sleepover. Cut out the shapes. Poke two holes in the shape about two and a half inches apart, starting at the neck. Thread a straw through the two holes, and stand the cutouts in a cupcake or roll, or use them for a puppet show.

Decorated Scarves

Materials

- ★ White handkerchiefs
- ★ Puffy paints or permanent markers

Directions

Give each guest a handkerchief. Have the guests decorate the handkerchiefs with paints and markers. When the paint is dry, have the kids wear them for pirate scarves, mystery masks, or spy disguises.

Dough Critters

Use one of these recipes for artistic creations. The first recipe makes a fun dough for playing and creating and keeps well in the refrigerator, but doesn't really harden. The second recipe makes a nice baking dough and can then be painted and kept.

Salty Fun Dough Materials

- ★ 1 cup flour
- ★ 1 cup water
- ★ ½ cup salt
- ★ 2 teaspoons cream of tartar
- ★ 2 tablespoons oil
- ★ Liquid food coloring

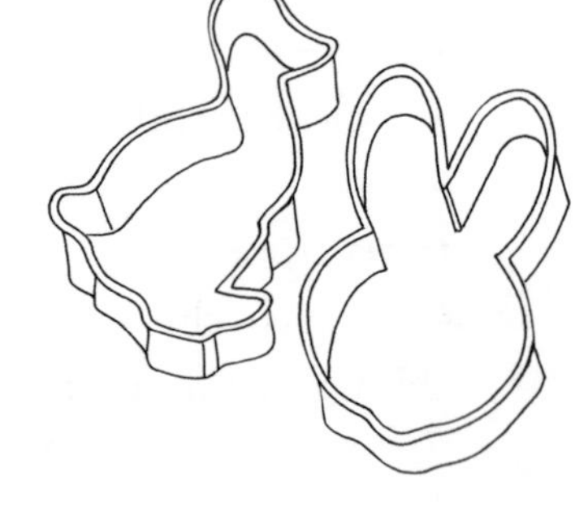

Directions

Mix all ingredients in a pan, including enough drops of food coloring to achieve the desired shade. Cook until thickened over low heat, stirring often. Cool dough and knead. Use cookie cutters or freely design farm animals, desert animals, reptiles, or horses. (This recipe makes about one and a half cups of dough. Try making two or three batches in different colors.)

Baking Dough Materials

- ★ 4 cups flour
- ★ 1 cup salt
- ★ 1½ cups water
- ★ Spoon
- ★ Cookie cutters
- ★ Fabric paint
- ★ Paintbrushes

Directions

Mix flour and salt; add water. Mix with a spoon until dough sticks together. Form a ball, and knead five to ten minutes. (If dough is too sticky, knead in up to a quarter cup more flour.) Use cookie cutters or create free-form animals. Roll and pinch pieces to add to the shape, or use a garlic press to squeeze small amounts of dough through to form animal fur or lion's manes. Bake on a cookie sheet for approximately one hour at 300 degrees. Check to make sure thinner creations are not getting too brown. Let cool and then paint with fabric paint. (This recipe yields about twelve to fourteen cookie-cutter shapes and fewer free-form shapes.)

Edible Jewelry

Materials

- ★ Round cereal pieces (e.g., Cheerios, Fruit Loops. Apple Jacks)
- ★ Shoestring licorice pieces

Directions

Thread the cereal pieces onto a strip of licorice long enough to go around a wrist or neck. Once the bracelet or necklace is complete, tie the ends together in a knot. Or try using two pieces of licorice at the same time. Holding the two ends together, thread a cereal piece on one strip; thread a cereal piece on the next strip at a different length. Twist the licorice one time, then thread more cereal. Keep threading and twisting until the necklace or bracelet is complete. Tie ends together.

Elephant Parade

Materials

★ Strips of ribbon, six feet long

Directions

Have the guests get on hands and knees on the floor. Give each child a strip of ribbon. Have the guest tuck the ribbon in the waist of his or her pants or pajamas. Line up the children in single file. Each guest holds the "elephant's tail" (end of ribbon) in his or her "trunk" (teeth). Parade around the house without letting go of the tails.

Face Painting

Materials

★ Face paints, available at toy or party stores
★ Polaroid camera (optional)
★ Cold cream for removing paints

Directions

Pair the children to apply paint to each other's faces to become leprechauns, circus stars, or silly kids. Take instant pictures of each guest to use as a place card for dinner or breakfast if you wish. Remove the paints with cold cream and a washcloth.

Feed the Birds

Materials

★ Plastic knives
★ Peanut butter
★ Cereal pieces
★ Sugar cones
★ Birdseed

Directions

Have the guests use plastic knives to spread peanut butter on the outside of the cone and press in cereal pieces. Spoon birdseed in the inside of the cone. Carefully carry the cones outside and wedge in tree branches or shrubbery to delight the neighborhood birds. Watch for visitors throughout the sleepover.

Fireworks Show

Materials

★ Helium-filled tank (check with your local party store)
★ Black balloons
★ Yarn
★ Glow-in-the-dark paint
★ Paintbrushes

Directions

Using helium, inflate the balloons and tie the ends closed with yarn. Tie the balloons to the back of a chair or something else stationary while painting. Use the glow-in-the-dark paint to make stars, pictures, or other designs on the balloon. Allow to dry completely. Release the balloons outside at the stroke of midnight and watch the "fireworks," or play with the balloons inside in a dark room.

Fruity Links

Materials

★ Clean scissors
★ Pressed fruit rolls

Directions

Cut the fruit rolls into seven-inch strips. Form a circle with the first strip, pressing the ends together gently. (If the ends do not stick, moisten finger with water; rub on one end of strip and press together.) Stick the next strip through the first loop, pressing ends together to form to chain links. Continue with other strips to form an edible chain to decorate the table. Use a theme-related flavor/color, such as strawberry for Valentine's decorations, or use a variety of flavors.

Funny Faces in a Frame

Materials

★ Scissors
★ Poster board
★ Markers
★ Stickers

Directions

Cut each sheet of poster board in half. Cut the inside out of each half, leaving a three-inch border for a frame. Let each guest decorate his or her frame with markers and stickers. When the guests have completed the frames, let each guest take a turn holding the frame in front of his or her face and making funny faces.

Fuzzy Fish

Materials

★ Mittens
★ Plastic cup
★ Puffy paints and fabric paints
★ Dried beans or stuffing beads
★ Thin ribbon

Directions

Give each child a mitten and a plastic cup. (Be sure to use a mitten, not a glove.) Have the child use the fabric paints to decorate the mitten to look like a fish, using the thumb covering as a fin. When the paint dries, fill the fish with dried beans or stuffing beads, leaving about two inches at the top. Use the thin ribbon to tie the mitten closed, forming the tail for the fish.

Gelatin Jewels

Materials

- Knife (not a sharp one)
- Four oranges
- Spoon or other fruit-scraping device
- Muffin pan
- One (three-ounce) package of Jell-O
- Gummy fish, dinosaurs, sharks, or theme-related treat

Directions

Cut the oranges in half and carefully scoop all the flesh out of the halves. Stand the empty skins in cups of a muffin pan. Meanwhile, make the Jell-O, following the directions on the package. Fill the orange skins halfway with the Jell-O, and place in the freezer for about fifteen minutes. Place gummy treats in each orange. Finish filling the skins with the remaining warm gelatin, and chill for several hours. Use blue gelatin for a swimming fish treat or green for a dinosaur fossil treat.

Get-Away Box

Materials

- Large appliance box
- Paints
- Paintbrushes

Directions

Let the guests work together to turn the appliance box into a spaceship, treehouse, barn, canoe, or toboggan.

Glowing Reviews

Materials

- Black T-shirts
- Glow-in-the-dark paint
- Paintbrushes

Directions

Give each guest a black T-shirt to decorate with glow-in-the-dark paint. Allow the paint to dry thoroughly, and then have the guests don the shirts, turn out the lights, and dance or do tricks. (*Hint:* Do this activity early during the sleepover so the paint has a chance to dry, and encourage the guests not to paint thick decorations.)

Happy Hands

Materials

★ Construction paper
★ Markers
★ Scissors
★ Tape

Directions

Choose colors of construction paper to match the theme of the party: fall colors for an autumn sleepover; red, white and pink for a February sleepover; or pastels for a springtime sleepover. Have the guests trace their hands on the construction paper. Let each guest make at least five shapes. Cut out the shapes. Have the guests write something or someone that they are thankful for on each shape. Tape to a bare wall or to a large tree or large heart attached to the wall.

Hearts and Lace

Materials

★ Construction paper, reds, pinks and whites
★ Heart-shaped cookie cutters or patterns
★ Paper doilies
★ Markers
★ Stickers
★ Glue
★ Heart-shaped candies

Directions

Have the guests use the materials creatively to make Valentine's cards for friends at the sleepover, neighbors, or family members.

Horse Parade

Materials

★ Folding chairs
★ Towels
★ Ribbons
★ Crepe paper

Directions

If enough are available, give each child a folding chair for a pretend "horse." If you do not have that many, let the guests work in pairs or take turns decorating the horse for the parade. Drape the towel over the seat to be the "saddle." Then weave and tie the ribbons and crepe paper on the chair for a decorated horse.

Hot Air Balloon

Materials

- ★ Balloons
- ★ Permanent markers
- ★ Yarn
- ★ Small boxes or empty plastic strawberry baskets
- ★ Tape

Directions

Have the guests inflate the balloons and use the markers to decorate them like hot air balloons. Tie yarn to four corners of the box or basket and tape the yarn to the balloon. Tape a strip of yarn to the top of the balloon and suspend the hot air balloons from the ceiling. (*Hint:* The baskets work best, as they are lighter. Often, you can get these from your grocer, with enough advanced notice.)

Leather Loops

Materials

- ★ Thin leather cords
- ★ Scissors (or other leather-cutting tool)
- ★ Beads

Directions

Cut the leather cords to necklace lengths, making sure to allow enough cord to tie at the end. Have the guests string beads on the cord and tie the ends together for a necklace. You may have the guests put the necklaces in a pile and draw numbers to choose a different necklace as a sleepover souvenir.

Miniature Art Show

Materials

- ★ Small piece of paper, measuring two by four inches, per guest
- ★ Colored pencils
- ★ Five-inch-long piece of string, per guest
- ★ Two clothespins with springs, per guest

Directions

Fold the piece of paper in half to get a two-inch square. Have the guest use the colored pencils to draw a picture on both sides of the fold. "Exhibit" the picture on the easel by stretching the string between the two clothespins, standing the clothespins upside down, and draping the paintings over the string.

Muddy Mess

Materials

★ One box of instant chocolate pudding per four guests, plus ingredients to complete the mix
★ Plastic tablecloth or newspaper
★ Baking sheets

Directions

Prepare the pudding according to the package directions. Cover a table completely with a plastic tablecloth or newspaper. Spread the pudding in layers on baking sheets. Place the sheets on the table, and let the guests "play in the mud."

Patriotic Footprints

Materials

★ Newspaper
★ Large white bed sheet or sheet of white bulletin board paper
★ Tape or weights
★ Blue and red paint
★ Shallow plastic or disposable containers
★ Wipes for easy cleanup

Directions

This activity is best completed outside! Cover the driveway with newspapers, then spread out the sheet or white paper. Weight or tape down the edges to keep the sheet in place. Pour paint into containers and let the children dip their hands in blue paint and make handprint "stars" in one corner. Then let the children step into the red paint and walk across the sheet to make red stripes. Let the sheet or paper dry thoroughly. Use wipes to clean up the guests. (*Hint:* Do this activity early during the sleepover so that the flag may be used as a party decoration later.)

Pin the Car on the Map

Materials

★ Large map of the United States
★ Car shapes cut from construction paper
★ Tape
★ Blindfold

Directions

Hang the map on the wall. Give each guest a car shape; have the guest write his or her name on the car. Place a rolled piece of tape on the back. Have the guests take turns being blindfolded and sticking the car on the map. Find out where each guest "traveled"!

Pom-Pom Puppets

Materials

- ★ Pom-poms
- ★ Small, wiggly eyes
- ★ Felt scraps
- ★ Fabric glue
- ★ Self-adhesive Velcro strips
- ★ Gloves, one per guest

Directions

Have each guest create animals, critters, or characters from five pom-poms using the materials provided. After the pom-poms have been decorated, cut small pieces of Velcro to attach to the back of each pom-pom puppet. Peel the backing and attach a matching strip of Velcro to each finger on the glove. When the puppets are completely dry, let the children attach the puppets to their gloved hand and put on a puppet show.

Poster Board Puppets

Materials

- ★ Poster paper, one sheet per guest
- ★ Scissors
- ★ Markers

Directions

Give each child a sheet of poster paper. Help the child cut a hole for his or her head near the top and two armholes in the appropriate places. The child should be able to insert his or her arms through the holes and hold up the poster board in front of his or her face. Have the child use the markers to create a costume to match the sleepover theme. Encourage the child to create a leprechaun, alien from outer space, or mystery, spy, or fairy-tale character. After all the children have created their costumes, have them put on a play with their characters.

Resolutions and Rhymes

Materials

- ★ Notebook paper
- ★ Pens

Directions

Give each guest a sheet of notebook paper. Have the guest tear the paper in half. Have each guest write two resolutions, with rhyming words, for a new year or new month. Resolutions may be serious or silly. Give an example, such as, "I resolve to clean my room, before my mom sends me to the moon."

Silly Socks

Materials

- ★ Two white socks, all identical, for each guest
- ★ Fabric paints
- ★ Paintbrushes

Directions

Give each guest two socks to decorate using fabric paints. Allow the socks to dry overnight. Just before the sleepover ends, put all the socks in a pillowcase. Have each guest pull out two socks to take home for a "matching" pair.

Sleepover Times

Materials

- ★ Large sheets of blank newsprint
- ★ Markers and pens

Directions

Let the guests create a newspaper about an event, such as the sleepover, an outer-space trip, a bird-watching trip, or an Olympic event. Or have the guests make a pretend sports page for a newspaper or a tabloid fairy-tale paper.

Spyglasses

Materials

- ★ Paint
- ★ Paintbrushes
- ★ Empty paper towel tubes

Directions

Have each guest paint and decorate an empty tube for a pirate or secret agent's spyglass.

Sticky Balloons

Materials

- ★ Balloons

Directions

Choose a color of balloons to match the sleepover theme (e.g., blue balloons for ocean bubbles, white s for snowballs, or pastel balloons for spring ...vers). Inflate the balloons. Have the children rub the balloons in their hair to get static electricity and stick the balloons to the wall for added decorations.

Superhero Cape

Materials

- ★ Sewing materials
- ★ One yard of material per guest
- ★ Two-inch-wide ribbon strips, forty-eight inches in length, per guest
- ★ Paintbrushes
- ★ Fabric paints

Directions

Before the sleepover, hem the edges of each piece of material. Fold over two and a half inches of the top edge and sew to make a casing. Thread the ribbon through the casing so that even lengths extend from both ends. Sew the ribbon in place in the middle of the casing. For this activity, have each guest decorate his or her superhero cape with the fabric paints. Let dry completely. Don the capes and "save the world!" (*Hint:* Do this activity early during the sleepover to allow ample drying time.)

Sword Fighting

Materials

- ★ Cardboard wrapping paper tubes
- ★ Markers

Directions

Let each child decorate his or her "sword" with the markers. Then have pretend sword fights with the tubes, reminding children to hit only each other's cardboard tubes.

TV Time

Materials

- ★ Exacto knife
- ★ Cardboard box
- ★ Dowel rods
- ★ Rubber bands
- ★ Freezer paper
- ★ Markers or colored pencils
- ★ Tape

Directions

Have an adult cut off the flaps of the top of the box. Turn the box on its side so that the opened side is the "viewing screen" of the television. Cut holes through the top panel and bottom panel, on the left and right sides for the dowel rods. The dowel rods should be the length of the viewing screen plus about four inches. Insert both dowel rods; wrap rubber bands around the dowel rods on either end, just outside the box edge to keep the dowel rods from slipping through. Cut a long strip of freezer paper the width of the "viewing screen." Have the children mark off sections the size of the screen and create a television show about the theme of the sleepover, such as a fairy tale, baseball game, or Valentine's love story. Once the story is complete, tape each end to a dowel rod. Roll all of the story onto the second dowel rod, then roll the first dowel rod to "watch" the show.

Tree Trimming

Materials

- ★ Brown paint (washable)
- ★ Construction paper
- ★ Wipes or rags
- ★ Glue
- ★ Cotton balls, tissue paper, or colored pasta

Directions

Have each child make a tree to match the theme of the sleepover: Paint each child's arm and hand with brown paint. Have the child make a print of his or her arm, hand, and outstretched fingers onto a large sheet of construction paper. (The fingers become the branches; the arm, the trunk.) While the paint is drying, use wipes or soap and water to clean up the guests. For a winter sleepover, have the child glue cotton balls onto his or her tree for "snow." For an autumn party, glue crumbled bits of fall-colored tissue paper on the tree branches. And for a spring or rain forest party, glue pasta noodles or rice that has been colored with green food coloring onto the tree.

Vegetable Landscapes

Materials

- ★ Broccoli stalks
- ★ Celery stalks
- ★ Leafy lettuce pieces
- ★ Green Styrofoam base, available in department or craft stores
- ★ Coconut, tinted green with food coloring

Directions

Push the vegetables into the Styrofoam base to form a forest. Cover the forest floor with coconut "grass."

Vehicle Boxes

Materials

- ★ Cardboard boxes for each guest
- ★ Markers
- ★ Paper plates
- ★ Paper cups
- ★ Construction paper
- ★ Glue

Directions

Have each guest use the materials provided to make and decorate a transportation vehicle. Use paper plates for tires and steering wheels, cups for headlights, and so on. When the marker and glue are dry, have the guests step into their cars and "drive" around the house.

Chapter 7

Catnap Cuisine

Super Snacks and Suppers

Let them eat cake"—and lots of other goodies! A sleepover provides opportunities for a fun evening meal, a delightful wake-up breakfast, and loads of snacks and goodies in between.

Plan your menu well in advance. List the grocery items you will need, and shop for them at the same time you're looking for decoration and favor supplies. Some foods may be frozen several weeks ahead or prepared two to three days before the party.

Be creative with your food, just as you were creative with the other ingredients of the sleepover. Some of the suggestions in this book lend themselves to being made by the guests, therefore doubling as party activities.

Serve the foods in fun ways—serve cold salads in beach pails, soup or stew in goldfish bowls, and snacks in baseball caps or doggie dishes. Eat with chopsticks or plastic utensils decorated with ribbons.

Choose the host's favorite foods or try some of the recipes presented here. Recipes are divided into entrée suggestions for evening meals or next-day lunches; desserts and snacks for any time of the sleepover; breakfast items for early- or late-morning eaters; and beverages, including milkshakes. Keeping your theme in mind, look over the suggestions and "get cooking"!

Asteroid Meat Muffins

Yield: 12 servings

Foil cupcake liners
1 egg
½ cup milk
¾ cup oatmeal
1 pound ground beef
1 teaspoon salt
½ cup grated cheese
¼ cup ketchup

Line a muffin pan with 12 foil cupcake liners. Very lightly grease the foil. Combine all ingredients except ketchup and mix well. Spoon the mixture into greased muffin cups. Bake at 350 degrees for 30 minutes. Remove from oven; spoon ketchup evenly over the cups. Return to oven and bake for 30 more minutes. Cool slightly before removing from muffin cups.

Baby Chick Rolls

Yield: 16 servings

2 packages active dry yeast
½ cup very warm water
1¼ cups buttermilk or plain lowfat yogurt
6½ cups all-purpose flour
½ cup softened butter
½ cup sugar
2 large eggs
2 teaspoons baking powder
1½ teaspoons salt
32 whole cloves for eyes

Lightly grease two cookie sheets. Sprinkle yeast over water in large mixing bowl. Stir until yeast is dissolved. Add buttermilk, 2½ cups flour, the butter, sugar, eggs, baking powder, and salt. Beat until blended. Gradually beat in as much of the remaining flour as needed to form a soft, sticky dough. Turn out on lightly floured surface. Knead 6 to 8 minutes until dough is smooth and elastic. Divide in 16 pieces. Cover with a damp kitchen towel when not actually working with dough. With floured hands, roll each piece of dough into a 12-inch-long rope. Carefully tie rope into a knot.

Place on cookie sheet. One end will form a tail. Slightly stretch other end; shape into head and beak. Center over body. With a floured toothpick, poke a hole in each side of head for eyes; insert cloves. Make two slits in tail to form tail feathers.

Repeat with remaining pieces of dough, placing them 3 inches apart on cookie sheet. Let rise in a warm place 40 minutes, until almost doubled.

Heat oven to 350 degrees. Bake 20 to 22 minutes until lightly golden. Remove to rack to cool completely.

Bach's Beef and Bow Ties

Yield: 6 servings

½ pound ground turkey breast
1 garlic clove, minced
1½ teaspoons vegetable oil
1 can (14½ ounces) chicken broth
2 cups uncooked bow tie pasta
1 can (14½ ounces) stewed tomatoes
1 tablespoon vinegar
¾ teaspoon sugar
½ teaspoon chili powder
½ teaspoon salt
2 tablespoons grated Parmesan cheese
1 tablespoon minced fresh parsley

In a large skillet or Dutch oven, brown turkey and garlic in oil. Remove the turkey and vegetables with a slotted spoon and keep warm. Add broth to the pan; bring to a boil. Add pasta; cook for 10 minutes or until tender. Reduce heat; stir in the tomatoes, vinegar, sugar, chili powder, salt, and turkey mixture. Simmer for 10 minutes or until heated through. Sprinkle with Parmesan cheese and parsley.

Calendar Creation

Yield: 9 servings

¼ cup butter
6 tablespoons mayonnaise
3 finely chopped hard-boiled eggs
¼ teaspoon paprika
¼ cup cream cheese
¾ cup grated Parmesan cheese
½ teaspoon salt
¼ teaspoon pepper
9 slices whole-wheat bread
9 slices white bread
Softened cream cheese (for frosting)

Beat the butter with the mayonnaise and divide into two bowls. Stir the chopped eggs and paprika into one, and mix the cheeses into the other. Season both mixtures with salt and pepper. Make four and a half sandwiches with whole-wheat bread and four and a half sandwiches with white bread, using both fillings for both sandwich types. Remove the crusts, and cut each whole sandwich into four squares and the half-sandwiches into two squares.

Cover a large cookie sheet or piece of cardboard with colored foil paper. Alternate the colors of bread and line the sandwiches to resemble a calendar: seven sandwiches across and five sandwiches down. Stir the cream cheese and put in a decorator tube with a large writing tip. Pipe numbers on each sandwich to match the calendar month of the sleepover.

Cheeseburger Pizza Pie

Yield: 4 servings

1 can (10 ounces) refrigerated pizza crust
½ pound ground beef
1 cup spaghetti sauce
1 cup shredded Cheddar cheese
¼ cup dill pickle slices

Grease a 12-inch pizza pan. Unroll crust. Place in greased pan. Starting at center, press out crust dough with hands, forming ½-inch rim. Bake at 425 degrees F for 7 to 9 minutes or until light brown. Brown ground beef in medium skillet until thoroughly cooked. Drain. Spread spaghetti sauce evenly over partially baked crust. Top with cooked ground beef and cheese. Return to oven; bake an additional 12 to 18 minutes or until bubbly and edges are golden brown. Top pizza with pickle slices.

Chicken Taco Wedges

Yield: 6 servings

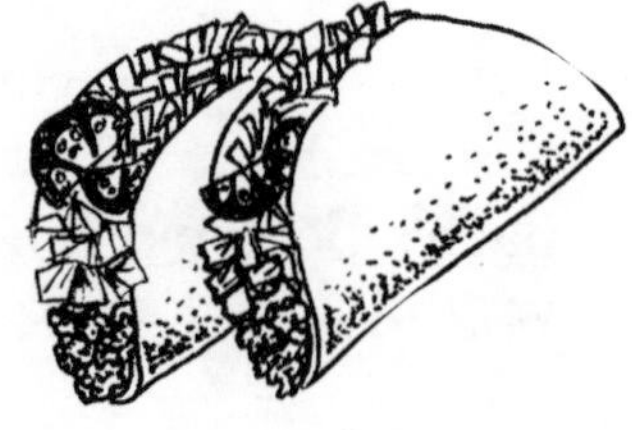

1 package (15 ounces) refrigerated pie crusts
¼ cup mayonnaise
¼ cup salsa
1 cup cubed cooked chicken
1 cup chopped tomato
1 cup shredded Cheddar cheese

Unfold pie crusts; place on ungreased large cookie sheet. Press out fold lines. In small bowl, combine mayonnaise and salsa; mix well. Spread mayonnaise mixture evenly over each pie crust. Sprinkle half of each crust with half of all remaining ingredients. Fold untopped half of each crust over filling; do not seal. Bake at 450 degrees F for 14 to 18 minutes or until golden brown. Cut into wedges to serve.

Cottage Cheese Face

Yield: 1 serving

1 leaf of lettuce, shredded
½ cup cottage cheese
Small slices of carrots
Small slices of celery
1 peach slice

1–2 olives
1–2 small cherry tomatoes
1 slice of American cheese, cut in strips
1–2 raisins

On a small plate, spread shredded lettuce in a thin layer. Spoon the cottage cheese on the shredded lettuce and flatten somewhat, forming a circle. Have the guest use the other ingredients to form a face on the cottage cheese.

Eggs in a Nest

Yield: 6 servings

½ cup chopped onion
¼ cup margarine
1 cup rice
1 teaspoon salt
2 cans beef broth
18–20 prepared meatballs
1 jar (16 ounces) brown gravy

Grease a large round casserole dish. Sauté onions in margarine in a small skillet. To prepared casserole dish, add onions, rice, salt, and beef broth. Bake covered at 375 degrees for 45 minutes, or until rice has absorbed all liquid. Meanwhile, warm meatballs according to package directions. When the rice is finished cooking, remove from the oven, uncover, and stir to mix all ingredients. Use the back of a large spoon to pack the rice around the bottom and sides of the bowl, forming a well in the middle. (The rice should resemble a nest.) Place the meatball "eggs" in the well of the "nest." Warm the brown gravy. Serve the guests rice and meatballs and pass the gravy to top the meat, if desired.

Fiesta Feast

Yield: 5 servings

1 pound ground beef
½ cup chopped onion
¾ cup salsa
1 can (11 ounces) corn and red and green pepper mixture
1 can (8 ounces) tomato sauce
1 teaspoon sugar
½ teaspoon garlic powder
½ teaspoon chili powder
⅛ teaspoon red pepper
2 tablespoons yellow cornmeal
½ teaspoon paprika
⅛ teaspoon garlic powder
1 can (12 ounces) refrigerated biscuits
1 tablespoon margarine, melted
1 cup shredded Cheddar cheese

Brown ground beef and onion in a large skillet. Drain. Stir in next seven ingredients. Bring to a boil. Reduce heat to low; simmer 10 to 15 minutes or until most of liquid is absorbed. Meanwhile, in small bowl, combine cornmeal, paprika, and garlic powder; mix well.

Separate dough into 10 biscuits. Cut each in half crosswise. Arrange biscuits, cut side down, around outer edge of hot beef mixture. Brush biscuits with margarine; sprinkle with cornmeal mixture. Sprinkle cheese in center over beef mixture. Bake at 375 degrees for 15 to 20 minutes or until biscuits are deep golden brown.

Forest Salad

Yield: 6–8 servings

8 cups torn lettuce
1 cup parsley, coarsely chopped
1 cup fresh mushrooms, chopped coarsely
1 large tomato, chopped
1 medium carrot, shredded
2 radishes, chopped fine
1 envelope Italian salad dressing mix
1 tablespoon minced fresh basil
1 garlic clove, minced

In a large bowl, toss the first six ingredients. Prepare salad dressing according to package directions; add basil and garlic. Pour over the salad and toss to coat.

Lasagna Casserole

Yield: 6–8 servings

1 pound ground beef
½ teaspoon salt
½ teaspoon pepper, divided
1 pound medium shell pasta, cooked and drained
4 cups shredded mozzarella cheese, divided
1 carton (24 ounces) small-curd cottage cheese
2 eggs, beaten
⅓ cup grated Parmesan cheese
2 tablespoons dried parsley flakes
1 jar (26 ounces) spaghetti sauce

In a skillet, cook beef until meat is no longer pink; drain. Sprinkle with salt and ¼ teaspoon pepper; set aside. In a large bowl, combine pasta, 3 cups of mozzarella cheese, cottage cheese, eggs, Parmesan cheese, parsley, and remaining pepper; stir gently. Pour into greased 3-quart baking dish. Top with the beef mixture and spaghetti sauce. Cover and bake at 350 degrees for 45 minutes. Sprinkle with remaining mozzarella. Bake, uncovered, 15 minutes longer or until the cheese is melted and bubbly. Let stand 10 minutes before serving.

Luau Kabobs

Yield: 1 serving per skewer

Cube or ball any or all of the following: cheese; cooked turkey, chicken, beef, ham; melon; pineapple; tomatoes; cooked potatoes; green pepper; red pepper; onion; and broccoli. Have the children thread the food pieces onto wooden skewers for their own kabob meal.

One-Pot Barbecue

Yield: 6 servings

¼ pound ground beef
¼ pound sausage
1 can (28 ounces) baked beans
2 tablespoons brown sugar
¼ cup ketchup
6 wieners, sliced thin

In a large Dutch oven, brown beef and sausage. Drain if necessary; then return meat to pot. Add remaining ingredients. Reduce heat; simmer for 15 to 20 minutes. Stir often.

Pinwheel Sandwiches

Springy Pinwheels

Yield: 32 pinwheels

4 slices whole-wheat bread, crusts removed
3 ounces cream cheese
1 tablespoon mayonnaise
Salt and pepper
2 drops red food coloring
1 celery stick

Roll out the bread lightly with a rolling pin; set aside. Beat the cream cheese with the mayonnaise and salt and pepper to taste. Add red food coloring and stir. Cut the celery into four ¼-inch sticks, the same length as the bread. Spread each slice of bread thickly with cheese filling. Place a stick of celery across one end of each slice. Roll up tightly, pressing the edge down firmly. Wrap in plastic wrap and chill. Cut the rolls into ½-inch slices to serve.

Green Pinwheels

Yield: 32 pinwheels

4 slices white bread, crusts removed
4 tablespoons mayonnaise
3 finely chopped hard-boiled eggs
2 drops green food coloring

Roll out the bread lightly with a rolling pin. Mix the next three ingredients. Spread on the flattened bread. Roll up tightly, pressing the edge down firmly. Wrap in plastic wrap and chill. Cut the rolls into ½-inch slices to serve.

Orange Pinwheels

Yield: 32 pinwheels

4 slices whole-wheat bread, crusts removed
½ cup prepared pimento cheese spread

Flatten bread lightly with rolling pin. Spread two tablespoons of cheese spread on each piece of bread. Roll up tightly, pressing the edge down firmly. Wrap in plastic wrap and chill. Cut the rolls into ½-inch slices to serve.

Snailshell Pinwheels

32 pinwheels

4 slices white bread, crusts removed
¼ cup peanut butter
¼ cup grape jelly

Flatten bread lightly with a rolling pin. Stir together peanut butter and jelly. Spread on flattened bread. Roll up tightly, pressing the edge down firmly. Wrap in plastic wrap and chill. Cut the rolls into ½-inch slices to serve.

Pizza-Chicken Roll-Ups

Yield: 4 servings

4 boneless skinless chicken breast halves
12 pepperoni slices
8 mozzarella cheese slices, divided
1 can (15 ounces) pizza sauce
4 precooked, prepared meatballs

Flatten chicken to ¼-inch thickness. Place three slices of pepperoni and one slice of cheese on each. Roll up tightly; secure with toothpicks. Place in a greased 11 by 7 by 2-inch baking dish. Spoon pizza sauce over roll-ups. Cover and bake at 350 degrees for 35 to 40 minutes. Uncover. Drape the remaining cheese slices on top of the rolls, like a blanket over a sleeping bag. Place a meatball at the top of each chicken roll, to resemble the "head" of a person in the roll. Bake 5 to 10 minutes longer or until cheese is melted.

Potato Planets

Yield: 4 servings

4 medium baking potatoes
2 tablespoons margarine
1–2 tablespoons milk
½ teaspoon salt
¼ teaspoon pepper
1 tablespoon Parmesan cheese

Clean, pierce, and bake potatoes at 425 degrees F for 50 minutes. Cut a lengthwise slice from the top of each baked potato; discard skin from slice. Reserving potato shells, scoop out the insides and add to potato portions from top slices; mash. Add margarine. Beat in just enough milk to make a stiff consistency. Add salt, pepper, and cheese. Mix well. Use a melon ball scoop to form small, rounded potato balls. Place back in the reserved shells. Bake 2 to 3 minutes longer.

Sailing Sandwiches

Yield: 12 servings

1 can (7 ounces) tuna, drained and flaked
3 tablespoons mayonnaise
1 hard-boiled egg, mashed
Salt and pepper
12 small bridge rolls
3 slices of American cheese
12 small pretzel sticks

Put the tuna in a bowl and mash with a fork. Add the mayonnaise and mashed egg; season with salt and pepper. Mix until smooth. Halve the rolls; spread evenly with the tuna mixture. Cut each slice of cheese diagonally both ways to make four triangles. Thread a pretzel stick through the straight edge of a triangle to make a sail. Stand the pretzel in the top of the sandwich.

Sloppy Joes and Janes

Yield: 6 servings

1 can (15.5 ounces) prepared sloppy joe sauce
1 pound ground beef or turkey
6 hamburger buns

Decorations: green olives, ripe olives, banana pepper slices, carrot curls, red pepper, parsley sprigs, pretzel sticks, potato sticks, and raisins

Prepare sloppy joe sauce as instructed on can. Spoon meat mixture onto bottoms of buns. Lay top bun next to bottom bun on plate. Let child use decorations to make a face on the top bun.

Stuffed Tomato Salad

Yield: 1 serving

2 cherry tomatoes
4 teaspoons cottage cheese
1 drop blue food coloring (for patriotic theme only)

Wash cherry tomatoes; slice off the tops. Carefully scoop out the seeds and pulp. Fill the tomato with two teaspoons of cottage cheese. Repeat with other tomato. (For the patriotic theme, fill one tomato with two teaspoons of cheese. Then stir blue food coloring into the remaining two teaspoons of cheese. Fill the second tomato with blue cottage cheese.)

Sunny Rice

Yield: 6 servings

1 package (10 ounces) yellow rice, plus ingredients to prepare rice
Nonstick cooking spray
1 pound baby carrots, steamed

Prepare yellow rice according to package directions. Spray an 8-inch round cake layer pan with cooking spray. Pack the hot rice firmly into the cake pan. Let stand 10 minutes. Invert dish onto serving platter; gently shake to loosen rice, if necessary. Place the steamed carrots around the outside of the rice, to resemble sun's rays.

Sunny Sandwiches

Yield: 1 serving

2 slices bread
2 tablespoons butter
2 slices American cheese
1 large carrot, cut into strips

Spread one slice of bread with ½ tablespoon butter. Top with one slice of cheese. Spread ½ tablespoon butter on the other slice of bread and place buttered-side-down on the cheese. Melt remaining butter in skillet. Place sandwich in skillet; turn sandwich to coat both sides with butter. Cook until brown and cheese begins to melt. Turn sandwich. Place other slice of cheese on top. Cook until bottom browns and top slice of cheese melts somewhat. Remove from skillet, place on a serving plate, and use a serrated knife to round the edges, forming a circle. Place carrot strips around the outside of the sandwich for "sun's rays."

Train Track Vegetables

Yield: 4–5 servings

4 celery branches, cleaned and cut in half lengthwise
4 carrots, washed, peeled, and cut in 2½ by ¼-inch strips
1 small bunch broccoli florets

Line up four celery pieces, end to end. Line up the other four celery pieces end to end parallel to the first row, leaving about 2 inches between rows. Place the carrot strips atop the celery pieces to resemble a train track. Lay the broccoli florets next to both sides of the track for shrubs and bushes.

Twisty Corn Dog

Yield: 8 servings

1 can (11½ ounces) refrigerated cornbread twists
8 hot dogs
1 tablespoon butter, melted
1 tablespoon grated Parmesan cheese
¼ teaspoon dry mustard

Unroll dough into one long sheet. Seal crosswise center perforations. Separate dough into eight long strips (two cornbread twists each). Wrap one strip around each hot dog; place on ungreased cookie sheet with ends of dough tucked under hot dog. Brush each with butter. Stir together the cheese and dry mustard. Sprinkle mixture over each corn dog. Bake at 375 degrees for 12 to 16 minutes or until light golden brown.

Desserts and Snacks

Bat Cake

Yield: 2 bat cakes, 10 servings

1 box chocolate cake mix (plus ingredients to complete mix)
1 can (16 ounces) chocolate frosting
2 crème-filled sponge snack cakes
4 miniature candy-coated chocolate pieces
2 black gumdrops
Shoestring black licorice pieces

Bake cake according to package directions, using two 8-inch round cake pans. Cut one circle in half. Cut three "bites" out of the straight edge of each half of the cake, using a round biscuit cutter. Notch one end of a sponge snack cake, forming a point. This will be the bat head and body. Place the head on a cake board and position the two wings on either side of the head, with the cutout section pointing down. Frost the cake and head with chocolate icing. Add candy-coated chocolate pieces for eyes. Roll a gumdrop flat with a rolling pin. Cut two ears from a gumdrop and attach in place. Add licorice strips to form the wing outlines. Repeat with other cake layer.

Birds in the Nest

Yield: 1 dozen

12 chewy caramel candies coated in milk chocolate
12 pieces candy corn
24 miniature candy-coated chocolate pieces
1 container frosting, any flavor
3 slices of cookie dough from 1 package (20 ounces) refrigerated chocolate chip cookie dough

Cut slit into side of one caramel candy using sharp knife. Carefully insert the large end of one piece candy corn into slit. Repeat with remaining caramel candies and candy corn. Attach miniature chocolate pieces to caramel candies to resemble "eyes" using frosting as glue.

Grease 12 miniature muffin cups. Slice three 1-inch slices of cookie dough. (Save the rest of the dough to make cookies according to package directions.) Cut each slice into four equal sections. Place one section of dough into each muffin cup. Bake 9 minutes. Remove from oven and immediately press one decorated caramel candy into center of each cookie. Repeat with remaining ingredients. Remove to wire racks, cool completely.

Butterfly Cake

Yield: 2 butterfly cakes, 12 servings

1 box white cake mix (plus ingredients to complete mix)
1 can (16 ounces) vanilla frosting
Food coloring
4 crème-filled sponge snack cakes
Assorted sprinkles, candy-coated chocolate pieces, candies, and gumdrops
Two 12-inch shoestring licorice pieces

Bake cake as directed on box, using two 8-inch round layer pans. Cool completely. Cut one round layer into two halves and put them back to back. Notch two sponge cakes, forming a V, to use for the body of the butterfly. Place one sponge cake at the top of the two halves and the other sponge cake at the bottom of the two halves. Color the frosting with desired color of food coloring. Spread frosting over both halves of the layer and both pieces of sponge cake. Decorate the butterfly with candies, sprinkles, or gumdrops. Cut one piece of licorice into two 6-

inch pieces. Curl one end of each piece and put in place to be butterfly antennae. Repeat with remaining ingredients.

Camp-Out Tent

Yield: 1 serving

¼ cup coconut
3 drops green food coloring
1 tube chocolate icing
2 graham crackers
2 thin pretzel sticks

Place coconut in a small resealable bag. Squirt three drops of green food coloring in bag. Seal and squish until coconut is colored evenly. Open bag and sprinkle coconut on the bottom of a small paper plate. Let dry for 15 to 20 minutes. Squirt a line of chocolate icing down one long side of a graham cracker. Lean the second cracker against the first cracker at the line of icing to form a tent. Place the tent on the "grass-covered" paper plate. (If necessary, squirt thin lines of icing on the plate to help hold the crackers in place.) Place pretzel sticks at either end of the graham cracker to serve as the poles to hold the tent up.

Candied Apples

Yield: 14 servings

14 wooden craft sticks
14 medium apples
1 pound dark brown sugar
3 ounces margarine
2 teaspoons white vinegar
6 ounces water
2 tablespoons light corn syrup

Grease a baking sheet and set aside. Push a wooden craft stick into the core of each apple. Heat the remaining ingredients gently in a large saucepan until the sugar has dissolved. Bring to a boil and boil for 5 minutes, without stirring. Remove from the heat and set the pan in a large pan of cold water to stop the mixture from cooking. Dip the apples one at a time into the mixture. Lift each apple out and twirl over the pan until evenly coated. Place on greased baking sheet until candy mixture has hardened.

Caramel Apples

Yield: 5 servings

Nonstick cooking spray
5 medium apples
5 wooden craft sticks
1 bag of individually wrapped caramels
2 tablespoons water

Cover a baking sheet with waxed paper. Grease the waxed paper with cooking spray. Wash the apples and remove the stem. Insert a wooden craft stick into the core of each apple. Unwrap the caramels and put them in a microwave-safe bowl. Add the water. Microwave on high for 3 minutes, stirring every minute, until smooth. Dip the apples in the caramel. Turn to coat evenly. Stand the apples on the greased waxed paper.

Caramel Popcorn

Yield: 4 servings

Nonstick cooking spray
3 quarts popped popcorn
3 cups unsalted peanuts
1 cup packed brown sugar
½ cup light corn syrup
½ cup margarine
½ teaspoon salt
½ teaspoon vanilla
½ teaspoon baking soda

Spray large shallow roasting pan with cooking spray. Combine popcorn and nuts in pan; place in 250-degree oven while preparing glaze. In heavy 2-quart saucepan, combine brown sugar, corn syrup, margarine, and salt. Stirring constantly, bring to boil over medium heat. Without stirring, boil 5 minutes. Remove from heat; stir in vanilla and baking soda. Pour syrup mixture over warm popcorn and nuts, stirring to coat. Bake at 250 degrees for 60 minutes, stirring occasionally. Remove from oven. Cool; break apart. Store in tightly covered container.

Chocolatey Treats

Yield: 20 treats

2 cups semisweet chocolate chips
½ cup light corn syrup
¼ cup margarine
7 cups crispy rice cereal

Cover baking sheets with waxed paper; set aside. Combine chips, corn syrup, and margarine in medium saucepan. Cook and stir over low heat until chips are melted and mixture is smooth. Place cereal in large bowl. Pour chocolate mixture over cereal;

stir to coat evenly. Lightly butter hands. Shape about ½ cup cereal mixture into desired shape. Place on prepared baking sheets.

Football Chocolatey Treats

Cereal mixture from above
2 tubes white decorator frosting

Shape ½ cup cereal mixture into a football shape. Use decorator frosting to pipe lines and laces. Repeat with remaining cereal.

Bird's Nest Chocolatey Treats

Yield: 20 treats

Cereal mixture from above
Candy-coated chocolates with peanuts

Shape ½ cup cereal mixture into a bird's nest shape. Put four or five peanut candy-coated chocolates in the nest for eggs. Repeat with remaining cereal.

Lizard Chocolatey Treats

Yield: 12 treats

Cereal mixture from above
Almond slivers, cut in half
Miniature candy-coated chocolate pieces

Shape ¾ cup cereal mixture into a lizard shape. Add almond slivers for claws and chocolate pieces for eyes.

Spider Treats

Yield: 2½ dozen

Half the cereal mixture from above
Chow mein noodles
Miniature candy-coated chocolate pieces

Drop cereal mixture by rounded tablespoonfuls onto waxed paper–lined baking sheets. Insert chow mein noodles for legs and add candies for eyes.

Cinderella Cake

Yield: 12 servings

1 box white cake mix (plus ingredients to make mix)
1 can (16 ounces) of vanilla frosting
Food coloring
Sprinkles, assorted candies, assorted candy hearts, cinnamon candies

Prepare cake according to directions on package, baking in a 12-cup Bundt pan. Invert the cake on a covered baking sheet or cake board. Stand a 10- or 12-inch dress-up doll in the hole of the cake. Frost the cake to look like the skirt of the doll's dress.

Color the frosting to fit the theme. Add sprinkles and decorations to make the dress look like a princess, bride, or Valentine gown.

Cinderella's Pumpkin Bread

Yield: Three 1-pound loaves

⅔ cup shortening
2⅔ cups sugar
4 eggs
1 can (16 ounces) pumpkin
⅔ cup water
3⅓ cups flour
½ teaspoon baking powder
2 teaspoons soda
1½ teaspoons salt
1 teaspoon cinnamon
½ teaspoon ginger
¼ teaspoon cloves
⅔ cups nuts

Cream shortening and sugar; add eggs, pumpkin, and water. Sift flour, baking powder, soda, salt, cinnamon, ginger, and cloves together. Add to creamed mixture and mix well. Stir in nuts. Pour into three greased 1-pound coffee cans. Bake at 350 degrees for 1 hour.

Clock Cake

Yield: 12 servings

1 box white or chocolate cake mix (plus ingredients to complete mix)
1 can (16 ounces) chocolate frosting
1 tube decorator frosting, any color

Prepare cake according to directions on box, baking in two 8-inch round pans. Cool completely; frost with chocolate frosting. Use the decorator tube to pipe numbers and clock hands on the top of the cake. (If using for New Year's Eve Party, have the clock hands show midnight or just before midnight.)

Coated Pretzel Logs

Yield: 12 logs

8 ounces chocolate candy coating
12 pretzel rods
3 ounces white chocolate candy coating
Assorted sprinkles

Line baking sheet with waxed paper. Melt chocolate candy coating. Dip pretzel rods into chocolate, spooning chocolate to coat about three-fourths of each pretzel. Place on prepared baking sheet. Refrigerate until chocolate is firm. Melt white chocolate. Dip coated pretzels quickly into white chocolate to coat about one-fourth of each pretzel, forming a white tip. Place on baking sheet. Immediately top with sprinkles. Refrigerate until chocolate is firm.

Colored Popcorn Balls

Yield: 12 balls

9 cups popped popcorn
¼ cup margarine
1 package (10 ounces) large marshmallows
Food coloring

Place popcorn in a large bowl; set aside. In a saucepan, melt margarine and marshmallows over low heat. Stir in enough drops of food coloring to achieve desired color. Pour over popcorn and toss to coat. When cool enough to handle, lightly butter hands and quickly shape mixture into balls.

Constellation Cookies

Yield: 2 dozen

1 roll (18 ounces) refrigerated sugar cookie dough
Yellow candy sprinkles

Roll refrigerated dough according to package directions. Use a star-shaped cookie cutter to cut dough. Sprinkle with yellow sprinkles and bake as directed.

Country Crows

Yield: 12

1 box brownie mix (plus ingredients to make mix)
12 candy corn pieces
24 miniature candy-coated chocolate pieces

Bake brownies according to package directions, baking in a 9 by 13-inch pan. When cooled, use a biscuit cutter to cut 12 circles from the brownies. From the scraps, cut 24 crescent shapes for the wings. Give each child a circle and two crescent shapes. Have the guests put the wings on either side of the circle to form a crow. Insert the candy corn for a beak and two colored chocolate pieces for the eyes.

Doggie's Delight

Yield: 12 servings

1 box cake mix, any flavor (plus ingredients to complete the mix)
1 can (16 ounces) chocolate frosting

Prepare the cake as directed on package. Bake in a large metal dog dish. Cool completely, leaving cake in dish. Using chocolate icing, frost the cake in uneven strokes, to resemble a bowl of dog food. Use a permanent marker to write a message on the dog dish, if desired.

Dressed-Up Bananas

Yield: 6 servings

Nonstick cooking spray
½ cup chocolate chip pieces
½ cup butterscotch pieces
6 bananas
6 wooden craft sticks
½ cup honey
½ cup peanut butter
Chopped nuts
Assorted sprinkles
Miniature chocolate chip pieces
Raisins
Miniature candy-coated chocolate pieces

Line a baking sheet with waxed paper; lightly grease the paper with cooking spray. Melt the ½ cup chocolate chip pieces and ½ cup butterscotch pieces together in a microwave-safe bowl for 2½ to 3½ minutes, stirring after every minute, until smooth. Give each guest a banana. Have them insert a wooden craft stick into one end of the banana. Let each guest dip half of his or her banana into the chocolate/butterscotch mix or honey or spread half of his or her banana with peanut butter. Then let the guest add one or more toppings. Place on greased waxed paper. Refrigerate until firm.

Drum Cake

Yield: 12 servings

1 box white cake mix (plus ingredients to prepare mix)
1 can (16 ounces) vanilla frosting
10–12 flat-sided lollipops

Prepare the cake as directed on the box, baking cake in two 8-inch round layers. Cool completely. Frost the top of one layer of the cake sparingly. Now top the cake with the other layer and frost completely on all sides. Just before serving, unwrap the lollipops and arrange in triangles on the side of the cake. Top the cake with real drumsticks or two chopsticks.

Fishbowl Gelatin

Yield: 6–8 servings

1 box (6 ounces) blue gelatin (and water to prepare mix)
Gummy fish
1 can whipped topping spray

Prepare gelatin according to package directions. When the gelatin is completely chilled, spoon the gel-

4 chocolate wafers
4 green gumdrops
2 black gumdrops
Black shoestring licorice

Prepare cake as directed on box, baking in two 8-inch round layer pans. Cool completely. Tint frosting yellow with food coloring. Frost one layer. Surround layer with vanilla wafers, pushing edge of wafer just under cake somewhat. Cut the edges of two chocolate wafers to form a straight edge. Lay the wafers in place for the ears. Press two green gumdrops flat with a rolling pin. Use for eyes. Press one black gumdrop flat with a rolling pin. Cut a triangle for the nose. Use the licorice to form a mouth and whiskers. Repeat with the remaining ingredients to make another lion.

Mud Dunkers

Yield: 1½ cups

⅔ cup light corn syrup
½ cup whipping cream
1 package (8 ounces) semisweet chocolate chips

In medium saucepan, stir corn syrup and cream. Bring to boil over medium heat. Remove from heat. Add chocolate; stir until completely melted. Serve warm as a dip for fruit, cake, or cookies.

Mystery Cake

Yield: 10 servings

½ cup flour
1 teaspoon baking powder
¼ teaspoon salt
4 egg yolks
½ teaspoon vanilla
⅓ cup sugar
4 egg whites
½ cup sugar
2 cups ice cream, any flavor
½ cup ice cream topping

Grease and lightly flour a 15 by 10 by 1-inch jelly roll pan. In a bowl, stir together flour, baking powder, and salt. In small mixer bowl, beat egg yolks and vanilla on high speed of mixer about 5 minutes or until thick. Gradually add the ⅓ cup sugar, beating until sugar dissolves.

Thoroughly wash beaters. In large mixer bowl, beat egg whites with electric mixer on medium speed until soft peaks form. Gradually add the ½ cup sugar; continue beating till soft peaks form. Fold yolk mixture into egg whites. Sprinkle flour mixture over egg mixture; fold in lightly by hand. Spread batter evenly in prepared pan. Bake at 375 degrees for 12 to 15 minutes or until cake springs back, leaving no imprint when lightly touched. Immediately loosen edges of cake from pan and turn out onto a towel sprinkled with sifted powdered sugar. Starting with narrow end, roll warm cake and towel together; cool on a wire rack.

Soften ice cream. Unroll cake; spread the softened ice cream over surface of cake to within ½ inch of edges. Roll up cake and ice cream only; wrap and freeze at least 3 hours. To serve, place on a serving platter and drizzle a favorite ice cream topping over the top of the cake.

Note Bread

Yield: 10 servings

1 can (12 ounces) refrigerated biscuits (10 biscuits)
2 cans refrigerated breadsticks (use 10 breadsticks for recipe)
2 tablespoons butter

Lightly grease baking sheets. Cut two biscuits into four equal pieces. With floured hands, roll each piece into a 3-inch rope. Place a whole biscuit on the baking sheet. Place a breadstick next to the biscuit, pressing the biscuit dough into the side of the breadstick. (This should look like a letter *d.*) To the top of the breadstick, attach one end of the rolled rope. Swag the rope to make the top of the musical note. Continue with other biscuits, leaving 3 inches between each musical note. Melt the butter and brush each note with it. Bake according to package directions.

Photo Cake

Yield: 12 servings

1 box white cake mix (plus ingredients to make mix)
1 can (16 ounces) vanilla frosting
½ cup chocolate frosting

Prepare cake mix as directed on package, baking in a 13 by 9-inch pan. Cool completely. Frost sides with vanilla frosting. Frost the top of the cake with vanilla frosting, leaving a 2-inch border all around the edge of the cake. Frost the border of the cake with chocolate frosting, to resemble a picture frame. For extra effect, enlarge a head-shot photo of the sleepover host and gently lay the picture on top of the cake, inside the frame.

Pineapple-Banana Salad

Yield: 1 serving

1 lettuce leaf
1 pineapple slice
¼ cup cottage cheese
1 small banana
1–2 maraschino cherries

Place cleaned lettuce leaf on a plate. Place pineapple slice on lettuce leaf. Spoon cottage cheese around the outside of the pineapple. Cut the banana flat on the bottom to stand straight. Stand the banana upright in pineapple hole. Place one cherry on top of the banana. You may need to cut the cherry somewhat to have it fit.

Candlelight Salad: Follow above directions.

Spaceship Salad: Follow above directions. Cut small strips from the second cherry. Place the strips around the pineapple, in the cottage cheese, to look like fire.

Pretty Pretzels

2 cups white flour
1 tablespoon vegetable oil
1 tablespoon dry yeast
¾ cup lukewarm white grape juice
¼ cup evaporated milk
Coarse salt

Mix the flour, oil, yeast, and juice. Knead the dough for 3 to 5 minutes. Have the guests tear off small pieces of dough and roll them to make long ropes. Form the ropes into letters or shapes. Place the forms on a lightly greased baking sheet and let rise for 30 minutes. Lightly brush the pretzel shapes with the milk. Then sprinkle them with salt. Bake at 450 degrees for 15 minutes or until golden brown.

Rainbow Cake

Yield: 12 servings

1 box white cake mix (plus ingredients to prepare mix)
Food coloring in three colors
½ cup powdered sugar
1½ teaspoons milk
Rainbow-colored decorator candies

Prepare cake according to package. Divide batter evenly into thirds; add a different food coloring to each. Pour one color in the bottom of a prepared Bundt pan. Carefully pour another color on top of the first color. Finally, pour the third color on top. Bake 33 to 38 minutes, or until a toothpick inserted in center comes out clean. Cool 10 minutes in pan; invert onto serving dish. Cool completely. Mix powdered sugar and milk; drizzle over top of cake. Sprinkle rainbow-colored decorator candies on top of icing.

Rainbow Kabobs

Yield: 12 servings

4 packages (3 ounces each) of gelatin of differing flavors (plus water to complete mix)

Follow package instructions, stirring in ¾ cup cold water instead of 1 cup cold water. Pour liquid into a shallow plastic tray. Refrigerate until firm. Cut into cubes. Repeat with each packet of gelatin. Have the guests thread the cubes in a rainbow pattern onto wooden skewers.

Resolution Cookies

Yield: 3 dozen

Pretyped resolutions
⅓ cup all-purpose flour
6 tablespoons sugar
1 tablespoon cornstarch
⅛ teaspoon salt
⅓ cup water
¼ cup vegetable oil
1 egg white
1 teaspoon vanilla
Assorted paste food colors

Type resolutions on small strips of paper, approximately 2 inches by ½ inch. Combine flour, sugar, cornstarch, and salt in small bowl. Add water, oil, egg white, and vanilla; stir until smooth. Divide into three bowls. Use ⅛ to ¼ teaspoon of paste food coloring in each bowl to achieve the desired color.

Grease small skillet. Heat over medium heat. Spoon 1 tablespoon batter into pan, spreading to 3-inch circle with back of spoon. Cook 5 minutes or until golden brown on bottom. Turn over; cook 1 minute. Remove cookie from skillet and place, darker side up, on flat surface. Immediately place prepared resolution in center of cookie. Fold cookie in half, crescent-shaped. Fold straight edge of cookie over edge of bowl, so that it drapes and resembles a fortune cookie. Repeat with remaining batter.

Sandy Pudding

Yield: 4 servings

1 package (3.4 ounces) instant vanilla pudding (plus ingredients to prepare mix)
8 oblong, crème-filled vanilla cookies

Prepare pudding as directed on package. Spoon into individual serving dishes. Give each guest two sandwich cookies and a plastic resealable bag. Have the guests use a rolling pin, an empty bottle, or the side of a wooden mallet to crush the cookies. Then sprinkle the "sand" on top of the pudding.

Snowman Cupcakes

Yield: 15 snowmen

1 package (18.5 ounces) white cake mix, plus ingredients to prepare mix
2 cans (16 ounces each) vanilla frosting
4 cups flaked coconut
15 large marshmallows
15 miniature chocolate-covered peanut butter cups, unwrapped
Miniature candy-coated chocolate pieces
Pretzel sticks
1 tube of green frosting
1 tube of red frosting

Line 15 regular-size (2½-inch) muffin pan cups and 15 small (about 1-inch) muffin pan cups with paper liners. Prepare cake mix according to package directions. Spoon batter into prepared muffin pans. Bake 10 to 15 minutes for small cupcakes and 15 to 20 minutes for large cupcakes. Cool in pans on wire rack 10 minutes. Remove to racks; cool completely.

Remove paper liners. For each snowman, frost bottom and side of one large cupcake; coat with coconut. Repeat with one small cupcake. Attach small cupcake to large cupcake with some frosting. Attach marshmallow to small cupcake with frosting. Attach inverted peanut butter cup to marshmallow with frosting. With frosting, attach candies for buttons and pretzels for arms. Pipe faces with tubes of tinted green and red frosting.

Spaceship Dessert

Yield: 8 servings

14 chocolate sandwich cookies
1 cup canned vanilla frosting
Food coloring
1 sugar cone
Candy-covered chocolate pieces
5 vanilla crème-filled wafer cookies
1 can whipped topping
1 10-inch strip of pressed fruit roll, cherry flavor

Stack cookies together, securing with a dab of frosting in between each cookie. Let dry completely. Carefully stand in center of serving plate. Tint remaining frosting with desired color of spaceship, or leave white.

Spread cone and outside of cookie tower with frosting. Press candies into frosting around open edge of cone and in a line on the tower. Secure cone with frosting to top of rocket. Trim ends of wafers diagonally; press into frosting around base of rocket, spread evenly. Surround rocket ship with mounds of pressurized whipped topping for clouds.

Cut fruit roll into two 5-inch strips. Then cut each strip lengthwise into narrow strips. Curl one end and place the "fire trails" in the whipped topping as if shooting out from bottom of rocket.

To eat, remove the cone from the top and use a spatula to separate cookies from top to bottom. Have the guests dip the cookies in the whipped topping, if desired.

Sun Cookies

Yield: 2½ dozen cookies

1 package (18 ounces) refrigerated sugar cookie dough
1 egg, beaten
Thin pretzel sticks
2 cups powdered sugar
2–3 tablespoons milk
Yellow food coloring

Slice cookies and place on baking sheet as instructed on package. Brush cookies with beaten egg. Arrange pretzel sticks around edge of cookies to resemble sunshine rays; press gently. Bake according to package or until lightly browned. Remove to wire racks; cool completely. Mix powdered sugar, 2 tablespoons of milk, and enough drops of yellow food coloring to achieve desired shade of yellow. If necessary, add more milk, one teaspoon at a time, to make an icing with spreadable consistency. Frost the underside of the cookie, turning the cookies over such that pretzel sticks are on the bottom. Let stand 1 hour or until dry.

Sunflower Cookies

Yield: 8 cookies

1 package (20 ounces) refrigerated peanut butter cookie dough
⅓ cup flour
¼ cup semisweet chocolate chips
¼ cup butterscotch chips
½ cup unsalted sunflower seeds
2 cups powdered sugar
2–3 tablespoons milk
Yellow and green food coloring

Remove dough from wrapper according to package directions. Combine dough and flour in large bowl; mix well with wooden spoon. Divide dough into eight equal sections. For each sunflower, divide one dough section in half. Roll one half into ball; flatten on ungreased cookie sheet to 2½-inch thickness. Roll other half into 5-inch long rope. Cut 2 inches from rope for stem. Cut remaining 3 inches into 10 equal sections; roll into small balls. Place stem below cookie ball and arrange small balls around large ball to form a sunflower. Repeat with remaining dough. Bake 10 to 11 minutes or until lightly browned. Cool 4 minutes on cookie sheets. Remove to wire racks; cool completely.

Melt chocolate and butterscotch chips together. Spread melted chip mixture in center of each cookie; sprinkle with sunflower seeds. Mix powdered sugar and milk until a piping consistency is achieved. Add yellow food coloring to about two-thirds of the frosting and green food coloring to the remaining one-third of the frosting. Pipe yellow frosting on the petals and green frosting on the stem.

Supercool Pie

Yield: 8–10 servings

1 package (8 ounces) cream cheese, softened
1 jar (7 ounces) marshmallow crème
2 cups sherbet, any flavor, softened
2½ cups whipped topping
1 graham cracker crust
Candy sprinkles (match color of sherbet)

In a mixing bowl, beat cream cheese and marshmallow crème until smooth. Stir in sherbet. Fold in whipped topping. Pour into crust. Freeze until firm. Remove from the freezer 10 minutes before serving. Sprinkle with candy sprinkles just before serving.

Tiger Cake

Yield: 2 tiger cakes, 12 servings

1 box white cake mix (plus ingredients to prepare mix)
1 can (16 ounces) vanilla frosting
Yellow and red food coloring
4 vanilla wafers
Black and yellow gumdrops
Black shoestring licorice

Prepare cake according to box, baking in two 8-inch round layers. Cool completely. Color frosting with yellow and red food coloring to get desired shade of orange. Cut edges of two vanilla wafers to make straight edges. Frost one layer and the two vanilla wafers. Place the coated wafers at the top of the cake for the ears. Roll black gumdrops flat and cut into triangles. Place triangles around tiger's face, excluding the bottom fourth of the cake. Use one triangle for nose. Roll two yellow gumdrops flat for eyes. Use the licorice for mouth and whiskers. Repeat with remaining ingredients.

Transportation Cake

Yield: 12 servings

1 box cake mix, any flavor (plus ingredients to prepare mix)
1 can (16 ounces) vanilla frosting
1 cup chocolate frosting

Prepare cake according to box, baking in 13 by 9-inch pan. Invert onto serving platter and cool completely. Frost with vanilla frosting, then add a road with chocolate frosting. Place toy cars or vehicles along the road.

Breakfasts

Breakfast Bread Score

Yield: 4 servings

4 slices of white bread
1 tablespoon margarine
½ cup grape jelly
4 powdered minidoughnuts

Spread bread with margarine; toast. Spread grape jelly over toast. Cut each piece of bread into four strips. Arrange the strips on a prepared cake board to resemble a musical score. Horizontally place five strips of toast about one inch apart. Place another five strips end to end with the first row; place another five strips end to end with the second set of strips. Place the minidoughnut "notes" on top of the toast "staff."

Breakfast Casserole

Yield: 8 servings

6 eggs
6 slices bread, cubed
2 cups milk
1 teaspoon salt
1 teaspoon dry mustard
1 pound sausage, browned and drained
1 cup grated Cheddar cheese

Beat eggs well; add bread cubes, milk, salt, and mustard. Stir well. Add sausage and cheese; stir. Pour into greased 9 by 9-inch baking dish. Refrigerate several hours or overnight. Bake at 350 degrees for 45 minutes.

Breakfast Pizza

Yield: 6–8 servings

1 tube (8 ounces) refrigerated crescent rolls
1 pound bulk pork sausage
1 cup frozen shredded hash brown potatoes, thawed
1 cup (4 ounces) shredded sharp Cheddar cheese
3 eggs
¼ cup milk
¼ teaspoon white pepper
¼ cup grated Parmesan cheese

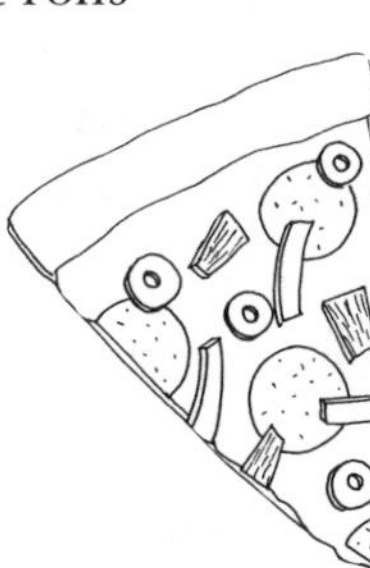

Unroll crescent dough and place on a greased 12-inch pizza pan; press seams together and press up sides of pan to form a crust. In a skillet, brown sausage over medium heat; drain and cool slightly. Sprinkle sausage, hash browns, and Cheddar cheese over crust. In a bowl, beat eggs, milk, and pepper; pour over pizza. Sprinkle with Parmesan cheese. Bake at 375 degrees for 28 to 30 minutes or until golden brown. Let stand 10 minutes before cutting.

Cheese Grits

Yield: 8 servings

2 cups milk
2 cups water
½ teaspoon salt
¼ teaspoon white pepper
1 cup white quick grits
1½ cups shredded sharp Cheddar cheese
2 eggs, slightly beaten
1 tablespoon margarine

Grease 1½-quart casserole. Heat milk, water, salt, and pepper to boiling in 2-quart saucepan. Gradually add grits, stirring constantly; reduce heat. Simmer uncovered, stirring frequently, about 5 minutes or until thick. Stir in cheese. Stir one cup of the hot mixture into eggs. Stir into remaining hot mixture in saucepan. Pour into casserole. Dot with margarine. Bake uncovered 35 to 40 minutes or until set. Let stand 10 minutes.

Spicy Cheese Grits

Cook as above, adding 3 tablespoons chopped jalapeño peppers when adding cheese.

Fruity Animals

Yield: 2 servings

1 grapefruit or orange
Cubes of melon, pineapple, grapes, and strawberries

Cut grapefruit or orange in half and turn upside down on serving plate. Have guests put fruit cubes on toothpicks and push other end of toothpick into grapefruit or orange half to create hedgehogs, porcupines, birds, or other animals.

Patriotic Puffs

Yield: 8 servings

1 can (17.3 ounces) refrigerated buttermilk biscuits
2 tablespoons butter, melted
4–5 tablespoons sugar
1 cup whipping cream
2 tablespoons powdered sugar
¼ teaspoon vanilla
4 cups strawberries, diced
4 cups blueberries
Powdered sugar

Separate dough into eight biscuits. Dip top and sides only of each biscuit in butter, then in sugar. Place, sugar side up, 2 inches apart on ungreased cookie sheet. Bake at 375 degrees for 13 to 17 minutes or until golden brown. Cool slightly.

In small bowl, beat whipping cream until soft peaks form. Gradually add powdered sugar and vanilla, beating until stiff peaks form. To serve, split biscuits; place on dessert plates. Layer biscuit with strawberries, blueberries, and whipped cream. Dust with powdered sugar; serve right away.

Pumpkin Muffins

Yield: 2 dozen muffins

1 can (16 ounces) pumpkin
1⅔ cups sugar
⅔ cup vegetable oil
2 teaspoons vanilla
4 eggs
3 cups flour
2 teaspoons baking soda
1 teaspoon salt
1 teaspoon ground cinnamon
½ teaspoon ground cloves
½ teaspoon baking powder

Grease bottoms only of 24 medium muffin cups. Mix pumpkin, sugar, oil, vanilla, and eggs in large bowl. Stir in remaining ingredients. Fill cups about three-quarters full. Bake 20 to 25 minutes or until tops spring back when touched lightly.

Red Riding Hood Muffins

Yield: 2 dozen

½ cup butter
1½ cup sugar
½ teaspoon salt
4 well-beaten eggs
1½ cup sour cream
1 teaspoon baking soda
2¾ cup flour
¼ cup sugar
½ teaspoon cinnamon

Mix butter, sugar, and salt until light. Add eggs, sour cream, baking soda, and flour; mix thoroughly. Fill muffin tins about half full. Mix together the sugar and cinnamon. Sprinkle tops with mixture. Bake at 425 degrees for 15 minutes.

Skillet Solar System

Yield: 6 servings

6 eggs, divided
6 bacon strips
6 cups frozen cubed hash brown potatoes
1 teaspoon salt
¼ teaspoon pepper
½ cup shredded Cheddar cheese

Scramble one egg; set aside. In a large skillet over medium heat, cook bacon until crisp. Remove bacon; crumble and set aside. Drain, reserving 2 tablespoons of drippings. Add potatoes, salt, and pepper to drippings; cook and stir for 2 minutes. Cover and cook, stirring occasionally, until potatoes are browned and tender, about 15 minutes. Make six wells in the potato mixture, one in the center and five surrounding. Break one egg into each of the surrounding wells. Cover and cook on low heat for 4 minutes. Add scrambled egg into center well. Cover and cook another 4 minutes on low heat, or until eggs are completely set. Sprinkle with cheese and bacon.

Spyglass Bagels

Yield: 1 serving

½ bagel
2 tablespoons cream cheese
1 breadstick

Use a sharp knife to enlarge the hole of the bagel. Spread cream cheese on the outside of the bagel and on the breadstick. Place the breadstick below the bagel to resemble a magnifying glass.

Waffle Sandwiches

Yield: 4 servings

8 frozen waffles
½ cup peanut butter
⅓ cup jam or jelly

Toast waffles as directed on package. Stir peanut butter and jam together. Spread four waffles with mixture. Top with remaining waffles; press slightly.

New Year's Waffles

Yield: 4 servings

Toast waffles as above and spread four waffles with peanut butter. Top with remaining waffles. Place on individual serving plates. Put jelly in a squirt bottle or cake decorator's tube and pipe the numbers for the new year on top of each sandwich.

Artist's Waffles

Yield: 4 servings

Prepare sandwich as for New Year's Waffles. Put a variety of flavors and colors of jelly in squirt bottles. Let each guest create an artistic design on top of his or her waffles using the jellies.

Wagon Wheels

Yield: 8 servings

1 tube (8 rolls) cinnamon rolls with icing
8 dried prunes
Raisins

Bake and frost cinnamon rolls according to package. Let each guest put a prune in the middle of the cinnamon roll and use raisins to make wheel spokes.

Beverages

Seven Dwarf Float

Yield: 1 serving

8 ounces 7-Up
1 scoop vanilla ice cream

Pour the 7-Up into a clear serving glass. Drop the scoop of ice cream in and serve immediately with a spoon.

Fizzy Sherbet

Yield: 1 serving

8 ounces ginger ale
Sherbet, any flavor

Pour ginger ale into a clear serving glass. Let guest put two scoops of sherbet into his or her drink. Serve a variety of flavors for children to choose from, or choose a sherbet in a color to match the sleepover theme.

Frothy Juice

Yield: 4 cups

1 can (6 ounces) juice concentrate, frozen
1 cup milk
1 cup water
½ cup sugar
8 to 10 ice cubes

Choose the host's favorite juice or select a juice with a color to match the sleepover theme. Combine all ingredients in a blender; cover and process until drink is thick and slushy.

Magic Juice

Yield: 4 servings

1 cup juice, any color
32 ounces white grape juice

Choose a favorite juice or juice with a color that fits the theme of the sleepover. Divide the cup of juice evenly into a plastic ice cube tray. Freeze the juice. To serve, pour 8 ounces of room-temperature white grape juice into four clear serving glasses. Drop three cubes of frozen juice into each glass. (For a rainbow or spring theme, use three different flavors of juice cubes for each glass.)

Milkshakes

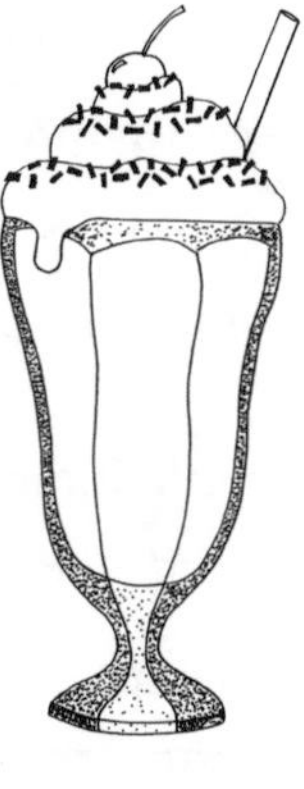

Chocolate Chip Shake

Yield: 1 serving

¼ cup milk
1 cup vanilla ice cream
1 teaspoon vanilla flavoring
1 tablespoon miniature chocolate chips

Combine all ingredients in a blender and blend until smooth.

Chocolate Cow Shake

Yield: 1 serving

¼ cup milk
1 cup chocolate ice cream
1 heaping tablespoon powdered chocolate flavoring
1 teaspoon vanilla flavoring

Combine all ingredients in a blender and blend until smooth.

Milk and Honey Shake

Yield: 4 servings

1 pint vanilla ice cream
½ cup milk
¼ cup honey

Combine all ingredients in a blender and blend until smooth.

Pink Flamingo Fluff

Yield: 2 servings

¼ cup milk
1 cup strawberry ice cream
1 medium firm banana, sliced
1 teaspoon honey

Combine all ingredients in a blender and blend until smooth.

Rain Water Shakes

Yield: 3 servings

2 cups cold milk
1 package (3 ounces) blue gelatin
2 cups vanilla ice cream
1 teaspoon honey

Combine all ingredients in a blender and blend until smooth.

Snowball Shake

Yield: 1 serving

¼ cup milk
1 cup vanilla ice cream
1 teaspoon vanilla
½ cup vanilla ice cream, scooped with melon ball scoop into small balls

Combine first three ingredients in a blender and blend until smooth. To serve, pour shake into clear serving glass. Add melon-ball-size ice cream scoops to glass. Serve with a spoon.

Palomino Pony Drink

Yield: 1 serving

8 ounces milk
½ cup chocolate ice cream, scooped with melon ball scoop into small balls

Pour milk into glass. Add small ice cream scoops to milk. Serve with a spoon.

Pink Lemonade

Yield: 1 serving

8 ounces lemonade
1 tablespoon cranberry juice

Let the guest combine the two ingredients to get a pretty pink drink.

Swamp Water

Yield: 10–12 servings

1 quart pineapple juice
1 quart orange juice
2 packages (14 ounces each) powdered lime-flavored drink mix
1 quart water
1½ cups sugar

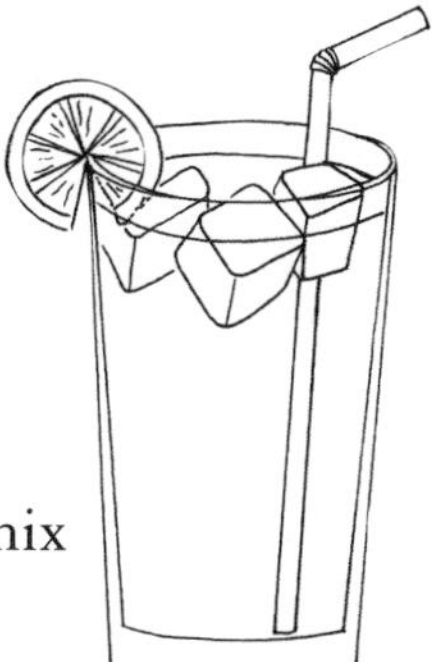

Combine all ingredients and mix well. Serve chilled.

Chapter 8

Sandman Surprises

Farewell Favors for Favorite Friends

The party may be over, but the memories of a sleepover's fun times and special bonds of friendship should not be forgotten. Purchase or make creative sleepover favors that will have your host and guests dreaming of this sleepover for days to come.

Keep the sleepover theme in mind as you search for inexpensive, store-bought items. Find a creative way to personalize the bought items, with permanent markers, puffy paints, ribbons, or bows. Or, use your own imagination to create homemade thank-you favors. Attach a note to the favor, perhaps cut out in a shape related to the party's theme, that says, "Thank you for coming to my sleepover." You may also attach a small trinket, toy, or bag of candy to each note.

Many of the suggestions described here can be made during the sleepover, as part of the entertainment, and then taken home as remembrances of the sleepover. Whatever form they take, make the sleepover favors fun, creative and personal!

Airplane Announcements

Send your guests home with these after-party treats, and they will have hours of fun playing with their slumber party favors.

Materials

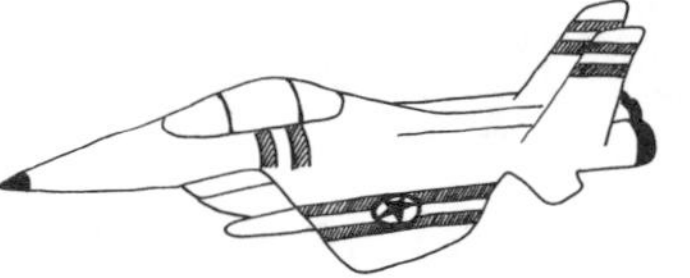

★ Airplane cookie cutter
★ Typing paper
★ Colorful markers
★ Assembly-required airplanes, one per guest (The least expensive of these are the balsa-wood planes found in many department stores, some dollar stores, and most hobby stores.)
★ Airplane stickers

Directions

Using the airplane cookie cutter as a guide, trace and cut out airplane shapes on the typing paper. Write a note to your guest that says, "Thanks for choosing [your name]'s Airlines for your sleepover. It was a first-class party!" Decorate with colored markers. Make a batch of cut-out cookies in airplane shapes. Include the airplane-shaped note, airplane-shaped cookies, the balsa-wood plane, and airplane stickers in a gift bag.

Basket of Goodies

Let your guests make their own goodie baskets. Ask your grocer for these strawberry baskets several weeks before the party to be sure you can get them in time for the sleepover.

Materials

★ Strips of construction paper in a variety of colors
★ Green plastic strawberry baskets, one per guest
★ Colorful pipe cleaners
★ Individually wrapped candy pieces and snack-sized candy bars

Directions

Have each guest weave strips of construction paper in the holes of the fruit basket. Make a handle for the basket by wrapping both ends of a pipe cleaner on opposite sides of the basket. Before the guests leave the party, fill the baskets with candies.

Beaded Bookmarks

Your guests will enjoy making this sleepover saver during the party and will treasure it as a keepsake.

Materials

- ★ Oaktag, cut into rectangles measuring 1½ inches by 6 inches
- ★ Colored or printed Con-Tact or self-adhesive paper
- ★ Hole punchers
- ★ Yarn
- ★ Beads

Directions

Give each guest a precut piece of oaktag. Carefully cover the oaktag with self-adhesive paper. (Because of the nature of self-adhesive paper, your guests may want to work in pairs to have additional hands for the job, or this step may require adult assistance.) Use the hole puncher to put a hole near the top of the bookmark. Thread a six-inch piece of yarn through the hole. Tie a knot to keep the yarn in place. Thread two or three beads onto each end of the yarn. Knot the ends to keep the beads from slipping off. In addition to the bookmark, you may choose to give a favorite book to each child as part of the slumber party souvenir.

Blooming Bouquets

Give this spring sleepover surprise to keep the guests remembering the party for the rest of the season.

Materials

- ★ Gift bags, one per guest
- ★ Flower stickers
- ★ Puffy paints
- ★ Small pair of garden gloves for each guest
- ★ Package of flower seeds for each guest
- ★ Trowel for each guest
- ★ Colorful markers

Directions

Decorate one gift bag for each guest using the flower stickers. Use the puffy paints to personalize and decorate a pair of garden gloves for each child. When the paints are dry, place the gloves, seed packet, and trowel inside the bag. Write a thank-you note on the outside of the gift bag with the markers.

As an alternative, have each guest decorate his or her own bag and gloves during the course of the slumber party. The next day, before the guests leave, fill the party bags with the gloves, trowel, and seed packs.

For an even more personal party favor, give the guests the opportunity to plant their own seeds. (You will need to provide potting soil and small planters.)

Candy-Coated Necklaces

Make these yummy sugary snacks that are sure to please all guests!

Materials

★ Yarn

★ Individually wrapped candies with twisted paper or plastic ends

Directions

Use small pieces of yarn, about 3 inches in length, to tie candy pieces together. Tie the ends of the candy papers together by tying the yarn into a knot. Continue tying candies together until the necklace measures about 2½ or 3 feet in length. Then tie the first and last pieces of candy together to form a completed circle. Give the guests these candy leis just before they leave the party.

Circus Sweets

Use this slumber party favor to show thanks for being a part of "the greatest show on Earth."

Materials

★ Elephant pattern

★ Gray construction paper

★ Marshmallow circus peanuts, small pack of peanuts, bag of cotton candy, or small box of popcorn

Directions

Enlarge the pattern of the elephant on this page to use as a pattern. Trace the elephant onto gray construction paper. Cut a trunk from gray construction paper. Attach the trunk in place on the elephant's face. Glue one of the listed treats onto the end of the elephant's trunk. Write a thank-you note on the elephant's face, telling your guest that you were glad he or she joined you for the circus slumber party.

Crayon Creations

Give your guests these unique favors to use for art projects at home.

Materials

★ Old crayons, paper removed

★ Cupcake pans

★ Foil cupcake liners

★ Small plastic bags, one per guest

★ Colorful ribbon

Directions

Break the crayons into small pieces. Line a cupcake pan with foil cupcake liners. Place broken crayon pieces in the liners. You may mix two colors to create a new color. However, if you mix too many colors in one container, you will only get a muddy shade of brown. Melt the crayons in an oven on a low setting, about 300 degrees. Check the crayons periodically. You may use a toothpick to swirl some of the colors as they begin to melt. When the crayons are melted, remove the pan from the oven. Allow the crayons to cool completely to enable them to harden again.

When the crayons are completely cooled and hardened, gently remove the foil cupcake liners. Place several chunky crayons in a small plastic bag and tie the top closed with a colorful piece of ribbon. Attach a note to the ribbon, thanking your guest for coming to the slumber party.

Cute Canteens

Keep the troops happy with these fun after-the-party treats. Use this idea for a military party, desert party, races and relays party, or all-occasion party.

Materials

- ★ One plastic canteen per guest
- ★ Stickers
- ★ Permanent markers
- ★ Thank-you card or typing paper
- ★ Twine or rope

Directions

Decorate and personalize the canteens for each guest with the stickers and markers. Write a thank-you note on the card or typing paper, thanking your guest for a fun time at the sleepover. Attach the notes to the canteens with the twine or rope. Fill the canteens with icy cold water and send the troops home!

Dough Delights

Here's a gift that the guests will enjoy long after the party is over. Remind the guests' parents that the dough can be kept for several weeks in the refrigerator.

Materials

- ★ 1 cup flour
- ★ 1 cup water
- ★ Several drops of food coloring
- ★ ½ cup salt

★ 2 teaspoons cream of tartar
★ 2 tablespoons oil
★ Resealable quart bag, one per guest

Directions

Mix the flour, water, desired shade of food coloring, salt, cream of tartar, and oil in a pan. Cook over low heat, stirring constantly, until the mixture has thickened. Cool, then knead until dough is smooth. The recipe makes enough for one guest to explore freely. Multiply the ingredients by the number of guests you will have. Or, make a different color for each guest. Place the dough in the resealable bag and give to each child to take home.

Fancy Fountains of Ink

These favors are fun to make and fun to use! The craft is simple, and you may want to let each child make more than one pen. Have several of each ink color available, in case the guests beg to do more!

Materials

★ Very small beads (found in craft stores or some department stores)
★ Double-sided tape
★ One or more ink pens per guest

Directions

On a cloth or paper towel, pour the beads carefully in a shallow pile. Have each guest wrap double-sided tape around his or her pen. Then roll the pen back and forth in the beads until the tape is coated. Press gently with your hands around the pen to make sure loose beads get attached.

Framed Favor

This is a personalized party favor that the guests can enjoy making at the party and can keep for some time to come!

Materials

★ Colored craft sticks
★ Craft glue
★ Small, bear-shaped crackers
★ Beads
★ Clear, spray acrylic
★ Polaroid camera

Directions

Have each guest glue four craft sticks together in a square. Then have them glue bear-shaped crackers and beads around the edges of the frame. Allow the glue to dry overnight. Early the next morning, spray the clear acrylic on the frame. Sometime during the sleepover, take a Polaroid snapshot of each guest with the host or enough shots of the whole group for each guest to have a picture. When the acrylic has had time to dry, cut the pictures to fit each frame and glue them into place.

Happy Hula Hoops

Show your guests that you had a "swinging" good time at your slumber party with these sleepover favors.

Materials

★ Ribbon in a variety of colors and widths
★ Craft glue
★ One hula hoop per guest

Directions

Working with short lengths of ribbon at a time, have the guests put a smear of glue along the ribbon as they wrap it around the hula hoop. Allow plenty of time for the glue to dry before using the hoops during the party.

Jump Rope Reminders

Here's a fun activity for the slumber party that is not only a piece of equipment for a party game but also a take-home favor!

Materials

★ One plastic toothbrush holder per guest (you will need the kind that comes apart in the middle and has two separate pieces)
★ Yarn in a variety of colors (you will need three pieces of yarn, each 7 feet in length, for each guest)

Directions

Have each guest take apart his or her toothbrush holder. Thread three pieces of yarn into the small hole at the top of one end of the toothbrush holder. Tie the three pieces of yarn into a knot to keep the yarn from coming out of the hole. Braid the three strands of yarn together, almost to the end of the yarn. Leave enough yarn to thread the ends into the hole at the top of the other end of the toothbrush holder. Tie the three strands in a knot to keep the yarn from pulling back through the hole. Use each end of the toothbrush holder as jump rope handles, and start jumping!

Kooky Cookie Cutters

Choose a selection of cookie cutters to go with your theme, and send your guests home with stencils for art projects, toys for play, or shapes to make cookies with Mom or Dad.

Materials

★ Cookie cutters, shaped according to the sleepover theme
★ Colorful ribbon
★ Thank-you note or typing paper
★ Colorful markers or pens

Directions

Tie a bundle of cookie cutters, related to your sleepover theme, with colorful ribbon. Write a note on the thank-you card or the paper with the markers or pens, thanking your guest for coming to the slumber party. Put the cookie cutter bundles in a small gift bag, along with a bag of homemade sugar cookies, cut from some of the included cookie cutters. Use the following cookie recipe or one of your own favorites:

Ingredients

2¾ cups all-purpose flour
½ teaspoon baking powder
½ teaspoon baking soda
½ teaspoon salt
⅔ cup margarine
1 cup sugar
1 egg, beaten
2 tablespoons milk
½ teaspoon vanilla

Directions

Sift the first four ingredients together. Cream margarine and sugar. Blend in egg, milk, and vanilla. Blend in dry ingredients. Chill in refrigerator for 2 hours. Roll dough ⅛-inch thick on lightly floured board. Cut into desired shapes using floured cookie cutters. Bake on an ungreased cookie sheet at 375 degrees for 10 to 12 minutes. Makes about three to four dozen cookies, depending on size of cookie cutter.

Magic Moments

Remind each guest what a magical time he or she had at the party with this special magician's cape and a deck of cards for future card tricks.

Materials

★ 1 yard of red cotton fabric for each guest

★ Black satin ribbon, approximately 1½ inches in width and 1½ yards in length
★ Fabric glue
★ Gold and silver glitter
★ Puffy paints or permanent markers
★ Deck of cards, per guest

Directions

Hem the edges of the red fabric. On one edge, fold the material over approximately 2 inches and sew in place, forming a casing. Leave both ends open. Attach a safety pin to the strip of ribbon for ease in threading the ribbon through the casing. Once the ribbon is threaded, make sure that there are equal lengths extending from each side to be used as a tie. Then stitch the ribbon to the cape in the very center, just to keep it from coming out of the casing. Remove the safety pin.

At this point, the host can decorate all of the capes, or the guests can complete them at the party and take them home as favors. Use the fabric glue to make a border of glitter around the edge of the cape. Spread glue near the edge; sprinkle gold or silver glitter onto the glue. Then use the permanent markers or paint to write "The Amazing [guest's name]" on the back of each cape. At the end of the sleepover, let each child take home his or her cape and a deck of cards.

Magnificent Magnifiers

Give these sleepover reminders for a mystery, detective, creepy-crawly, or all-occasion party.

Materials

★ Colorful markers
★ Thank-you note or small piece of typing paper
★ One magnifying glass, per guest
★ Colorful ribbon

Directions

Using the colorful markers, write a note on the thank-you card or typing paper that begins, "Thanks for coming to my sleepover. See you again soon!" Add personal notes about the guest or party to each note. Attach the notes to the magnifying glass with ribbon. (If you're using the magnifying glasses as part of the games or activities throughout the party, do not attach the notes until just before presenting the favors.)

Makeover Memories

Let each guest help make her own slumber party memory to take home when the party is over.

Materials

- ★ Yarn
- ★ Zippered makeup bag for each guest
- ★ Beads
- ★ A selection of some or all of the following for each guest: fake fingernails, makeup, small makeup brushes, fingernail polish, small mirror
- ★ Thank-you note or typing paper
- ★ Colorful markers

Directions

Cut a strip of yarn about 12 inches long for each guest. Thread the yarn through the hole of the bag's zipper and tie a knot. Then thread beads on each strip of yarn, leaving enough room on the very end to tie a knot. Tie a knot in each piece, large enough to prevent the beads from falling off. Before the guests leave, fill the makeup bag with makeup accessories and a prewritten thank-you note for joining the slumber party.

Mini Treasure Chests

This is a fun favor to make and is particularly appropriate for a makeover, fashion, pirate, or beach party.

Materials

- ★ Small, colorful decorative boxes, one per guest (these can be found in craft or hobby stores)
- ★ Seashells (these can be found in craft stores, also)
- ★ Beads
- ★ Craft glue
- ★ Toy jewelry, small toys, or candy

Directions

Have each child glue on seashells and/or beads to decorate the jewelry box. Allow the glue to dry overnight. Before the guests leave, add toy jewelry items.

Munchies for the Munchkins

Make a sack of goodies for each child. Choose snacks that relate to the sleepover theme or snack favorites of the sleepover host.

Materials

- ★ Gift bag or colored lunch-sized paper bag
- ★ Stickers
- ★ Colorful markers
- ★ Individually wrapped crackers, chips, or candies
- ★ Thank-you note or typing paper

Directions

Have the host decorate and personalize a gift bag or lunch-sized paper bag for each guest, using the stickers and markers. Fill the bag with snacks and goodies. Write a thank-you note on the card or typing paper that says, "Thanks for coming to my sleepover. It was so 'munch' fun."

Pail of Paints and Paste

Give a party favor that will keep a guest occupied for hours of artistic enjoyment!

Materials

- ★ Plastic pail, one per guest
- ★ Puffy paints
- ★ Permanent markers
- ★ Colorful marker
- ★ Small, colorful note pad or doodle pad, one per guest
- ★ Art supplies, such as paints, paintbrushes, paste, markers, sponges, or putty

Directions

Have the host decorate and personalize a pail for each guest using the puffy paints and permanent markers. Use a colorful marker to write a thank-you note on the first page of the pad. Put the pad and other art supplies in the pail, and present it to the guests as they leave the party.

Painted Paddles

Decorate these paddles for your guests, and then have a paddleball contest before the evening ends.

Materials

- ★ Paddleball and paddle, one set per guest
- ★ Puffy paints

Directions

Personalize and decorate a paddle for each guest with puffy paints. Play with the paddles and balls during the sleepover, and then be sure to take home this fun favor at the end of the party.

Paratrooper Treats

Recycle the parachutist invitations for permanent party favors. If you choose to use this idea, remember to ask the guests to bring their invitations to the slumber party.

Materials

- ★ Permanent black marker
- ★ White handkerchief, one per guest
- ★ Yarn or string
- ★ Toy figurine, one per guest
- ★ Gift bags, one per guest
- ★ Candies or cookies

Directions

Using the permanent marker, write a note of thanks to your guest on the white handkerchief. Begin the note by saying, "I'm glad you dropped by for my sleepover." Then add other personal words or thanks. Let dry.

If you choose to recycle the parachutist invitations, gather them from the guests at some point during the party. Clip the knots at the end of the yarn pieces attached to the handkerchief, on all four corners. Reattach the new handkerchief, using yarn or string. Refold the toy and parachute and place it in a gift bag with candy or cookie treats. (If you did not use the parachutist invitation, use scissors to cut small holes in the four corners of the handkerchief. Attach a strip of yarn or string about 10 inches long to each corner of the handkerchief. Tie the other ends of the string pieces to a small toy figurine.)

Pom-Pom Pals

Give each guest a new buddy to take home from the party!

Materials

- ★ Craft eyes
- ★ Scraps of felt material
- ★ Craft glue
- ★ One large, colorful pom-pom per guest
- ★ New pencils, one per guest

Directions

Let each child create a pom-pom buddy by gluing eyes and felt pieces for nose and mouth to a large pom-pom. Glue the pom-pom friend onto the eraser of a new pencil. These will need to dry completely before being handled much. Let the guests put on a puppet show the next morning with the pom-pom buddies and then take them home as sleepover favors.

Potpourri Pouches

Let your guests make these fragrant bags to take home as a reminder of the sleepover.

Materials

- ★ One rectangle per guest of cotton, muslin, or cheesecloth, measuring 9 by 11 inches
- ★ Stampers, in a variety of shapes
- ★ Stamp pads, in a variety of colors
- ★ Loose potpourri
- ★ Colorful ribbon

Directions

Fold each rectangle of material so that the short ends meet. Sew around three edges, leaving one open for stuffing. Hem the opened edge. Then turn the bag so that the seams are on the inside. Let each guest decorate his or her bag with stampers and stamp pads. When the ink is dry, have the guest add potpourri to his or her bag and tie the top closed with a strip of colorful ribbon.

Pretty Pads of Paper

Give each guest his or her own personalized stationery. You may choose to have the host prepare each child's stationery, or let the guests prepare their own as part of the sleepover activities.

Materials

- ★ One plain, colored pad of paper for each guest
- ★ Stickers
- ★ Stamp pads and stampers
- ★ Colorful markers
- ★ Glitter pens
- ★ Matching envelopes, one pack per guest
- ★ Stamps, one per guest

Directions

If you choose to let this be an activity for the party, give each child a pad of paper. Encourage the guest to create his or her own stationery by adding stickers, stamping pictures, or writing with the markers or glitter pens on each page in the pad. Make sure the guests decorate the borders of the pages and leave the inside section blank to be used for letter writing at a later date. You may also have the guests decorate matching envelopes, if desired.

Before finishing the activity, address one envelope from each guest's package with the host's address. Affix a stamp, also. Ask the guest to write a note in the next week or two, using the handmade stationery and the preprinted envelope, and drop it in the mail. Your child will love getting letters from his or her friends in the upcoming weeks!

Rainy-Day Rainsticks

Save empty wrapping paper tubes to make these fun favors.

Materials

★ One empty wrapping paper tube per guest
★ Spoon
★ Dried beans, peas, or rice
★ Masking tape
★ Colorful paints
★ Paintbrushes

Directions

Tape one end of the wrapping paper tube closed using the masking tape. Have each guest use a spoon to put about a cup of dried beans, peas, or rice into the tube. Seal the other end closed with masking tape. Then use the paints and paintbrushes to decorate the rainstick.

Riveting Ribbon Skirts

Make these hula skirts for your guests to enjoy at the party and to continue enjoying at home.

Materials

★ Strips of cotton material
★ Velcro strips
★ Colorful ribbon, 2 inches in width

Directions

Measure your child's waist. Use that measurement for the length of the cotton material, plus or minus a few inches. (Keep the size of your guests in mind as you make these skirts.) Cut the material 3 inches in width. Hem the edges of the material. Add Velcro strips to both ends of the material, allowing extra inches for a better fit. Cut the ribbon into strips about 2 feet long. Sew strips of ribbon in a rainbow of colors along the top edge of the waist material. Sew ribbon completely around the material. Have the guests dress in their hula skirts and dance to tropical music.

Sand and Sea Symbols

Show your guests you had a "whale of a time" at the sea creature slumber party with this goody-filled sand bucket.

Materials

★ Puffy paints
★ Permanent, colorful markers

- ★ Plastic pail and shovel, one set per guest
- ★ Goodies and treats for the inside of the pail, such as cookies, candy, sunglasses, balls, pencils, and floating toys
- ★ Thank-you note or typing paper
- ★ Colorful markers
- ★ Colorful ribbon or yarn

Directions

Use the puffy paints and permanent markers to personalize and decorate each child's pail and shovel. Create beach scenes or ocean scenes around the outside of the sand pail. Write the guest's name on the shovel. Then fill the pail with trinkets and snacks, preferably ones related to the party theme. Write a thank-you note on the card or typing paper with colorful markers, and attach it to the handle of the pail, using the ribbon or yarn.

Space Samples

Tell each guest that he or she is "out of this world" with this party favor.

Materials

- ★ Star cookie cutter
- ★ Yellow construction paper
- ★ Small gift bag per guest
- ★ Glow-in-the-dark paints
- ★ Paintbrush
- ★ Small spaceship toys, such as miniature astronauts, space stickers, glow-in-the-dark stars

Directions

Using the cookie cutter as a pattern, trace and cut out star-shaped thank-you notes from the yellow construction paper. Write this note on the star: "You are out of this world! Thank you for coming to my sleepover!" Decorate and personalize the outside of the gift bag, using the glow-in-the-dark paint and paintbrush. Then fill the bag with space toys and stickers. Be sure to include a thank-you star in each gift bag.

Spray Bottle Sensations

Give these slumber party favors at any time of the year. Spring and summer guests will enjoy dressing in bathing suits and spraying cool water on each other. Fall guests can spray water into the air on a sunny day and try to "capture" a rainbow. Winter guests can add a small dab of liquid, washable paint to the water and spray onto snow creations for dazzling effects.

Materials

- ★ One spray bottle per guest
- ★ Puffy paints
- ★ Permanent markers

Directions

Have the host decorate and personalize a spray bottle for each guest before the party, using puffy paints and permanent markers. Allow plenty of time for the paints to dry before the slumber party begins. See above explanations for how to use these favors during the sleepover.

Striking Straws

Keeping your sleepover theme in mind, look for cute straws in department stores, grocery stores, or dollar stores.

Materials

- ★ One or more straws per guest
- ★ Colorful ribbon
- ★ Fruit juice pouches

Directions

Choose one or more straws to go with the theme of your party. Use the ribbon to bundle the straws together and tie the straws to a juice pouch. Give the straw and juice treat to your guests as they are departing.

Sunny Sun Visors

Use these party favors for a summertime sleepover. Let each guest make his or her own bright-colored visor, and let the outside play begin!

Materials

- ★ Sun visors, one per child
- ★ Puffy paints
- ★ Yellow construction paper
- ★ Thank-you note or small piece of typing paper
- ★ Colorful markers
- ★ Yellow ribbon

Directions

Have the host personalize and decorate each sun visor with puffy paints in advance, to allow time for the paint to dry. Give the sun visors to the guests for outdoor play. Prior to the party, cut large circles from the yellow construction paper. Write a thank-you note on the note or typing paper with colorful markers to each child, beginning with, "Thank you for brightening my slumber party." Before the guests leave, attach the note to the visor with the yellow ribbon.

Tick-Tock Take-Home

Give your guests a gift that "keeps on ticking."

Materials

- ★ Inexpensive watch or miniclock
- ★ Colorful markers
- ★ Thank-you note or small piece of typing paper
- ★ Colorful ribbon

Directions

Most dollar stores and many department stores sell inexpensive watches and miniclocks. (Look for small clocks with the children's key chains.) Write a note using colorful markers on the thank-you card or on the paper that begins, "Thank you for coming to my sleepover. I had a great time!" Attach the note to the watch or clock with a piece of colorful ribbon.

Toothy Treats

Here's a treat that will have the guest remembering the slumber party, both morning and evening.

Materials

- ★ Colorful ribbon
- ★ New toothbrush, one per guest
- ★ Travel-size tube of toothpaste, one per guest
- ★ Thank-you note or colorful typing paper

Directions

Wrap a strip of ribbon around one toothbrush and one tube of toothpaste. Attach a thank-you note to the dental set, using one end of the ribbon. Write something clever on the card or typing paper, such as "Thanks for being at my slumber party. It was tooth-iffic!" or "Thanks for bringing your lovely smile to my sleepover!"

Windy Wonders

Use these sleepover reminders as a treat for any season of the year.

Materials

(Choose one or more of the following as a sleepover favor.)

- ★ Small, battery-operated and hand-held fan
- ★ Pinwheel
- ★ Kite
- ★ Bottle of bubbles
- ★ Windsock

Directions

Choose one or more of the gift items above for each guest. You may choose to give each guest a different item from the list or a basket with several of each item.

Winning Windsock

Make this beautiful windsock for your guest to hang inside his or her room as a constant reminder of special friendships. (You'll need to start collecting these oatmeal boxes in advance!)

Materials

- ★ One oatmeal box per guest
- ★ 2-inch-wide ribbon in a variety of colors
- ★ Craft glue
- ★ Stapler and staples
- ★ Hole punchers
- ★ Yarn

Directions

Cut the top and bottom out of each oatmeal box. Wipe out the excess oatmeal from the boxes. Have the guest choose colors of ribbon to use on his or her windsock. Wrap and glue ribbon around the outside of the oatmeal box, covering the entire box. Then cut strips of ribbons, 2 feet in length each. Staple the strips onto one opened end of the oatmeal box. On the other end of the box, punch two holes directly opposite of each other. Attach a 1-foot-long strip of yarn to the holes, tying each end of the yarn in one hole. This will be the handle of the windsock.

Winter Warmers

Give these heart-warming favors for a winter slumber party treat.

Materials

- ★ Pair of mittens or scarf in solid color, one per guest
- ★ Puffy paints in a variety of colors
- ★ Thank-you note or white typing paper
- ★ Colorful markers

Directions

On each pair of mittens or scarf, use the puffy paints to personalize and decorate the winter item. You may choose to spell out the guest's name on the mittens or scarf and then add flowers, squiggly lines, stars, or other shapes and patterns. Write a thank-you note using colorful markers to include with the favor.

As an alternate option, let each guest design and decorate their own pair of mittens and/or scarf at the party and then take them home the following day as a party remembrance.

Wooden Spoon Someones

Make a wooden buddy for each guest to enjoy at the party and afterward.

Materials

- ★ Large wooden spoon for each guest
- ★ Paint
- ★ Paintbrushes, large and small
- ★ Craft glue
- ★ Bits of yarn

Directions

Have each guest paint his or her own spoon and add facial features. When the paint is dry, use craft glue to add yarn bits for hair. Allow the wooden buddies to dry completely. Then put on a puppet show with the new friends. Send these wooden buddies home with each guest. You may add more delight to the treasure by giving each guest a small potted plant. Push the end of the spoon into the soil with the plant to watch over the growth process!

Chapter 9

Perfect Plans for Partiers

A Dozen Delightful Themes for Drowsy Dwellers

The previous chapters of this book grouped sleepover ideas in the following categories: themes, invitations, decorations, games, activities, food, and favors. This chapter is designed to show you how to pull all the ideas together to create a memorable sleepover. I've given suggestions for twelve sample sleepovers, from start to finish. Choose one of these parties for your sleepover or look back through the book and make selections of your own, following the format in this chapter for an exciting, fun-filled sleepover.

Alaskan Adventures

Go North, Young Man! (or Woman!)

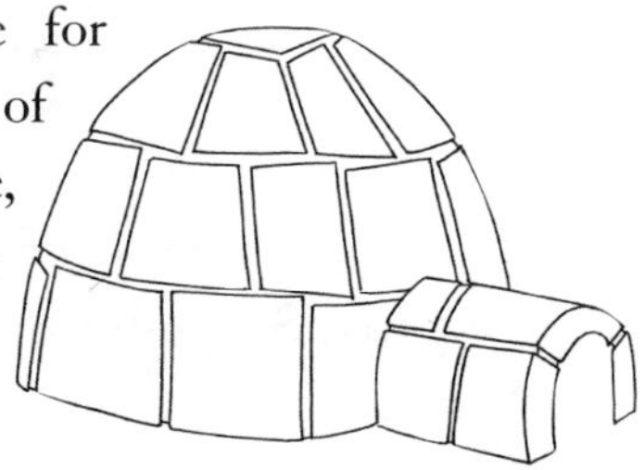

Invite your guests to this unique sleepover with one-of-a-kind snowflake invitations. Use coffee filters, folded in half and then in quarters. Make snips and cuts to create a different snowflake for each guest. Write the details of the sleepover on the snowflake, using a silver pen. You might choose to add white glitter around the edges of each snowflake. When the snowflake is dry, refold carefully and place in an envelope. Mail to your guests one to two weeks before the party.

Forecast: Snow, Snow, and More Snow!

Use coffee filters to make snowflakes to decorate one or more rooms in the house. Fold each coffee filter in half, then in quarters. Use scissors to snip and cut around the edges. Add glue and white glitter to both sides of the snowflake, allowing the first side to dry completely before working on the other side. Hang the snowflakes from the ceiling using fishing line or white yarn and thumbtacks. Hang the snowflakes at varying levels to give the impression of snow falling from the sky. Also use snowflakes in as many rooms as you'd like to decorate.

In the room that you will use for game time, pour white Styrofoam packing pieces on the floor.

Snowplay!

Choose one or more of the following games to play at the party. Suggestions are given for outdoor and indoor games.

Outdoor Games

Snowball Battle

Before the party, use felt and dried beans to make snowball beanbags. Cut the felt into circles, four inches in diameter. Sew together two circles, leaving an opening about one inch in length. Use a funnel or small spoon to fill the snowball with dried beans. Sew the opening closed. (You can use a hot-glue gun to make the snowballs instead of sewing. Make sure an adult uses the glue gun, as it can get very hot.) Make enough beanbags for each guest to have at least five.

To play the game, place a long rope on the ground. Stand the balloon-filled snowman (from the activity section) on the line. Divide the guests into two teams, one team on each side of the line. Have each child use white typing paper wadded into "snowballs" to form a circle on the ground, large enough for a child to stand in. This will be an "igloo." Give each child five beanbag snowballs to put inside his or her igloo.

To begin the game, say, "Truce." Each child runs around on his or her team's side of the line. When the caller says, "Attack!" each child finds an igloo and begins to throw snowballs at the snowman. After each child uses all of the ammunition in his or her igloo, a casualty count is taken. The team who has moved the snowman the farthest into the opposing team's territory is the winning team.

Gather the snowballs, give each player five snowballs to place in an igloo, and have another battle round.

Iditarod Racers

Before the party, set up five stations in the yard. At each station, place toys or candy surprises, one for each team that you will have. Use stakes with a piece of typing paper to number the stations.

On the day of the party, divide the guests into groups of two or three. (You can determine this by the number of children at the sleepover.) If there are two in each group, have the children decide who will be the "sled dog" and who will be the "racer." If there are three in each group, select two children to be the sled dogs and one child to be the racer. The sled dogs will run on all fours, and the racer will run behind, holding onto the dog's leash.

Using safety pins, attach two strips of yarn, each about six feet in length, to the sled dog's clothing at the shoulders. The racer will hold the other ends of the yarn leash. Give the racer a backpack.

The object of the game is for the sled-dog team to race to each station, collect one prize from each station, store the prizes in the backpack, and get back to the starting gate. Each team races separately, with someone timing the race. The team completing the race in the shortest amount of time is the winning team.

Indoor Games

Collecting Snowflakes

Play this game in the room with the packing pieces on the floor. Give each player a plastic bag and a garden glove. With a gloved hand, each player tries to pick up as many packing pieces as possible in two minutes. At the end of the two minutes, count to find a winner. Continue until all of the pieces are picked up! At this point, you may choose to vacuum the remaining pieces to prevent packing shreds from being scattered all over the house.

Snowball Surprises

Before the party, place small, individually wrapped pieces of candy into many white balloons, one per balloon. Use a funnel to add confetti to each balloon. (Use a hole puncher and white paper to make the confetti. Another messy but fun addition is white glitter!) Inflate each balloon and tie the end.

For the game, put the balloons on the floor. On the word "Go," have each guest try to pop as many "snowballs" as possible, collecting the candy as the balloons are popped. (Once again, you'll probably want to vacuum right after this game!)

Warm as Toast!

Gather a pile of winter clothes: sweatshirts, sweatpants, coats, sweaters, socks, mittens, gloves, scarves, and so on. Make a large pile on the floor. Choose two players. On the word "Go," each child puts on as many clothes from the pile as he or she can in one minute. At the end of one minute, count the clothing items. The child who donned the most clothing articles wins. You may choose to establish points for each item. For example, a sweatshirt, taking more time to put on than a scarf, could count for three points and the scarf only one point. Then total up the points for each child.

Alaskan Activities

Do one or more of the following activities in the order that best suits your party.

Stuffed Snowman

Inflate white balloons to use as stuffing for the snowman. For the bottom of the snowman, use a large white kitchen trash bag. Fill the bag with balloons and tie the top closed. Fill a smaller white bag with balloons, then tie closed. Fill an even smaller bag with balloons for the snowman's head, then tie closed. (To make the "snowballs" rounder, tape down each corner.) Attach two sections by knotting yarn around the tied ends. Then poke small holes and use yarn to attach the third section. (The snowman will be floppy; move some of the balloons around inside the bag to make the snowman stand.)

Use markers to add facial features or staple construction paper pieces in place. Add a hat and scarf for the finished product.

Soapsuds Snow

This is messy, but oh, so fun! Beat two parts of soap powder to one part of water with a mixer. Give each child a heavy piece of cardboard to use as a base. Then let each child scoop the "snow" onto his or her board and create a snow scene. Build snowmen, make snow forts, or create a hill for skiing. Let this dry overnight.

To add skiers to the scene, give each child colored pipe cleaners, colored craft sticks, and colored toothpicks. Begin with an eight-inch strip of pipe cleaner. Bend the top three inches over and wrap the end to form a circle for the head. Slightly bend the pipe cleaner two and a half inches from the bottom to form one leg. Cut a strip two and three-quarters inches long. Wrap one end at the top of the first leg to form the second leg. Bend up the ends of both legs to form feet. Lastly, twist a four and a half-inch pipe cleaner strip in place to form two arms. Wrap the end of each arm around a colored toothpick for the ski poles. Cut or break the colored craft stick in half for skis. Glue each foot on half of the stick. You'll need to prop the skier upright so that the feet will stay in place long enough for the glue to dry. Let this dry overnight. Then in the morning, let the skiers ski on the soap slope!

Home, Sweet Igloo

Let the guests create a sweet igloo using sugar cubes. Give each guest a white paper plate to work on. Have the children use white decorator frosting as glue to secure the cubes in place. For an igloo top, carefully place a coconut marshmallow-covered chocolate cupcake with cream filling on the glued cubes.

Polar Bear, Polar Bear

Use a long jump rope to play this favorite game. Have the children chant as they jump, replacing "teddy bear" with "polar bear."

Warm Your Nose and Fingers and Toes

As the guests begin to get drowsy, use the following idea to help settle them into rest time:

- Have the guests gather their sleeping bags and form a circle, with the head of the sleeping bag at the inside of the circle. You could add sticks and logs and torn strips of red, yellow, and orange tissue paper to form a pretend fire in the middle of the circle. Encourage the guests to warm by the fire and sing a song. Sing "Build a Snowman" to the tune of "Found a Peanut." Use verses along these lines:

  Build a snowman, build a snowman,
  Build a snowman in my yard.
  Build a snowman, build a snowman,
  Build a snowman in my yard.
  Add a carrot, add a carrot,
  Add a carrot for a nose.
  Add a carrot, add a carrot,
  Add a carrot for a nose.

- Encourage the guests to create new verses to complete the snowman.

Snowy Cuisine

To warm the hearts and tummies of the Alaskan guests, try this supper.

Snowman Pie

Yield: 6–8 servings

1 pound ground beef
2 tablespoons chopped onion
1 teaspoon salt
½ teaspoon pepper
3 cups mashed potatoes (prepared with a small amount of milk to be somewhat stiff)
½ cup grated Cheddar cheese
1 small carrot
16 whole black peppercorns
24 green peas
American cheese

In a skillet, brown ground beef, onion, salt, and pepper; drain. In a bowl, stir together the meat mixture and 1 cup of mashed potatoes. Spread into the bottom of a slightly greased, 9-inch pie plate. Top with grated Cheddar cheese. Using the remaining two cups of potatoes, form eight snowmen on top of the pie. Use 1 tablespoon of potatoes for each head and 3 tablespoons of potatoes for each body. Bake uncovered at 350 degrees for 20 minutes.

Meanwhile, with a sharp knife, cut the small carrot into eight strips. After removing the pie from the oven, place two peppercorns in each snowman for eyes, insert a carrot strip for a nose, add three peas to each body for buttons, and a narrow strip of American cheese between the head and body to form a scarf. Serve while warm; remind children to remove peppercorns before eating.

Snappy Snowmen

Yield: 6 snowmen

40 gingersnap cookies
6 tablespoons dark corn syrup
4 tablespoons creamy peanut butter
1 cup powdered sugar
6 wooden skewers
⅓ cup vanilla frosting
6 chocolate wafers
12 chocolate sandwich cookies
6 pieces of red shoestring licorice (12 inches each)
12 brown candy-coated chocolate candies
6 pieces of candy corn
30 miniature chocolate chips
18 semisweet chocolate chips

Place cookies in a resealable plastic food bag; crush finely with a rolling pin. Combine corn syrup and peanut butter in a medium bowl. Add the crushed gingersnaps; mix well. The mixture should hold together without being sticky. Add an additional tablespoon or two of corn syrup if the mixture is too dry.

Have each guest roll three "snowballs" of dough in descending sizes. (One ball should be about 1 inch in diameter, one ball about 1½ inches in diameter, and one ball about 2 inches in diameter.) Roll the three balls in powdered sugar. Cut the skewers slightly shorter than the height of the snowmen; insert through the center of each snowball to secure them. Using frosting as glue, place a chocolate wafer on the top ball to form a hat brim. Place a dollop of frosting on top of one sandwich cookie; top with the second cookie. Attach to chocolate wafer with frosting to create the hat. Carefully tie licorice around the snowman for a scarf. Use frosting to attach chocolate candies for eyes, candy corn for nose, miniature chips for a smiling mouth, and semisweet chips for buttons. (Remind the guests about the skewer before they eat the snowmen.)

Snowball Milkshakes

Yield: 1 milkshake

¼ cup milk
1 cup vanilla ice cream
1 teaspoon vanilla
2 scoops vanilla ice cream

In a blender combine the first three ingredients; blend until smooth. After pouring into a serving glass, add two scoops of vanilla ice cream "snowballs."

For breakfast, serve powdered sugar doughnut holes and milk. (If you can't find these at a bakery or grocery store, purchase glazed doughnut holes and roll them in powdered sugar.)

For an Alaskan snack, serve slushies by adding fruit juice to shaved ice.

Warm Remembrances

If you choose to give party favors, you might decide to give each guest a pair of mittens with a matching scarf. Before the party, have the host personalize the scarves using puffy paints. Fill both mittens with small individually wrapped candies, a pack of Winterfresh gum, and a snowman cookie cutter. Pin each mitten to one end of the scarf with a large safety pin

Alaskan Adventure reminder to
: she leaves the sleepover.

lphabet Antics

ver Fun from A to Zzzzzz

Use letter-shaped cookies, pasta, or cereal to create this slumber invitation. Glue the letters onto colored oaktag to spell out the party information. For a less time-consuming alternative, glue only the letters of the guest's name on the oaktag card and write the remaining details with a marker. Carefully place the invitation in a large manila envelope and hand-deliver one to two weeks before the party.

As Easy as A-B-C

Decorate the house using alphabet letters. Draw large letters on colored oaktag or poster paper. Cut out; use fishing line or yarn to hang from the ceiling. Hang the letters in several rooms and at varying heights.

Pick a Letter, Any Letter

Choose one or more of the following games to play at the party. Suggestions are given for outside games and inside games.

Outdoor Games

Alphabet Scavenger Hunt

Before the party, trace your child's foot to make a footprint pattern. Make many footprints from colored construction paper. Also collect small prizes, one for each letter of the alphabet. (Check dollar, department, party, or grocery stores for small, inexpensive toys or food items.) Put each letter's prizes in a small paper bag with that letter written on the outside of the bag with a thick marker. Write a question or riddle for each letter on an eight-inch by ten-inch sheet of colored oaktag. The answer to the riddle or question could be the prize itself or another word with that letter. For example, at the "D" station, the riddle could be "We lived a long time ago on land and sea. Some of us ate meat; some ate trees. Some were fierce and very tall—some were nice and kinda small. What are we?" The prize in the paper bag would be a small dinosaur toy. Or the question could be unrelated to the prize, such as "I am a sweet food with a hole in the middle. What am I?" And the answer, obviously, is doughnut.

Staple the oaktag to a stake with the letter written at the top.

Set up twenty-six stations, one for each letter. Set the stake in the ground with the question and place the bag with the prizes near the stake.

Place footprints on the ground, leading to each letter, in alphabetical order. The object of the game is for each child to follow the footprints, answer the question correctly, and reach in the bag for a prize. Give each player a party bag to put each of his or her toys in as he or she follows the footprint maze.

Animal Charades

Before the sleepover begins, write animal names from *A* to *Z* on slips of paper. Put the slips in a basket. Have a child draw a slip of paper and pretend to be that animal. Tell the children the letter it begins with and have the guests try to guess the animal.

Indoor Games

Letters in the Air

Have the guests gather in one of the rooms with the letter decorations. Play music and have the children dance or skip around the room. When the music stops, each child must find a letter to star neath. Ask a question, such as, "Can you na etable that begins with your letter?" Each then respond with a vegetable beginning with the letter that is above his or her head.

Alphabet Bingo

Before the party, make alphabet cards, one per guest, using oaktag. Draw sixteen squares on each card and fill in with alphabet letters. Write the letters with a marker, or glue alphabet cookies in place. To play the game, give each guest a card and small markers, such as quarter-sized circles cut from oaktag, buttons, or checkers. Put the remaining cookies in a cookie jar. Let each guest take a turn pulling out a cookie, without looking, and calling out that letter. That guest gets to eat the cookie, and all the guests check their cards for that letter. The players put a marker on that letter, if found. The first person with four in a row, horizontally, vertically, or diagonally wins the round. (If you let the guests eat the cookies as they call out the letters, make sure you have enough to continue playing the game.)

Numbers and Letters

Before the party, make two large dice. Buy gift boxes at a department store or mailing boxes at a mail store.

The boxes could be from six to ten inches in width and length, but make sure they are square. If the boxes are not white, cover the boxes with white freezer paper. Draw large dots on each side of one die with a black marker. On the other die, write a large letter on each of the six sides.

To play the game, let a guest roll both of the dice. The player has to name as many words as there are dots on the die, beginning with the letter shown on the other die.

Alphabet Activities

Dreaming of Letters

Before the party, purchase letter-shaped sponges, usually found in the craft or school section of a department store. Also purchase fabric paints in a variety of colors and one white pillowcase per guest.

On the day of the party, cover a table with newspapers. Give each guest a white pillowcase. Cut cardboard, poster paper, or oaktag the size of the pillowcase. Slip one piece into each pillowcase to prevent the paint from bleeding through to the back. Pour paint into shallow containers and have the sponges and paintbrushes handy. Encourage each guest to stamp his or her name onto the pillowcase. Then let each guest add other decorations with paintbrushes.

Allow the pillowcases to dry, then remove the board inside the pillowcase. Use each child's pillowcase for a favor bag at the end of the sleepover.

Body Language

Have the children work in pairs or groups of three to make letters on the floor, using their bodies to form the letters.

Pudding Pictures

Use one box of instant pudding for every four guests. Prepare the pudding ahead of the party and chill. When you are ready for this activity, have each person wash his or her hands with soap. Give each person a paper plate with a half cup of pudding. Have the guests spread the pudding with a finger to a thin layer on the plate. Call out a letter; have each guest draw a picture of something that begins with the letter in the pudding. Give the "artists" plenty of time to work, then have them smear their pudding to prepare for the next letter. Call out as many letters as the guests' interest allows.

Pretzel Letters

Prepare the dough before the sleepover and refrigerate.

1½ cups warm water
1 package yeast
1 teaspoon salt
1 tablespoon sugar
4 cups flour
1 egg, beaten
Salt

Pour warm water into a large bowl. Sprinkle on yeast and stir until soft. Add salt, sugar, and flour. Mix and knead dough with hands.

Give each child a small amount of dough. Have the guest roll the dough and form the first letter of his or her name. (If this would cause identical letters, you may choose to use a favorite letter or a last name.) Place the letters on a greased cookie sheet. Brush each letter with the beaten egg; sprinkle with salt. Bake 12 minutes at 350 degrees.

Sounds of Silence and Snores

As the guests begin to get drowsy, use the following idea to help settle them into rest time:

- Have the children place their sleeping bags on the floor to form letters and then crawl inside their bag. Decide who will start the Alphabet Soup game and the order in which the other players will follow. The first person says, "I'm making alphabet soup. I need to add _________." The first person fills in the blank with an *A* word. The next person repeats exactly what the first person says and adds another *A* word. Each person continues to add an *A* word until each person has had a turn. (The words do not have to be food items—the sillier the answer, the better!) Once all the players have had a turn with letter *A*, the game starts over again with letter *B*.

Soup's On!

Alphabet soup, that is. Serve this hearty alphabet pasta soup, as well as the other yummy recipes here, to your letter-loving guests.

Alphabet Soup

2 cans (13¾ ounces) chicken broth
4 cups cold water
1 cup uncooked alphabet pasta

1 cup thinly sliced carrot pieces
3 cups chopped cooked chicken
Saltine crackers
Squirt cheese

In large saucepan, combine broth, water, pasta, and carrots; bring to a boil. Cover; simmer 15 minutes. Add the chopped chicken and cook 5 additional minutes.

Serve the soup with crackers and squirt cheese. Let each child write letters, using the squirt cheese, on his or her crackers during the meal.

Alphacakes

For breakfast, serve prepared pancakes and syrup. Before the party, make two or three small pancakes for each child. Use a pancake mix to prepare the batter. With a funnel, carefully pour a small amount of batter onto the hot griddle, in the shape of a letter. (Use each guest's first initial, last initial, or spell out the entire name.) *Note:* You will have to make the letter backward in order for it to turn out correctly on the pancake! After the batter has had a short time to cook, pour more batter on top of the letter, forming a round pancake. Continue to cook, following the directions on the package. The letter you wrote will be a tad browner and will show up on the top of the pancake. If the pancakes are prepared a day ahead, refrigerate until the morning of the party. The pancakes may also be made one to two weeks ahead and frozen. Let thaw in refrigerator the night of the sleepover. To serve, warm the pancakes in a microwave or on a cookie sheet in a warm oven.

A Final Note

To remind each guest of the fun had at this alphabet party, put prizes and surprises in his or her stamped pillowcase from the activity time. Put each child's prizes from the footprint maze in his or her pillowcase, along with a pack of sponge alphabet letters, an alphabet book, and/or a bag of alphabet cookies.

Beach Blasters

Invite your landlubber friends to join you for a beach sleepover.

Ahoy, Mate!

Purchase a plastic pail and shovel for each guest. Have the host use puffy paints to personalize each child's pail. Write the slumber party details on a sheet of paper. On the notes, ask your guests to bring their pails to the party. This way, you can add goodies to the pail at the end of the slumber party as parting favors. Roll the paper and tie with a string or piece of yarn. Place the party info inside the pail and hand-deliver the invitations to the guests.

Surf's Up!

To decorate for the party, place opened beach umbrellas on the floor, spread beach towels in various rooms, and lay seashells on the floor. (Seashells can be found at some department stores, party stores, or linen and bathroom stores that carry home decorations.)

Beach Bash

Choose one or more of the following games to play at the party. Suggestions are made for outside games and inside games.

Outdoor Games

Swim, Friends, Swim!

Mark off a rectangular play area about fifteen feet by twenty feet. Two of the guests are "lifeguards" and stand along the twenty foot sidelines, one on each side. Each lifeguard holds an inflated life ring. The rest of the guests stand along one of the fifteen foot sidelines. When a caller yells, "Swim, friends, Swim!" the swimmers run to the opposite side of the rectangle. The lifeguards throw the life rings like Frisbees, aiming for the swimmers. If a swimmer is hit, he or she trades places with the lifeguard and play begins again.

Bouncing Beach Ball

Inflate a beach ball. Give the guests a sheet to hold, with a guest at each corner and others scattered around the sheet. The children stand with the sheet held about waist-high and pulled taut. Place the ball on the sheet. On "Go," encourage the children to wave the sheet up and down to bounce the beach ball. Time the play to see how long the guests can keep the ball bouncing on the sheet.

Indoor Games

Pass the Life Ring

Divide the guests into two teams, and have them form lines. Give each guest a stick pretzel. Have each guest hold the pretzel stick between his or her lips. Place a Lifesaver candy ("life ring"!) on the pretzel of the first player of each team. On "Go," the first person on each team turns around to face the next person on the team. He or she passes the Lifesaver to the next person; neither player may touch the candy with his or her hands, and the pretzels must stay in the mouths. The Lifesavers are passed down the line, and the first team to pass the life ring to the end is the winning team.

Surfboard Stunts

Place a surfboard or plywood plank between two chairs. Play on a carpeted area and line the floor around the plank with pillows. Have the children take turns pretending to surf, doing stunts and tricks on the surfboard. Have the other guests judge each child's performance.

Crabwalk Relay

Show the guests how to walk like a crab, by placing their feet on the floor, arching their backs, and placing the palms of their hands on the floor. Divide the guests into two teams. Have the first "crab" from each team walk on a given path, then come back and tag the next player. When all the children from a team have followed the path and returned, those players are the winners.

Atlantic (or Pacific!) Activities

Do one or more of these activities in the order that best suits your party.

Rainbow Sand

Add powdered gelatin to sand to make a variety of colors. Provide a small jar for each child (preferably plastic) with a lid. Let each child use spoons and small funnels to fill the jar with colored sand. Demonstrate how to pile the sand in varying depths to make an interesting design on the outside. You can also poke a toothpick into the edges of the sand next to the glass to form neat patterns. Fill the jar to the very top to prevent the sand from shifting if tilted. Secure the lid.

May I Have Your Footprint?

Let the guests create a special party favor for the host.

Purchase a very large beach towel in a solid color. Pour fabric paint into shallow containers. Have each guest step into the paint, then carefully make a footprint on the towel. Support the guest so that he or she will not fall or smear the footprint. Help the child remove the paint from his or her foot, then have the guest use a paintbrush to sign his or her name on the towel, also.

Zucchini with a Bikini

Have each guest create a zucchini beachcomber. Give each child a zucchini squash, four golf tees (for arms and legs), whole black peppercorns (for hair), scraps of material, and thumbtacks. Have each child add the arms, legs, and hair. Then cut the material into a bathing suit shape and secure in place with thumbtacks. To add facial features, use a knife to scrape off the peeling for eyes, nose, and mouth. Fill in the indentions with colored frosting, if desired.

Beach Blanket Bingo

Give each person a beach towel or large towel to spread on the floor. Playing beach music, have the guests do swimming dances to the music.

The Lull of the Waves

As the guests begin to get drowsy, use the following idea to help settle them into rest time:

- Give each child a beach towel or large towel to spread on the floor. Tell the guests that they will be sleeping on the beach! Then have each child lay his or her sleeping bag on top of the towel. Play this thinking game while lying in the sleeping bags: Have each child say the following rhyme. At the end of the rhyme, each guest should name something that lives in the ocean. "I went swimming in the deep blue sea. Here's what I saw swimming next to me: ______."

Captain's Feast

Prepare these sea-themed treats for the sleepover guests.

Fish Food

Prepare tuna salad in a bowl. Make a fish-shaped sandwich for each child. Spread the tuna salad between four slices of bread to make two whole sandwiches. Cut a V shape from the bottom left of one sandwich to form a fish's mouth. Cut the other sandwich into two triangles. Place one triangle on the right side of the other sandwich, with the point of crust touching the edge of the sandwich. (Use the other triangle for the next fish shape.) Add a sliced olive for an eye.

Fishy Gelatin

Prepare blue gelatin as directed on the box. When firm, scoop the gelatin out in large spoonfuls and fill a clean, glass goldfish bowl. Add gummy fish to the "ocean water" as you are filling the bowl. Top with whipped topping for waves. To serve the "ocean water," place a lettuce leaf on each child's plate with the sandwich. Tell the guest that this is the kelp plant. Then scoop some of the blue gelatin on top of the leaf.

Sand Pudding

Prepare vanilla pudding according to the directions on the box. Spoon one-half cup into a serving dish for each guest. Top the pudding with crushed, vanilla cream-filled cookies.

Life Ring Bagels

For breakfast, color cream cheese with food coloring to make a variety of colors. Have each child use plastic knives or spoons to decorate the flat portion of a bagel cut in half to resemble a life ring. Drink milk tinted with blue food coloring for "ocean water."

Party Pails

Use the decorated plastic pails that were personalized for sleepover invitations for the party favors. Fill each guest's pail with surprises such as sunglasses, suntan lotion, Chapstick, sea creature toys, fish-shaped crackers, and the sand jars and zucchini person made during the activity time.

Community Kids

Invite your guests to be a part of your town with this clever sleepover idea.

Employees Needed!

Several weeks before the sleepover, ask each guest's parent for a small head shot of the child. On oaktag, prepare an identification card for each child. Glue the picture on one side of the four by two-inch card. Write the child's name and "occupation" on the card—banker, service station attendant, grocery store owner, restaurant owner, and so on. Then laminate the cards.

On the front of a sheet of folded typing paper, draw buildings and stores. At the top, write, "Come spend an evening in Lavendertown." (Use the host's name to create a silly city name.) On the inside, write the sleepover details. Tell the guest to bring his or her identification card to the party. Ask each guest to bring items related to his occupation to the party. Tuck the ID card inside the invitation, insert the invitation in a small manila envelope, and mail to the guests one to two weeks before the sleepover.

The Big City

Before the party, locate enough large appliance boxes for each guest and the host to have one. Tape the top and bottom closed. Cut out one side of the box. On the opposite side, cut a window. Line the boxes up along the wall. When the guests arrive, they will complete the "buildings" of the city. String Christmas lights around the room to be streetlights. (If the boxes will take up too much room for the children to sleep in that room, string lights in another room for the children to sleep.)

Let the Games Begin!

Choose one or more of the following games to play at the party. Suggestions are given for outdoor and indoor games.

Outdoor Games

Banker's Delight

Divide the children into two groups and form two lines. About fifteen feet away, place two large piggy banks (or a basket). Give each child five or more play coins. On "Go," the first person in each line runs to the "bank" and puts his or her first coin in. Then that person runs back to the line and tags the next person. That person runs to the bank next. Play continues with each person depositing one coin at a time until all the coins have been deposited. The first team with all of its coins in the bank is the winning team.

Cops and Drivers

Choose one player to be the "police officer"; the other players are the "drivers." The game is played like tag, with the police officer chasing the drivers. Once a player is tagged ("given a ticket"), he or she must park the car and stand still for one minute. Have the player count to sixty, then resume driving. Once a player receives three tickets, that player becomes the police officer. Establish three locations for "gas stations"—these are the bases, and children may not be tagged while on base.

Indoor Games

Stocking the Shelves

Make a collection of boxes, plastic jars, small cans, and other nonfragile food items. Divide the children into two teams. Set a timer for three minutes. Let each team use the items to build a tower. See which team can build the tallest tower and which team can use the most items.

Like a Kid in a Candy Store

Fill two baskets with a variety of candies, including suckers and individually wrapped candy pieces. Divide the group into two teams. Give the first person in each line a ruler. On the word "Go," the first person scoops out one piece of candy with the ruler. The player may not touch the candy with his or her hands but may lean the basket, if necessary to help get the candy on the ruler. The player then walks to another basket and puts the candy inside. The first player returns to the line and passes the ruler to the next person. The game continues until a team completely empties their basket into the other basket. The first team to transfer all the candy is the winning team.

Clothing Store Customers

Make two piles of clothing. Divide the children into groups of two. Let each child hide a marble in one pile of clothing, without the other person seeing where the marble is hidden. Give both players a shoehorn. On the word "Go," the players search for the marbles, each child searching in the pile in which the other person hid the marble. The players may not touch the clothing with their hands; he or she must use only the shoehorn to move around the articles of clothing. The first person to find the marble is the winner of that pair. Continue until each person has had a turn. Mix the kids into new pairs and repeat the game.

Build a Community

Do one or more of these activities in the order that best suits your party.

Open for Business

Let each child choose a large box for his or her store. Provide markers and crayons and have the children decorate and name his or her building.

May I Help You?

Give the children toy money for the bank, candy for the candy store, cans and boxes for the grocery store, and so on. Then allow the children to use their imaginations and "play" in their community.

The Candy Jar

Provide a large Styrofoam cone, found in department stores or craft stores. Let the children use the suckers from the game time and insert them into the cone, stick first. Then provide baskets or small jars; let the children sort the candy pieces from the game time into the baskets. The children may decide to sort by color or type. After the candy has been displayed nicely on the shelf, let the children "shop" for candy. Give each child a small paper bag (a white lunch-size bag will work nicely). Let each child have a turn rolling a die. The child chooses pieces of candy, according to the number on the die. Continue until each child has a nice selection of candy.

Driving Delight

Use a store-bought road map or create one on a large sheet of bulletin board paper. (Bulletin board paper may be purchased at teaching supply stores.) Draw roads, buildings, shops, parks, and so on, using markers. Provide small cars and vehicles, and let the children's imaginations get in high gear!

Closed!

As the guests begin to get drowsy, try this idea to help settle them into rest time:

- Have the guests form a circle with their sleeping bags, with their heads facing the inside of the circle. Place all the ID cards in the center of the circle, face down. Let the first child draw a card, without letting the other guests see whom it belongs to. That person must describe or tell a true story about the owner of the ID card. The other children try to guess whose card has been drawn. After each child has had a turn, you may choose to play the game again. This time, make up silly stories about the person whose ID is drawn.

Fast-Food Fare

For your busy community workers, serve typical fast food. Serve up burgers, french fries, and soda for supper. For breakfast, don shoes and go to the local doughnut store in pajamas.

Favorite Favors

Before the party, purchase inexpensive favors at a department store or dollar store. Give each child some of the coins used in the banker's game. Have the host sit inside one of the stores at the window. Let a guest give the host one of his or her coins, and have the host choose a prize for the guest. Do this as often as your budget allows. Let the children put their goodies in a small colored paper bag. (Before the party, write a personalized thank-you note to each guest on the outside of the bag. Thank him or her for visiting your town, and ask that friend to visit again soon!)

Construction Crews

Inspire the future architects, city planners, and construction workers in your group with this fun sleepover idea.

Reach for the Sky!

Use one sheet of white paper for two invitations. Starting close to the bottom, draw a three-and-one-half inch square. Center a three-inch square on top of that one. Center a two-and-one-half inch square on top of that and end with a two-inch square centered on the very top. Let the party host add a door and windows to complete the skyscraper. Cut out the entire skyscraper. Then add these words to the back of the invitation: "Construction Workers Needed: Apply in person at [address of party] on [date and time of party] for an all-night construction session. Please bring a sleeping bag."

Finally, cut the skyscraper apart carefully at each floor to have four squares of ascending size. Place the squares in an envelope with these instructions for the recipient: "Construct a skyscraper to read the message."

Hard-Hat Area!

Prepare your den for the construction zone with these decorations. Several days before the party, cut apart cardboard boxes, leaving two sides intact. Stand the cardboard to form an upside-down V. Let the party host use paint to turn the cardboard into construction signs that read, "Kids Working—Slow Down," "Work Zone Ahead," and "Construction Site Ahead."

Use large sheets of white bulletin board paper or several sheets of freezer paper to create a skyscraper backdrop for the slumber area. Use rulers and markers to create a skyline of tall, window-filled buildings.

On the day of the party, tape the skyscraper scene in the room where the guests will sleep. Scatter construction signs throughout the house. You can even place one of the signs at the front door with helium balloons attached if desired. Use toy hard hats (usually found at department stores or party stores) and construction-type vehicles to complete the decorations.

Kids at Play!

Choose one or more of the following games to play at the party. Suggestions are given for outdoor and indoor games.

Outdoor Games

Construction Crew Collection

Gather various tools and items that might be seen at a construction site, such as hammers, screws, small rakes and shovels, buckets, thermoses, and small coolers. Divide the guests into two teams. Divide the items equally, making sure there is at least one item per guest. Make a pile of items at the front of each line. The first person in line runs with one of the items to a basket about fifteen feet away, places the item in the basket, runs back to the line, and tags the next person. That person takes another item from the pile and does the same thing. The first team to have all of their supplies in the basket is the winning team.

Water for the Crew

Place two empty thermoses on a table. Divide the guests into two teams and have them line up about fifteen feet from the table. Place a bowl of water and a quarter-cup measuring cup beside each team. The object of the relay is to fill the Thermos with water as quickly as possible. The team filling the thermos first is the winning team.

Indoor Games

Heads Up!

Take turns tossing screws into an upturned h d hat. Start with the hat about four feet away. A child has a turn tossing screws into the hat. hat farther away. See who can get the mo the hat at the farthest distance.

Timber!

Use soup cans, small cereal boxes, small wooden blocks, books, or boxes for this game. Divide the guests into two teams. See which team can build the tallest tower before the tower topples. (Soup cans would best be used with older children in case the cans fall near the guests.)

Construction Crew Statues

Play music, and ask the guests to pretend to be at work on a construction site. Tell them that when the music stops, they must freeze in that position. Stop the music in various places and have the guests observe the silly statues.

Awesome Architects!

Do one or more of these activities in the order that best suits your party.

Build a City

Before the party, make or purchase frosting to use as "glue" for this building activity. Let each child use six graham cracker squares to build a house, four for the sides and two for the roof. While the houses harden a bit, build skyscrapers. Use sugar cubes, frosting for glue, and graham cracker squares to build tall buildings. Add a train track to your city: Use large pretzel rods, small pretzel sticks and frosting to build a track. Add a train by stacking two small brownie squares onto a larger brownie rectangle. Put a dab of frosting on four mini cookies and attach the "wheels" to the train. Now that the graham cracker houses have had time to harden, add candy decorations to each house using frosting as glue.

Hard-Hat Helpers

Give each child a hard hat, small paintbrushes, and paint to design a personalized hard hat. Place the hats aside to dry when each child is finished.

Sandcastle Construction

This is probably an outside activity, due to the mess! Multiply this recipe by the number of children attending. Stir together one-third cup of flour and two tablespoons of sugar in a saucepan. Gradually add one cup of water, stirring vigorously. Cook and stir over low heat until clear. Cool slightly, then add this mixture to six cups of sand. Add more water gradually, until the sand becomes claylike. The mixture should pack firmly into containers.

Give each child a large piece of cardboard to work on and lots of containers of varying sizes in which to pack the sand. Encourage the children to start with a large base and add smaller shapes. Use a spoon to cut out windows and doors. Let the castle harden overnight.

Construction Crews Crashing

As the guests begin to get drowsy, use the following idea to help settle them into rest time:

- Have the children "build" a home by arranging their sleeping bags on the floor and crawling inside. Play "I'm building a building!" to settle down before going to sleep. The first person starts by saying, "I'm building a [choose something to construct]. I'm taking a [name a tool or other item—items can be serious or silly]." The next person has to repeat what the first person said and add another item to the list. Each person must repeat everything said prior to his or her turn, then add an item.

Build a Meal

Serve your construction workers meals they can enjoy building on their own.

Slumber Supper

Give each child a small sub roll. Let the guests add sliced meats, sliced cheeses, lettuce, tomatoes, pickles, mayonnaise, or mustard to construct a submarine. Add olives and cheese cubes to pretzel sticks. Attach these to the top of the submarine. Give each child a square of blue gelatin for his or her "ocean" and goldfish crackers to eat along with the sub.

Pancake Skyscrapers

Before the party, make pancakes and refrigerate or freeze until needed. Make pancakes such that each child can have pieces of descending size when stacked. The morning of the party, warm the pancakes. Then let each child build a pancake pyramid, starting with a large base, then stacking descending-sized pancakes on top. Top with syrup and enjoy!

Hats Off to a Great Party!

Let each child take home his or her personalized hard hat for a party favor. Add candy and/or small construction vehicles to the hat, if desired.

Optional party favor: If hard hats cannot be located or are too expensive, purchase water bottles for each child and have him or her personalize a bottle. Then fill the bottle with candy for a take-home treat.

Insect Investigators

Have fun "bugging" your friends at this sleepover!

Ladybug, Ladybug, Fly to My Home

Create this cute critter invitation for your insect-loving guest. For each invitation, paint a small paper plate and a large paper plate red. Cut black circles from construction paper and glue spots on the ladybug's body. Cut red wings from red construction paper. Attach each wing to the body using paper fasteners. Staple or glue the head to the body. Write the party invitations, beginning with, "Buzz on over to my house for a sleepover," on a small sheet of white paper. Glue the paper to the back of the ladybug, or write the party details on the back of the paper plate. Put the ladybug invitation in a large manila envelope and address it to a party guest.

I Spy a Critter!

Hang flyswatters around the house and place plastic, toy insects in each room of the house for sleepover decorations.

Flying Things and Gnat Games

Choose one or more of the following games to play at the party. Suggestions are given for outdoor and indoor games.

Outdoor Games

Mosquito Tag

Have sheets of red sticker dots for all players. Give one person three stickers. That person is the "mosquito," who chases the other players. To tag a player, the mosquito puts a red sticker "bite" on that person. When a mosquito gets rid of all his or her dots, another person takes a turn as the mosquito. After each person has had a turn being the mosquito, count to see how many bites each player has.

Fly Swatter Relay

Divide the guests into two teams. Give the first person in each line a fly swatter and each person one raisin. Place pails or trash baskets about twenty feet away from each team. On "Go," the first person from each team places his or her "fly" (raisin) on the flyswatter. The players move quickly to the trash can, trying not to drop the raisin. If the raisin falls, the person may pick it up with his or her hands and place it back on the flyswatter, but may not hold the raisin while it is on the flyswatter. When the players reach the trash can, they dump the fly in the can and run quickly back to the next player. The next player takes the flyswatter, places his or her fly on the swatter and takes off! The first team to "trash" all their flies is the winning team.

Indoor Games

Anthills and Ants

Divide the guests into pairs or groups of three. Let each team build an anthill by stacking pillows on the floor. Then each team places "ants" (marbles) on the anthill. The object of the game is to get the most ants on the hill without them rolling off the pillows. The team who places the most ants on their hill is the winning team.

Roach Race

Purchase large black buttons, with at least two holes in the middle, for each player. Use a needle to wrap several strands of thread around the holes in the middle. Use a different color of thread for each button. Add a small magnetic strip to the back of the button. (Magnetic strips with sticky backing are available in craft stores or department stores.) Draw paths on a sheet of poster paper with markers. You may choose to use a different color for each path.

On the day of the party, give each child a "roach" (black button). Set the poster paper between two chairs to allow accessibility to the bottom of the poster board. On the word "Go," a child places his roach at the beginning of a path and holds a magnet under the poster board. The child makes the roach move by slowly moving the magnet underneath the button. Have the roach follow the path to the other end. If you choose to do so, you can time each person's roach race. The fastest roach wins!

One Less Bug

Play this altered version of the old-fashioned card game called "Spoons." Gather some of the plastic toy insects used as decorations for the sleepover. Place one less critter on the table than number of children playing the game. Give each person four cards. The object of the game is to collect four of any number or face card. The dealer picks a card from the deck and decides to keep or pass the card. If he or she keeps the card, the dealer must pass one of his or her own cards. The next player picks up that card and makes the same decision. The game is played quickly, with people picking and passing cards simultaneously. When a person has four of a kind, he or she quietly takes one of the insects from the middle of the table. As soon as one insect is taken, the other players immediately snatch an insect. The person without an insect receives a letter of the word *insect*. The first person to spell the entire word is out of the game.

Going Buggy!

Do one or more of these activities in the order that best suits your party.

Uninvited Ants

Let the guests create the tablecloth to be used for supper. On a white paper tablecloth, have the children make red and black ants. Let each child dip his or her pinkie finger in black and red stamp pads. For each ant, have the child stamp three small circles, touching, for the head and body parts of the ant. Then let the child use a thin-lined red or black marker to add six legs and two antennae to each ant.

Beautiful Butterflies

Give each child a large coffee filter. Let the guests use eyedroppers to drop a dot or two of food coloring onto his or her paper. Drop several colors all over the filter. Allow the filter time to dry. Then scrunch up the middle of the filter to form two wings. Use a clip-style clothespin for the body of the butterfly. Clip the clothespin onto the scrunched part of the filter, having a wing on each side of the clothespin. Glue curled pieces of pipe cleaner to each side of the top of the clothespin for antennae.

Flea-Ridden Cookies

Let the sleepover friends prepare their own snacks. Give each child a small amount of prepared sugar cookie dough on a small square of floured waxed paper. Have the child flatten his or her dough, then use an animal-shaped cookie cutter to cut out a cookie. Place each cookie on a cookie sheet to bake. Before cooking, let each child add a few miniature chocolate chips to his or her animal. Now it is a flea-ridden pet! Bake the cookies according to directions. Carefully remove the warm cookies, giving each child his or her cookie on a small paper plate. Let the child use a small strainer or sifter to dust his pet with "flea powder" (i.e., powdered sugar) to rid the animal of fleas.

Insect Scavenger Hunt

Give each child a magnifying glass, plastic jars with lids, and small plastic tweezers. (Often these scientist-type kits can be found at toy stores or educational stores.) Have the children explore the back yard to find and collect insects. Instruct the guests to gently pick up the critters and place them in the jar. Also, remind the children not to try to capture bees, wasps, or other stinging or biting insects. A good rule would be not to handle anything with the hands, but use only the jar and tweezers to collect. After you have studied and examined the critters, release them as close to where you found them as possible.

Buzzzzing into Bed

As the guests begin to get drowsy, try this idea to help settle them into rest time:

- Have the children stretch their sleeping bags out on the floor. Encourage the kids to climb in their sleeping bags and give each child a flashlight. Turn out all the lights and let the children make "fireflies" on the ceiling. Let the children tell firefly stories or let the fireflies dance across the ceiling.

Flying Food and Food with Legs!

Serve up a butterfly supper with chips and other treats.

Butterfly Sandwiches

Make chicken salad prior to the party. When it's time to eat, have each child spread some salad between two pieces of bread. Cut the bread into two triangles. Give each child a raw carrot cut lengthwise. Have the child place his or her carrot in the middle of a paper plate. Place each triangle on either side of the carrot for the butterfly wings. Give the children pickle slices and pimentos to decorate the butterfly's wings. Add two celery curls for the antennae. Serve a green juice or punch to drink, and call it "bug juice."

Ladybug Cookies

Prepare slice-and-bake sugar cookies. Give each child round, baked cookies to make ladybugs. Add red food coloring to prepared frosting. (Liquid red food coloring doesn't make a very dark red, but rather a pink color. For a true red, purchase food-coloring paste in the craft section of a department store or at a craft store.) After the children have frosted the cookies with red, have them add miniature candy-coated chocolates or miniature chocolate chips for the spots. Then add small snips of black licorice strips for legs.

Eggs with Bug Sauce

For breakfast, give your little insect investigators an anthill complete with "ants." Before the party, fry one egg per child in a tad of butter. Fry the egg slowly, without flipping the egg, and leave the yolk intact. This is the anthill. Carefully place the anthills on a waxed-paper-lined cookie sheet and refrigerate until needed. Prepare the following sauce prior to the party, also.

Bug Sauce

3 egg yolks
1 tablespoon lemon juice
½ cup firm butter

Stir egg yolks and lemon juice vigorously in a 2-quart saucepan. Add ¼ cup of the butter. Heat over very low heat, stirring constantly with wire whisk, until butter is melted. Add remaining butter. Continue stirring vigorously until butter is melted and sauce is thickened. The butter should melt very slowly to allow time for the eggs to cook thoroughly.

On the morning of the sleepover, allow the sauce to come to room temperature, toast an English muffin for each guest, microwave the eggs just enough to warm, and place the egg on top of a muffin. Place the egg-topped muffin on a serving plate and pour one tablespoon of "bug sauce" on top. Let each child sprinkle a tablespoon of bacon bits ("ants!") on the anthill and enjoy!

Ants on a Log

For a midnight snack, give each child a pretzel log and a handful of raisins. Let the guests smear peanut butter on the pretzel, then press raisins in the peanut butter.

Creepy-Crawly Take-Homes

As a reminder of the buggy fun had at the sleepover, give each guest a magnifying glass, box of "roaches" (raisins!), and his or her coffee-filter butterfly made during the activity time.

Manicures and Makeovers

Invite your favorite females to a manicure and makeover sleepover.

A Hand-y Invite

Trace the party host's hand; cut out and use as a pattern. Trace the hand onto pale colored oaktag or poster paper. Cut out. Use polish to paint each nail. When the polish is dry, write the party details on the back of the hand. On the palm, use a marker to write, "Come to my manicures and makeover sleepover." Then on the five fingers with a fine-line marker, write the who, where, when, what to bring and the response phone number. (You may want to ask each guest to bring a favorite color of nail polish to the party to have a variety of colors for the sleepover activities.) Add a toy dress-up ring to one of the fingers, then hand-deliver (pardon the pun!) or place in a padded envelope and mail one to two weeks before the sleepover.

Dazzling Decor

Dress up the sleepover area with lots of mirrors and silver and gold streamers hung from the ceiling. If you really want to "roll out the red carpet," add a long strip of red bulletin board paper (found at teacher supply stores) or a large red towel to the floor near the doorway.

Makeover Moves

Choose one or more of the following games to play at the party. Suggestions are given for outdoor and indoor games.

Outdoor Games

Hairy Races

Divide the guests into two teams and form two lines. Place a rope about twenty feet from the lines to designate the stopping place. Give the first person in each line a hairbrush. The player should place the brush on top of her head. The object is to race as quickly as possible to the rope without holding onto the brush and without losing the brush. Once the person reaches the rope, she tags the rope with a foot, removes the brush, and runs quickly to the next team member. That player puts the brush on her head and races to the line. After each player on a team has completed the relay with a brush, start over again with a comb, clips, hair rollers, or other "hairy" items. The first team to complete the relay with all the designated items is the winning team.

Beauty Salon Relay

For this game, you will need at least two wigs. These can be found at party stores, beauty supply stores and clothing rental stores. You'll also need ten hair clips or bows.

Divide the guests into two teams; form two lines. Use the same boundaries as the previous game. Place two chairs across from each team along the rope line. One player from each team is the beautician and stands behind the chair for her team. On "Go," the first player in line puts on a wig, and races with ten clips to the beautician. The player sits in the chair; the beautician quickly puts the ten clips in the wig. When all ten clips are in the wig, the player runs back to the next team member. The team member removes the clips and transfers the wig to her head. That player then races to the beautician. When each player on the team has had her hair "styled," the game is over; the first team to complete the game wins.

Indoor Games

Evening Gown Competition

Provide colored rolls of toilet tissue and clear adhesive tape. Divide the guests into pairs. Let one child in the pair use the toilet paper to create a lovely evening gown on the other player in the pair. After each pair is finished, judge the evening gown competition. If the children desire, let the pairs switch positions so that each child has a turn creating an evening gown.

Wigworks

Divide the guests into two teams. Give each team a wig and many hair accessories. Set a timer for five minutes. Have the teams create a unique hairdo, using the provided accessories. Then compare and judge the "do's." Make new teams and do another do!

Before the Makeover

Divide the children into two teams. One team will compete at a time. Have someone use a watch with a second hand to time the team. The team with the shortest relay time wins.

On "Go," the first player uses clips and ponytail holders to put all of her hair up. The player then puts on a shower cap, tucking hair underneath. The player runs to a provided chair, sits down, and poses for a picture. An adult uses a Polaroid or instant camera to take a picture. Once the picture has been taken, the player runs to the next person on her team and gives that player the cap and clips. Once each player has had a "before the makeover" picture made, the game is over. (Save the pictures to make a "Before and After" poster.)

Beautiful Friends

Do one or more of these activities in the order that best suits your party.

The White Glove Treatment

Give each guest a white glove. (An elbow-length glove would work best.) Let the guests stuff the hand part of the glove with spoonfuls of small colored candies. Tie the top closed with a colorful ribbon. Then let the manicurists add fake glue-on nails to the hand. Give the "client" rings and bracelets, too.

Polish Pointers

Before the sleepover, make two spinners using square pieces of cardboard. Cover the cardboard with white Con-Tact or self-adhesive paper. Then draw lines on each spinner. Make enough lines on one spinner to write each guest's name in a section. Make enough lines on the other spinner to put polish colors in sections. Use oaktag to make two arrows. Make a hole in each arrow so that it will spin around a pin. Attach the arrows in the middle of the spinner, using push pins.

Choose a person to be the first spinner. Have the child spin the guest spinner to determine the first recipient of polish. Then the child spins the polish spinner to determine what color of polish to use first. The child who did the spinning will then use the color shown on the spinner to paint one fingernail or toenail of the guest whose name is shown on the spinner. This play continues until each child has all ten fingernails and all ten toenails painted a variety of colors.

Bright Barrettes

Give each child a hair barrette and several strips of colorful ribbon, each strip twelve inches long. Provide small beads. Show the children how to tie one end of each ribbon strip onto the barrette. Then have the guests braid the ribbons or tie on beads to make a brightly colored hair barrette.

Makeover Moments

Invite a beauty consultant or a makeup distributor to come to the sleepover and give the guests a face and hair makeover. After each guest has had a makeover, allow them to put on dress-up clothes and jewelry. Have the guests give a fashion show, with music playing in the background. (Let the guests use the "red carpet" from the decorations as a runway.) After the fashion show, take instant pictures of each girl.

Put the "before" pictures taken during game time and these "after" pictures on a poster for the guests to admire.

Beauty Secrets and Slumbers

As the guests begin to get drowsy, try this idea to help settle them into rest time:

- Have the guests snuggle into their sleeping bags, laid out in a circle on the floor with the guests' heads on the inside of the circle. Play "Pass the Microphone" to find out beauty secrets and answers. One guests holds a hairbrush ("microphone") and asks a question. The microphone is passed to each person to give an answer to the question. After everyone has answered the question, another guest gets to ask a new question. The questions can be about beauty secrets, makeup, polish, family, friends, and so on.

Tea for Two–or Three or More!

Serve the guests tea and finger foods on fancy china just after the fashion show so that the guests are still "dressed for the occasion."

Rich Tea

Using tea bags, follow the directions on the box for making hot tea. Pour one cup of hot tea in a china cup for each guest. Have the guests add one teaspoon of sugar and one tablespoon of sweetened condensed milk and stir gently.

Party Finger Sandwiches

Cut white bread into shapes with cookie or canapé cutters. Spread the bread with a thin layer of margarine to prevent the fillings from making the bread soggy. Make the fillings provided here, then spread onto each sandwich shape. Add tiny shrimp, diced vegetables, or fresh herbs as garnishes to each sandwich.

Chicken Salad Filling

1½ cups chopped cooked chicken
½ cup salad dressing
¼ teaspoon salt
¼ teaspoon pepper

Mix all ingredients.

Beef Salad Filling

1½ cups chopped beef
½ cup mayonnaise
¼ teaspoon onion salt
¼ teaspoon pepper

Mix all ingredients.

Egg Salad Filling

6 hard-cooked eggs, chopped
½ cup salad dressing
½ teaspoon salt
¼ teaspoon red pepper

Mix all ingredients.

Lady Fingers

Yield: about 3 dozen

2 sticks margarine
5 tablespoons sugar
1 teaspoon vanilla
2 cups self-rising flour
2½ cups nuts, chopped
¾ cup powdered sugar

Mix margarine and sugar. Add vanilla and flour. Add nuts. Roll in finger-shaped logs about two inches in length. Bake at 300 degrees for 35 minutes until brown. Roll in powdered sugar while warm. Let cool. Roll in powdered sugar again.

Bad Hair Day Open-Faced Ham Biscuits

½ biscuit
1 round ham slice (cut with a biscuit cutter)
1 cherry tomato, sliced in half
½ green olive
1 peel-apart string cheese log

Give each guest a small plate and the ingredients. Have each guest place the ham slice on the biscuit, then add the cherry tomato halves for eyes and the green olive half for a nose. Peel the string cheese into small strings. Use half of one of the strings to form a curved mouth. Use the rest of the strings to add hair to the face. Have the guests roll, curl, or braid the hair for an early-morning, "bad hair day" ham-face biscuit.

Makeover Memories

To have each guest remembering this sleepover for days to come, present each attendee with a personalized makeup bag. Use puffy paints to put each child's name on her bag. Then add yarn and beads to the zipper or handles of the bag. Fill the bag with polish, makeup, toy jewelry, or hair accessories. Be sure to include each child's gloved, candy-filled hand made during activity time and the before and after pictures taken with the instant camera.

Rainbow of Colors

Invite your friends to come over and make golden memories as you explore the colors of the rainbow.

Searching for Friends

On an eight and a half by eleven-inch piece of colored oaktag or poster paper, paint a rainbow across the top section, leaving about three inches on one side. Cut a black cauldron-shaped pot from construction paper. When the rainbow paint is dry, glue the pot at the end of the rainbow, leaving the top open. Write the sleepover details underneath the rainbow, beginning with something along the lines of this: "Come to my sleepover and we'll search for the pot of gold and play in the rainbow!" Just before sending the invitation, carefully insert one or two gold foil-wrapped chocolate coins in the black pot. Carefully slide the invitation into a large manila envelope and mail one to two weeks before the sleepover.

A Colorful Collection of Balloons

To decorate for the party, hang colorful, inflated balloons and colorful streamers from the ceiling.

Rainbow Races and Other Games

Choose one or more of the following games to play at the party. Suggestions are given for outdoor and indoor games.

Outdoor Games

Bowling for Bottles

Before the party, collect ten empty, clean plastic liter bottles. Wrap different colors of construction paper around each bottle; secure with tape. Determine the number of points each color will represent before the game. Set the bottles up like bowling pins. Give each child a turn to roll a ball toward the bottles. Tally up the number of points according to the bottles that the ball knocks down. Let the children bowl as long as time or interest permits. Keep a count for each child and total the scores when the game is over.

Rainbow Dances

Cut thirty-six-inch-long dowel rods for each guest. Cut three two-inch wide ribbons for each guest; each ribbon should be five feet in length. Use a variety of colors. Let each guest choose his or her colors and attach the three ribbons to the dowel rod with a rubber band. Then let the guests use the ribbon rods to perform ribbon dances to music. Have one guest perform a dance and the others must copy his or her dance. Then choose another guest to create a new dance to follow.

Indoor Games

Missing Balloons

Play this fast and fun balloon game. Inflate one less balloon than guests in each of six colors. Put all the balloons in the middle of the floor of a large room. Have the guests stand around the balloons in a circle. Write the colors of the balloons on strips of paper and put the strips in a basket. A caller chooses a strip of paper and calls out the color word. Each guest quickly grabs a balloon that color. The guest without a balloon gets the first letter of the word *rainbow*. Continue playing, giving a letter from the word *rainbow* to the player without a balloon. The first player to spell rainbow is out of the game. To make the game more fun and to have all guests playing, start the lettering over rather than remove a player.

Every Color in a Pot

Purchase or make beanbags in a variety of colors. (To make a beanbag, cut felt or cloth into four-inch squares. Sew or hot-glue the four sides together, leaving a one-inch opening. Use a funnel to pour dried beans or stuffing beads, found in a craft store or department store, into the beanbag. Then sew or glue the bag closed.) Also before the party, locate a large black pot or cover a large container with black construction paper. For the game, give each color a representative number of points. Have each child toss one of every color beanbag into the pot. Total the number of points by tallying only the points for the beanbags that made it into the container. Keep a record of the scores. After each child tosses one of every color with his or her right hand, try these ways: left-handed, overhand while turned away from the pot, and right- and left-handed while blindfolded. Check the total number of points to find a winner.

Follow the Rainbow Path

Before this game, make a long path of construction paper sheets through several rooms in your home. Choose six colors, and use those same six colors over and over again. Draw or paint a rainbow on a sheet of poster paper. Put this at the end of the path. Make a playing die by covering a square box with white Con-Tact or self-adhesive paper. The box should be about six inches in width. Glue construction paper on each side of the die to correspond with the six colors you used on the path. Have the first player roll the die. The player walks along the path until he or she comes to the first sheet of construction paper that is the same color as is on the top of the die. The next player rolls the die and finds his or her place along the path. Play continues until one person reaches the rainbow poster at the end.

Colorful Creations

Do one or more of these activities in the order that best suits your party.

The End of the Rainbow

Before the sleepover, write clues on colored paper for a treasure hunt. At each spot, place a colored crepe paper streamer and the clue for the next spot. The last clue should send the guest to a black pot, filled with candy, especially lots of gold foil–wrapped chocolate coins. Have the children work as a team to follow the clues, collect the crepe paper streamers, and find the "pot of gold." When the pot is found, have the guests use the streamers to make a rainbow on the ground or floor.

Playing in a Rainbow

Cover a large area outside with newspapers. Place a white flat sheet on top of the newspapers. Pour paint into shallow containers near the sheet. On strips of paper, write the names of the colors of paint and actions, such as "hop on one foot," "jump with both feet," "skip," "walk on tiptoes," and so on. Put the color strips in one basket and the actions in another basket. Let each child remove their shoes and socks. One at a time, let the guests draw a color strip and an action strip. Have the guests step into the paint container of the color he or she drew. Then have the child follow the action across the sheet. For example, if "blue" and "walk on tiptoes" were drawn, have the child step into the blue paint and tiptoe across the sheet. Have paper towels and water available to clean painted feet! Let the children do this several times each to cover the sheet in multi-colored footprints.

Allow the sheet to dry overnight. In the morning, help the guests cut the sheet into a rainbow-shape of footprints.

Colored Candy Counting

Give each child a variety of colored candies in a jar. Have each child guess how many candy pieces are inside, and then count to find out the exact number. See who comes closest to the right answer.

Rainbow Wall Hanging

Cut oaktag or poster board into eight and a half by eleven-inch sheets. Add powdered paint to six to eight cups of sand. Use a different color for each cup of sand. Start with one tablespoon of paint; stir. Add more for a darker shade. (Precolored sand in more vibrant colors can be purchased at craft stores and educational stores.) Give each child a paintbrush and liquid glue. Have the children paint a curved line of glue; shake small spoonfuls of one color of sand on the glue; then, shake off the excess sand. Continue with many colors to achieve a rainbow. Use a hole puncher to punch holes in the bottom of the paper. Tie ribbons in each hole in a variety of colors. Glue a twelve-inch piece of ribbon to the back of the rainbow picture for a hanger.

Rainbow Dreams

As the guests begin to get drowsy try the following idea to help settle them into rest time:

- Have the children stretch their sleeping bags in a circle or line. Give one person the die with the colored faces. Have him or her roll the die and call out a guest's name as he or she rolls. When the die lands, the person's name who was called must quickly name three things that can be that color. Continue the game, trying not to repeat anything that has already been mentioned.

Artistic Appetites

Concoct these colorful meals for your guests.

Rainbow Supper

Serve hot dogs and chips. Put ketchup and mustard in squirt bottles. Let each child squeeze a dollop of each onto his or her plate, swirl the colors with a spoon, then add the mixture to his or her hot dog. Also serve yogurt. Choose a pink- and a blue-colored yogurt. Let each child take a spoonful of each onto his or her plate and swirl the two together. Give each child a small cup of lemonade, a small cup of blue juice, and a larger cup to mix the two juices. Have the guests pour both juices into the large cup.

Rainbow-Topped Bagels

Cut a bagel in half. Then cut the half-bagel from top to bottom to get two rainbow-shaped pieces. Tint cream cheese in a variety of colors by adding and stirring in food coloring. Put each color of cream cheese in a decorator bag. Let each child squeeze the colors onto his bagel half to form a rainbow.

Rainbow Reminders

Fill a colorful gift bag full of rainbow favors for each party guest. Give each guest one or more of the beanbags and a covered liter bottle with instructions to play a tossing game with the two items. Also add an assortment of colored candies and some of the foil-covered chocolate coins from the treasure hunt activity. Be sure to include each child's rainbow wall hanging, too.

Stuffed-Animal Lovers

Animal lovers unite at this special sleepover party.

Lions and Tigers and Teddies, Oh My!

Make or use a turtle pattern. Cut two body parts from light green felt and one shell from dark green felt. Place a small amount of cotton batting on the top of the turtle's back; glue the shell over the batting. Allow some time for the glue to dry. Next, glue the two body pieces together, leaving a small opening. Use a funnel to add dried beans or small stuffing beads to the turtle. Glue the opening closed. Safety pin a note to the turtle that says, "Hurry on over to my sleepover. Bring your stuffed animals for a 'Stuffed Animal Menagerie Party.'" Add the details of the sleepover to the note as well.

Stuffed Full of Animals

Using the host's stuffed animals and the stuffed animals brought by each guest, set up a stuffed animal menagerie or zoo to decorate your home.

Lots of Stuff To Do

Choose one or more of the following games to play at the party. Suggestions are given for outdoor and indoor games.

Outdoor Games

Stuffed Kids

Divide the guests into two teams. Give the first player on each team an adult-sized sweatshirt and adult-sized pair of sweatpants. Give each team five towels, also. To play the game, the first person dons the adult-sized clothes and stuffs the five towels inside the shirt and pants. Once the towels are stuffed inside, the player turns cartwheels, jumps, skips or some other action as decided beforehand, to the other end of the playing area. The player then runs back to the next person on the team, removes the towels and adult clothes and that person "stuffs" him- or herself and follows the same action. The first team of "stuffed kids" to complete the relay wins.

Animals in a Basket

Divide the children into two teams. Have each child place his or her favorite stuffed animal on a sheet placed at the other end of the play area. Give each team a laundry basket. On "Go," the first person in each line pushes the basket to the sheet, picks out his or her stuffed animal and returns to the team. The next person does the same thing. The first team to collect and return with all of their animals wins.

Indoor Games

Animals from A to Z

Divide the group into pairs. Have the children search through the stuffed animal zoo to find an animal for each letter of the alphabet. If there is no animal present for a letter, the pair should make up an animal. Two points are given for each animal that is at the party, one point for animals not at the party. Stop the game after five minutes; add up the points to see which pair found the most animals.

Musical Animals

Place chairs in a line as you would for musical chairs. Put a stuffed animal in each chair. (Remember, there will be one less chair and animal than number of players.) Play music. When the music stops, each guest picks up an animal and sits down in that chair. The person without a chair chooses one of the animals to remove for the next round. Remove the chair, also. That child dances with the stuffed animal while the music is playing and the other guests repeat the game. Repeat this procedure until only one guest is left.

Taking Care of Baby

Have each guest choose a favorite stuffed animal. Place one of each of the following on two chairs, side by side: baby bottle, cloth diaper or burp cloth. Also place a disposable diaper for each player on the team on each chair. Divide the guests into two teams. To start the game, the first player of each team runs to the chair, diapers his or her stuffed animal, "feeds" the stuffed animal, burps the stuffed animal, and rocks the stuffed animal to sleep. The player then runs back to the line to tag the next person. That person does the same with his or her stuffed animal. The first team to take care of all its animals is the winning team.

Terrific Teddies and Other Stuffed Animals

Do one or more of these activities in the order that best suits your party.

Stuffable and Lovable

Purchase a large teddy bear cookie cutter to use as a pattern. Trace and cut two bears out of felt for each guest. Hot-glue the two pieces together, leaving an opening to stuff the bear. Have the children use puffy paints to decorate the front of the bear. Allow the bear to dry. Later during the sleepover or early the next morning, have each guest stuff cotton batting in his or her bear. Let an adult hot-glue the opening closed.

Friends in a Frame

Take an instant picture of each guest. Have the guest and the host sit among the stuffed animals for the picture. After the pictures are developed, give the pictures to the guests. Have them glue four colored craft sticks together the size of the picture for a picture frame. Let each guest add teddy bear–shaped crackers and beads to the frame, using craft glue. After the glue is dry, have an adult place the frames on newspaper and spray acrylic finish on each frame. Let the frames dry overnight, then glue the picture in the frame before giving it to each guest to take home.

Stuffed Animal Dress-Up

Give the guests scraps of material, scissors, needles and thread. Let each guest make a new outfit for his or her stuffed animal. (If the guests are younger, use felt scraps and large plastic needles with yarn.)

Animal Actors and Actresses

After the stuffed animals are dressed in their new outfits, have the guests put on a play.

Snoozin' with the Animals

As the guests begin to get drowsy, try this idea to help settle them into rest time:

- Have the guests form a circle with their sleeping bags. Choose an animal from the menagerie. Pass the animal around the circle to quiet music. Have someone be in charge of the music. When the music stops, the person holding the animal must tell a story about the animal he or she is holding. Repeat several times, then choose a different animal to pass around.

Food Fit for Teddies

Let each child "stuff" his or her own sandwich for supper and enjoy these other treats!

Bearwiches

Before the party, cut biscuit dough with a teddy bear cookie cutter. Make one teddy per person. Bake the bread ahead of time and refrigerate or freeze. Also use the cookie cutter to cut sliced meats and cheeses into bear shapes. (Save the meat and cheese scraps to use for breakfast sandwiches.) On the day of the sleepover, have the children "stuff" their teddy bears with meat and cheese and enjoy! Serve with chips.

Teddy Bear Wreath

Give each child a round butter cookie with a hole in the middle. Give each child several teddy bear–shaped cookies also. Let the children use a knife to spread frosting on the round cookie. Then stick the bears onto the wreath.

Breakfast Sandwiches

For breakfast, give each guest a croissant. Have him or her use the extra meat and cheese from last night's supper.

Stuffed Animal Souvenirs

Make a party favor bag by filling a gift bag for each child with the following: stuffed animal toys, and the frame and bear made during the activity time.

Tent Campers

Use these ideas to turn your home into a campground for a night of fun.

Calling All Campers!

Make this cute invitation in the shape of a tent. Cut brown construction paper in the shape of a tent. Add an extra piece of construction paper to make a tent flap. Write the party details on the back of the tent. (Each guest will need a flashlight; you can purchase each guest a flashlight as a party favor and use it during the evening or you can ask each guest to bring a flashlight with his or her sleeping bag and pillow on the invitation.)

Lights! Campers! Action!

Not many decorations are needed for this campout. In addition to the tent, however, strings of outdoor Christmas lights shed excitement and light to the sleepover. (Although this sleepover is held outside, feel free to decorate the kitchen and bathroom with such decorations as plastic bugs, toy snakes, and artificial trees and plants.)

A-Camping We Will Go

Choose one or more of the following games to play at the party. Suggestions are given for outdoor and indoor games.

Outdoor Games

Flashlight Tag

This game is played like tag, except instead of tagging the person, "it" shines a flashlight on that person. When a person is "shined," that person becomes "it."

Mosquito Bites

One guest is the "mosquito" for this game. Give him or her a page of red, sticky office dots. Choose two safety zones about fifteen to twenty feet away from each other. Also have outside boundary lines, forming a rectangle. The players stand at one safety zone with the mosquito in the middle. The mosquito yells, "Run, friends, run," and the players run from one zone to the other, staying within the outside boundaries. The mosquito tries to "bite" a player by sticking a red dot on his or her arms or clothing. Once all the players are in the safety zone, the play begins again. When a person gets three bites, that person becomes the mosquito.

Indoor Games

Sounds of the Night

Have the guests take turns making animal noises; friends try to guess what animal makes that sound.

Marshmallow Pickup

On a clean towel, spread one or two bags of miniature marshmallows. Give each child a pair of kitchen tongs and a drinking mug. (If you do not have enough tongs for each player, let one player do the game alone and use a stopwatch to time him or her. Keep up with each time to see who fills his mug in the least amount of time.) On "Go," the guests use the tongs to pick up the marshmallows. The first person to fill his or her mug is the winner.

Puppet Show

Divide the guests into pairs or groups of three. The guests plan a puppet show using only hands and a flashlight. Each team performs its puppet show on the side of the tent. Then the guests judge the shows and determine the winners. (Decide on enough categories so that each show will "be a winner." Choose prizes such as "Funniest Puppet Show," "Puppet Show with the Most Action," "Silliest Puppet Show," etc.)

Clever Campers

Do one or more of these activities in the order that best suits your party.

Worm Wiggle

Have the guests zip up inside their sleeping bags and wiggle around like worms!

Trail Mix Mixing

Place these snacks in bowls: pretzels, raisins, marshmallows, dried fruit, miniature chocolate chips, sunflower seeds, and yogurt-covered raisins. Give each guest a resealable plastic bag. Decide which snack item will be measured first. Let each child roll a die to determine how many tablespoons of that snack to put in his or her bag. Do this for each person, for each snack item. Once the trail mixing is complete, the child hangs onto his or her bag to snack on during the night.

Fishing Fun

Before the sleepover, cut lots of fish shapes from construction paper. Put a paper clip on each fish for a mouth. On each fish, write an action to perform. The actions may be silly or serious, such as "turn a cartwheel," "do a chicken dance," "square dance with another guest," and so on. Make fishing poles from dowel rods, fishing line, and a magnet for a hook.

Just outside the tent, place a small wading pool. Put the fish inside the empty pool, making sure to turn the messages on the fish face down. Let each guest fish. The guest must perform the action on the fish he or she catches.

Star Gazing

Give each child a sheet of black construction paper and gold or silver star stickers. Let each child create a constellation on his or her page. Then let the guest tell a silly myth about how his or her constellation came to be.

Cozy Campers

As the guests begin to get drowsy, try this idea to help settle them into rest time:

- Let the guests tell a cumulative ghost story. Start the timer and let the first guest begin and tell a ghost story for three minutes. When the timer rings, have the next person continue telling the story for the next three minutes. Continue until each person has told part of the story.

Over an Open Fire

For this sleepover, serve typical camping fare, cooked outdoors or indoors.

Wienie Roast

Let each child roast hot dogs, under adult supervision, and serve with chips and juice.

S'more Bites

Yield: 1 dozen

6 milk chocolate candy bars (1.55 ounces each), broken into pieces
1½ teaspoons vegetable oil
2 cups miniature marshmallows
8 whole graham crackers, broken into bite-size pieces

Coat the candy pieces with the oil; melt the chocolate and oil, stirring. Stir in marshmallows and graham crackers. Spoon into paper-lined muffin cups. Refrigerate until firm.

Tenter Take-Homes

Give each guest a camp-out memory. Suggestions for party favors are mess kits for each guest, canteens (these can be personalized before the party by the host), or flashlights.

Weather Forecasters

These sleepover ideas predict a fun time for all!

Come Rain or Shine

Cut an umbrella shape for each guest out of construction paper. Glue a pipe cleaner onto the umbrella and curl the end for a handle. Write this poem on front of the umbrella: "Whether rain, or sleet, or snow, or hail / My All-Weather Sleepover will prevail!" Then add the sleepover details on the back of the umbrella.

And the Forecast Is . . .

Decorate each room in a different forecast. Hang a large sun cut from yellow poster board in one room; add extra lamps to make it a really sunny room. In another room, hang clouds cut from white poster board and white streamers from the ceiling. Turn a fan on in that room and aim it toward the ceiling decorations. In another room, hang snowflakes from the ceiling. Let the host create unique snowflakes cut from folded coffee filters or paper doilies. Hang from the ceiling with fishing line.

Weatherworks

Choose one or more of the following games to play at the party. Suggestions are given for outdoor and indoor games.

Outdoor Games

Spring Showers

Divide the guests into two teams. For each team, provide a raincoat and a one-cup measuring cup. Also beside each team, place a bucket filled with water. Place another bucket, somewhat smaller than the first one, for each team fifteen feet away from the teams. On "Go," the first person in line puts on the raincoat and scoops up one cup of water from the bucket next to his or her team. The player runs quickly to the other bucket and pours the water into the bucket. The first team to fill the bucket is the winning team.

Tornado!

This game is an altered version of "Red Light, Green Light." One person is "it," and stands about twenty feet away from the rest of the players. The players should be spread out at least an arm's length away from each other. "It" turns away from the players and yells, "Tornado!" The players spin around and around, towards "it" until he or she yells "Stop!" and turns around. The players must stop immediately. Anyone who falls down or moves his or her feet must go back to the starting line. The first tornado to reach "it" becomes the next "it."

Indoor Games

Summer Swim

Use the summer beanbags made during the activity time for this activity. If you do not use that activity, make at least one beanbag for this game. Before the sleepover, make a swimmer beanbag by using a gingerbread boy or girl cookie cutter as a pattern. Trace and cut the pattern from felt. Make two pieces. Hot-glue the patterns together, leaving an opening. Fill the beanbag with dried beans or stuffing beads. Glue the opening closed. Use puffy paints to give the character a bathing suit. (As an alternative idea, use a store-bought beanbag. Use the puffy paints to draw a person wearing a bathing suit on one side of the beanbag. Another idea is to use a small stuffed doll or toy, wrapped in a washcloth for a bathing suit.)

Using blue bulletin board paper (available at a teaching supply store), number different areas with 5, 10, and 15. Have each child toss the beanbag "in the water." That person receives the score of the number closest to where his or her beanbag lands. Toss the "swimmer" several times and tally up the total score for each child.

Fall Festivity

Before the sleepover, cut leaf shapes from orange, brown, gold, yellow, and red tissue paper. For the game, place the leaves at one end of the table; spread the leaves around. Give each player a straw. Time each player to see how long it takes him or her to blow all the leaves to the other side of the table.

Catch a Cloud

Give each guest a nine-inch, round white balloon. Have the children inflate the balloons and hold the end closed. On "Go," each person holds his or her balloon high into the air and lets go. The object of the game is to catch the deflated balloon before it hits the ground. (A guest doesn't necessarily have to catch his or her own balloon. The fun begins when guests snag other guests' balloons.)

Climate Creations

Do one or more of these activities in the order that best suits your party.

Windsock Wonder

Give each child an oatmeal box that has been wiped clean with the top and bottom removed. Cover the oatmeal box with a piece of solid-colored Con-Tact or self-adhesive paper. Staple or glue crepe paper streamers around the bottom of the box. Punch two holes at the top of the box, and tie yarn through the holes to use as a hanger.

Unique Umbrellas

Give each guest a solid-colored umbrella. Provide puffy paints and permanent markers. Let the guests personalize and decorate his or her opened umbrella with the paints and markers. Let the opened umbrellas dry overnight.

Snowball Fight

For a year-round snowball fight, give each child five to ten sheets of typing paper. Have each child wad his or her paper to make "snowballs." On "Go," let the children have a snowball fight. Remind the children not to aim above the shoulders with the "snowballs."

Summertime Beanbags

Before the party, use a gingerbread boy or girl cookie cutter to cut from felt two shapes for each guest. Hot-glue the patterns together, leaving an opening. At the sleepover, let the guest use puffy paints to give the beanbag a bathing suit. Let the paints dry. Then fill the beanbag with dried beans or stuffing beads. Have an adult hot-glue the opening closed.

Create a Cozy Climate

As the guests begin to get drowsy, try this idea to help settle them into rest time:

- Have the guests snuggle into their sleeping bags. Choose one person to be the storyteller. That person will think of a story that involves lots of weather-related words. The rest of the guests will do the sound effects for the story. The guests make these sounds each time they hear these words: For "rain," the guests say, "drip, drip." For "wind," the guests say, "Phffeeewwww." For "sunny," the guests say, "Boy, is it hot!" For "thunder," the guests say, "boom, boom!" For "lightning," the guests say, "flash!" Let the guests tell a silly, scary or true story, but it must include lots of weather words. Let each child have a turn telling a story.

Warm as Toast

Serve this supper to warm your guests' hearts and tummies!

Kids in a Blanket

Canned biscuits, two or three per guest
Miniature wieners, two or three per guest

Let each guest flatten a biscuit somewhat with the palm of his or her hand. Place the miniature frankfurter on one edge of the biscuit. Roll the bread so that the wiener is inside. Let one end of the wiener extend just a tad from the blanket. Bake at 350 degrees, for 10 to 12 minutes until the bread is lightly browned.

For the supper, fill three squirt bottles with ketchup, mayonnaise, and mustard. Also provide squirt cheese. Have the guests use the cheese and other condiments to decorate the "blanket" (bread) before eating. Serve with warm beans and warm milk.

Snowballs

Give each child two or three rounded scoops of vanilla icing. Allow the guests to sprinkle chocolate or candy sprinkles on the "snowballs," if desired.

Eggs, Sunny Side Up

Yield: 1 serving

1 teaspoon butter
1 egg
1 slice of American cheese, cut into narrow strips

Melt the butter in a skillet. Crack the egg into the butter. Gently break the yolk. Fry the egg slowly so that the center has time to cook but stays intact. Just before the egg is done, lay the cheese strips around the yolk, like sun rays. Carefully take the "sunny egg" out of the pan with a flipper and place on a cookie sheet lined with waxed paper. Cover and store the eggs in the refrigerator until ready to use. On the morning of the party, place an egg on each child's plate. Warm slightly in the microwave and serve with toast and orange juice.

Rainbow Sherbet

2½ cups raspberry sherbet
2 cups orange sherbet
1¾ cups lemon sherbet
¾ cups lime sherbet

Line a 9-inch round pan with waxed paper. Firmly press the raspberry sherbet into a 1-inch ring around the edge of the pan. Smooth the inside of the ring with a butter knife. Quickly form rings with the orange and lemon sherbet. Fill in the center with the lime sherbet. Freeze overnight. Loosen the edge with a knife. Invert onto a 12-inch square of waxed paper. Remove waxed paper from top of sherbet. Cut in half. Press two halves together, forming a half circle. Smooth the rounded edge. Transfer the rainbow, cut side down, to a freezer-proof serving platter. Freeze until ready to use.

Forecast Favors

Give your guests a gift bag full of favors and reminders of the fun had at the all-weather sleepover. In a gift bag, put a guest's decorated umbrella, summer beanbag, and windsock. Add one or more of these fun surprises: kid's suntan lotion, a bottle of Sunny Delight citrus drink, Winterfresh gum, Rainblo bubble gum, or Ice Breakers gum.

Zany Zookeepers

Invite your friends to come be a part of your wild adventure!

Who's at the Zoo?

Fold a sheet of white typing paper in half lengthwise. Then cut that in half so that you have two folded notes, four and a half inches by five and a half inches. (Each sheet of paper will make two invitations.) Cut a piece of black construction paper to be four and a half inches by five and a half inches. Leave a half-inch border on all four sides. Cut rectangles out of the middle of the paper to resemble bars on an animal's cage. Put stickers on the front of the folded invitation. (You can also add a small photo of the sleepover host in the "cage," if you desire.) Then glue the bars in place

over the animals. Along the half-inch border of the black construction paper, use a silver pen to write, "Come to my wild sleepover!" Write the sleepover details on the inside of the invitation. Close the invitation and poke a small hole in the right side of the invitation, through the front and back. Use a small piece of yarn to tie the "cage" closed.

It's a Zoo Out There!

Decorate your home in wild animal décor, filling the rooms with stuffed animals or a variety of small plastic animals. (Large containers of small plastic animals can usually be found at department, toy, dollar, and educational stores.) As an alternate idea, try locating pictures of wild animals in magazines. Tear them out; frame them on black construction paper, and tape them to the walls.

Animal Antics

Choose one or more of the following games to play at the party. Suggestions are given for outdoor and indoor games.

Outdoor Games

Zookeeper, May I?

Play this game just like "Mother, May I?" The person who is "it" is the zookeeper. The zookeeper calls on a person and gives him or her animal-like instructions, such as "Hop like a kangaroo" or "Slither like a snake." The player must then request to proceed by asking, "Zookeeper, may I?" If the player forgets to get permission, he or she does not get to proceed. The first person to reach the zookeeper becomes the new zookeeper.

Elephants at Play

Divide the children into two teams, and line each team up along a horizontal line. Have the children get down on all fours and become "elephants." Place five peanuts in the shell in front of each elephant. (These peanuts are located in the produce or bulk foods section of a grocery store. Be sure to find out whether any of the guests are allergic to nuts. If this is the case, use the orange marshmallow circus peanuts found in the candy section of a grocery store.) On "Go," the first person of each team picks up a peanut using only his teeth and walks quickly on all fours to a bucket placed fifteen feet away. After dropping the peanut in the bucket, the elephant returns to the line and the next player takes his or her first peanut to the bucket. After each player has delivered his or her first peanut, the first person in line picks up his or her second peanut to deliver. Play continues in this manner until every person on the team has taken all five peanuts to the bucket. The first team out of peanuts is the winning team.

Indoor Games

Animal Charades

Write the names of common zoo animals on strips of paper. Place the papers in a basket. Divide the group into two teams. Have one person choose a slip of paper. The object is to get the other guests to guess what animal you have without saying the animal's name. The player may use noises, show actions, or describe what the animal looks like. The team of the person who guesses the animal correctly gets one point. The team with the most points after each person has acted out an animal is the winning team.

Lost Keys

Before the sleepover, write clues for a scavenger hunt, using various places within the house. At each one of those places, leave two keys. (You may make keys using construction paper or purchase plastic keys such as those found on baby rattles and teething toys.) At the sleepover, tell the guests that the zookeeper has lost the keys to the animal cages. Divide the group into two teams. The object of the game is to be the first team to find all the missing keys. Give each team a set of clues, mixed in different orders, or have only one team compete at a time and time both teams with a stopwatch.

Alligator Wrestling

Provide a green pillowcase for each guest's pillow. Put all but one pillow in a circle. Play music. When the music stops, each person should find a pillow to sit on. The person who didn't "wrestle an alligator" (find a pillow to sit on) is out of the game temporarily. Continue the game until you have a winning wrestler.

Awesome Animal Activities

Do one or more of these activities in the order that best suits your party.

Animal Faces

Provide construction paper, paper plates, markers, scissors, and glue. Have each child use the materials to create an animal mask. For example, make a lion mask by coloring a paper plate yellow and cutting eye holes. Then cut strips of yellow and brown construction paper. Glue the strips around the paper plate. Roll the ends around a pencil to give the mane a curl. To make an elephant mask, cut a band of gray construction paper large enough to fit around the child's head. Staple to fit. Cut very large ears to staple on each side. Cut several strips of gray paper and glue together to make a long trunk. Staple the trunk to the front of the headband. Wrap the end of the trunk around a pencil to give it a curl.

Animals Alive!

Using the masks made in the previous activity, put on a play about a zoo. All the children may work together, or you may choose to divide them into pairs or groups of three.

There's an Alligator in My Bed!

Take the green pillowcases (used during the game section) off of each pillow. Place a sheet of cardboard inside each pillowcase to prevent paint from bleeding through. Using black or dark green fabric paint, paint a child's hand and lower arm. Have him or her carefully print the arm and hand on the pillowcase, with the four fingers at the top and the thumb opened. (This will be the alligator's mouth.) Clean the child's arm and hand before continuing. Have the child use a paintbrush to add legs and a tail. Use white paint to add teeth and an eye. Let the pillowcases dry before removing the cardboard.

Trip Through the Zoo

Let the guests create a board game of their own. Use a sheet of freezer paper six feet in length for the playing board. Before the party, draw a path of three-inch squares from the beginning of the paper to the end of the paper. Make the path wind and turn to add more fun. At the end of the path, let the host draw a zoo cage with animals or use wild animal stickers. At the beginning of the path, draw a zookeeper.

At the sleepover, let the children work together to fill in every second or third square with directions, such as "Slipped on a banana peel; go back two spaces," or "Took a ride on an emu; skip ahead three spaces." Let the children take turns coming up with ideas. Those who are not writing may choose to illustrate zoo animals around the outside of the path. After the path is created, play the game. Give each player a plastic wild animal toy to use as a marker. Roll a die to see how many places to move.

The Zoo at Dark

As the guests begin to get drowsy, use the following idea to help them settle into rest time:

- Have each child snuggle into their sleeping bags for this thinking activity. Give each child a paper and pencil. Have each child write the alphabet, *A* to *Z* on his or her paper, leaving spaces between each letter. Have the guests write the names of as many animals as he or she can think of under the letter of which the name begins. After an allotted amount of time, see who has the most animals under each letter. You may choose to give a toy animal or sticker for the winner of each letter. (If the children are not capable of writing the animal names, do this activity differently. Starting with letter *A,* go around the circle and have each child name an animal that begins with that letter. When a child is stumped, go to the next letter. Continue until you make it through the alphabet.)

Time to Feed the Animals

The pizza is sure to gross out any adult and get giggles from any child!

Animal Poo Pizza

1 cheese pizza mix
½ pound ground beef, browned but left in big chunks
6 link sausages, cooked and cut into ¼-inch slices

Prepare pizza according to directions on box. On top of the cheese, add the chunks of ground beef and sausage slices. Bake according to package directions.

Brownie Cages

Before the sleepover, prepare a pan of brownies using a boxed mix. Cut each brownie to be the size of a graham cracker half (approximately 2½ by 2¼ inches). On the day of the sleepover, give each guest a cut brownie, a graham cracker half, stick pretzels, and a selection of animal crackers. You'll also need decorator frosting, preferably in a squirt tube. Let each guest make a cage for an animal by using the brownie as a base. Gently press one or two animal crackers into the middle of the brownie. Insert pretzels around the edges of the brownie for the bars. Use the squirt tube to squeeze frosting around the outside edge of the graham cracker. Turn the graham cracker over and very gently place it on top of the pretzels, such that the pretzels fit into the icing. Leave the cages for an hour or more for the frosting to harden.

Wild Wonders

Give each guest a wild treat to remember the slumber party. Put one or more of the following inside each child's alligator pillowcase: a box of animal crackers, small plastic toy animals, or a stuffed animal. Be sure to include each child's animal mask made during the activity time.

Index

C

D

E

S

T

About the Author

Julie Lavender was born and raised in Statesboro, Georgia. She lived in the same house from the day she was born until the day she married her husband, and never planned to leave her hometown. However, eight moves, five states, and four kids later, Julie realized that there's a big, wonderful world out there!

Julie received a master's degree in early childhood education and taught public school for six years before starting a family. She eventually decided to combine her teaching credentials with her desire to spend every possible moment with her children, and the result was eight years of homeschooling. Julie's "classroom" now consists of her four children: Jeremy, Jenifer, Jeb Daniel, and Jessica.

After she had her first child, Julie began her writing career. She has written many Sunday School lessons and coauthored six books for Group Publishing. She often writes preschool and elementary unit studies for *Homeschooling Today* magazine, and she has written articles, crafts, and devotions for *ParentLife* magazine, Frank Schaffer's *Schooldays Magazine*, *The Secret Place*, *Pathways to God*, and *Country Woman*.

Julie's husband, David, is a medical entomologist for the United States Navy. This career has enabled the Lavender family to call Florida, North Carolina, Virginia, California, and Washington "home." Julie greatly enjoys being a mom and spending time with her family.